A TEXT BOOK OF
OBJECT ORIENTED MODELING AND DESIGN

For
T.E. SEMESTER – VI
THIRD YEAR DEGREE COURSE IN COMPUTER ENGINEERING & INFORMATION TECHNOLOGY

As Per New Revised Syllabus of North Maharashtra University, Jalgon

Sambhaji Sarode
Assistant Professor,
Deptt. of Computer Engineering
MIT COE, Pune

Prachi Sarode
Assistant Professor,
Deptt. of Information Technology
MIT COE, Pune

N 3357

OOMD (TE COMP AND IT SEM. VI - NMU)　　　　　　　　　　ISBN : 978-93-5164-410-1
First Edition　　:　JANUARY 2015
© 　　　　　　 : **Authors**

The text of this publication, or any part thereof, should not be reproduced or transmitted in any form or stored in any computer storage system or device for distribution including photocopy, recording, taping or information retrieval system or reproduced on any disc, tape, perforated media or other information storage device etc., without the written permission of Authors with whom the rights are reserved. Breach of this condition is liable for legal action. Every effort has been made to avoid errors or omissions in this publication. In spite of this, errors may have crept in. Any mistake, error or discrepancy so noted and shall be brought to our notice shall be taken care of in the next edition. It is notified that neither the publisher nor the authors or seller shall be responsible for any damage or loss of action to any one, of any kind, in any manner, therefrom.

Published By :	Printed By :
NIRALI PRAKASHAN Abhyudaya Pragati, 1312, Shivaji Nagar, Off J.M. Road, PUNE - 411005 Tel – (020) 25512336/37/39, Fax – (020) 25511379 Email : niralipune@pragationline.com	**REPRO INDIA LTD,** **Mumbai.**

DISTRIBUTION CENTRES
PUNE

Nirali Prakashan
119, Budhwar Peth, Jogeshwari Mandir Lane
Pune 411002, Maharashtra
Tel : (020) 2445 2044, 66022708, Fax : (020) 2445 1538
Email : bookorder@pragationline.com

Nirali Prakashan
S. No. 28/25, Dhyari,
Near Pari Company, Pune 411041
Tel : (022) 24690204 Fax : (020) 24690316
Email : dhyari@pragationline.com
bookorder@pragationline.com

MUMBAI
Nirali Prakashan
385, S.V.P. Road, Rasdhara Co-op. Hsg. Society Ltd.,
Girgaum, Mumbai 400004, Maharashtra
Tel : (022) 2385 6339 / 2386 9976, Fax : (022) 2386 9976
Email : niralimumbai@pragationline.com

DISTRIBUTION BRANCHES

NAGPUR
Pratibha Book Distributors
Above Maratha Mandir, Shop No. 3, First Floor,
Rani Jhanshi Square, Sitabuldi, Nagpur 440012,
Maharashtra, Tel : (0712) 254 7129

BENGALURU
Pragati Book House
House No. 1, Sanjeevappa Lane, Avenue Road Cross,
Opp. Rice Church, Bengaluru - 560002.
Tel : (080) 64513344, 64513355,
Mob : 9880582331, 9845021552
Email:bharatsavla@yahoo.com

JALGAON
Nirali Prakashan
34, V. V. Golani Market, Navi Peth, Jalgaon 425001,
Maharashtra, Tel : (0257) 222 0395
Mob : 94234 91860

KOLHAPUR
Nirali Prakashan
New Mahadvar Road,
Kedar Plaza, 1st Floor Opp. IDBI Bank
Kolhapur 416 012, Maharashtra. Mob : 9855046155

CHENNAI
Pragati Books
9/1, Montieth Road, Behind Taas Mahal, Egmore,
Chennai 600008 Tamil Nadu, Tel : (044) 6518 3535,
Mob : 94440 01782 / 98450 21552 / 98805 82331, Email : bharatsavla@yahoo.com

RETAIL OUTLETS
PUNE

Pragati Book Centre
157, Budhwar Peth, Opp. Ratan Talkies,
Pune 411002, Maharashtra
Tel : (020) 2445 8887 / 6602 2707, Fax : (020) 2445 8887

Pragati Book Centre
Amber Chamber, 28/A, Budhwar Peth,
Appa Balwant Chowk, Pune : 411002, Maharashtra,
Tel : (020) 20240335 / 66281669
Email : pbcpune@pragationline.com

Pragati Book Centre
676/B, Budhwar Peth, Opp. Jogeshwari Mandir,
Pune 411002, Maharashtra
Tel : (020) 6601 7784 / 6602 0855

PBC Book Sellers & Stationers
152, Budhwar Peth, Pune 411002, Maharashtra
Tel : (020) 2445 2254 / 6609 2463

MUMBAI
Pragati Book Corner
Indira Niwas, 111 - A, Bhavani Shankar Road, Dadar (W), Mumbai 400028, Maharashtra
Tel : (022) 2422 3526 / 6662 5254, Email : pbcmumbai@pragationline.com

www.pragationline.com　　　　　　　　　　　　　　　　　　　　info@pragationline.com

PREFACE

It gives us immense pleasure to present this book of **"Object Oriented Modeling and Design"** for the Students of Third Year Degree Course in Computer Engineering and Information Technology of North Maharashtra University, Jalgaon.

The book is written strictly as per New Revised Syllabus which has been implemented from Academic Year (2015).

Although the book is written for student community, it will be also useful for the teaching faculty.

The objectives of this textbook are :

Unit I : It included Introduction to Object Oriented Modeling and (4 + 1) view architecture including Rational Unified Process (RUP).

Unit II : It included Introduction to UML and Object Constraint Language.

Unit III : It included Class Diagram and Composite Structure Diagram and Advanced Relationships.

Unit IV : It included Behavioral Diagrams, Communication Diagram, Sequence Diagram, Timing Diagram, State Chart Diagram and Activity Diagram.

Unit V : It included Package Diagram, Component Diagram, Development Diagram, It's Terms, Concepts and Common Modeling Techniques.

Our special thanks to publisher Mr. Dineshbhai K. Furia, Mr. Jignesh C. Furia, Mr. M.P. Munde and Mrs. Depali Lachake (Co-ordinator), all the team members namely Mrs. Neeta Kulkarni, Mrs. Pratibha Bele, Miss Mandakini Jadhvar and Mrs. Madhuri Khadgi of Nirali Prakashan, for their efforts in bringing out this book.

We are also thankful to **Shri P. M. More**, Branch Manager, Jalgaon Offfice for their valuable help and efforts for promotion of our book.

Thanks to all those who directly and indirectly helped us for completion of this book.

Any suggestions for the improvement of this book are always welcome.

January 2015   **Authors**

Pune

SYLLABUS

Unit 1 : Introduction of Object Oriented Modeling   (08 Hrs, 16 Marks)

Introduction : (a) What is object-oriented ? (b) What is Object oriented development? : Modeling Concept, Not Implementation, Object-Oriented Methodology, Three Models. (c) Object oriented themes.

Why We Model : (d) The Importance of Modeling, (e) Principles of Modeling, (f) Object-Oriented Modeling, 4+1 View architecture,

Architectural Approaches : Use case driven, Architecture-centric, Iterative and Incremental,

Rational Unified Process : (g) Characteristics of the process.

Phases and Iterations : (h) Inception Phase, (i) Elaboration Phase, (j) Construction Phase, (k) Transition Phase, (l) Iterations, (m) Process Workflows, (n) Artifacts, (o) Other Artifacts.

Unit II : Introduction to UML   (08 Hrs, 16 Marks)

(a) An Overview of the UML: Visualizing, Specifying, Constructing, Documenting, (b) Background, UML Basics, (c) Introducing UML 2.0

A Conceptual Model of the UML : (d) Building Blocks of the UML, (e) Rules of the UML, (f) Common Mechanisms in the UML: Specifications, Adornments, Common divisions, (g) Extensibility Mechanisms: stereotypes, tagged values, constraints.

Object Constraint Language : (h) OCL Basics, OCL Syntax, Advanced OCL Modeling.

Unit III : Class Diagram and Composite Structure Diagram   (08 Hrs, 16 Marks)

Object Diagram : (a) Terms and Concepts : Common Properties, Contents, Common Uses.

(b) Common Modeling Techniques : Modeling Object Structures.

Class Diagram : (c) Classes, Attributes, Operations, Abstract Classes,

(d) Relationships : Dependency, Association, Aggregation, Composition, Generalization, Association Classes, Association Qualifiers.

(e) Advanced Relationships : Stereotypes on Dependency, Stereotypes and Constraints on Generalization, Constraints on Association, Realization, (f) Interfaces, (g) Templates, (h) Class Diagram: Common Properties, Contents, Common Uses, (i) Common Modeling Techniques : Modeling Simple Collaborations, Modeling a Logical Database Schema, (j) Forward and Reverse Engineering.

Composite Structures Diagram : (k) Connectors, Ports, Structured classes and Properties.

Unit IV : Behavioral Diagrams   (08 Hrs, 16 Marks)

(a) Use case Diagram : Names, Use Cases and Actors, Use Cases and Flow of Events, Use Cases and Scenarios, Use Cases and Collaborations, Organizing Use Cases, Common Properties, Contents, Common Uses. **(b)** Sequence Diagram, **(c)** Communication Diagram, **(d)** Timing Diagram.

(e) State chart Diagram : Behavioral State Machines, States, Composite States, Submachine States, Transitions, Activities, Protocol State Machines ,Pseudo States , Event Processing.

(f) Activity Diagram : Common Properties, Contents, Action States and Activity States, Transitions, Branching, Forking and Joining, Swimlanes, Object Flow, Common Uses.

Unit V : Package Diagram, Component Diagram, Deployment Diagram
   (08 Hrs, 16 Marks)

Package Diagram : (a) Terms and Concepts : Names, Owned Elements, Visibility, Importing and Exporting.

(b) Common Modeling Techniques: Modeling Groups of Elements, Modeling Architectural Views.

Component :

(c) Terms and Concepts : Names, Components and Classes, Components and Interfaces, Kinds of Components.

Component Diagram : (d) Common Properties, Contents, Common Uses.

(e) Common Modeling Techniques: Modeling Source Code, Modeling an Executable Release, Modeling a Physical Database, Modeling Adaptable Systems, (f) Forward and Reverse Engineering

Deployment : (g) Terms and Concepts : Names, Nodes and Components, Connections.

Deployment Diagram : (h) Common Properties, Contents, Common Uses.

(i) Common Modeling Techniques: Modeling an Embedded System, Modeling a Client/Server System, Modeling a Fully Distributed System, (j) Forward and Reverse Engineering.

CONTENTS

Unit I : Introduction to Object Oriented Modeling — 1.1 to 1.22

Unit II : Introduction to UML — 2.1 to 2.24

Unit III : Class Diagram and Composite Structure Diagram — 3.1 to 3.38

Unit IV : Behavioral Diagrams — 4.1 to 4.80

Unit V : Package Diagram, Component Diagram, Deployment Diagram — 5.1 to 5.28

- **Case Studies** — CS.1 to CS.36

UNIT - I
INTRODUCTION TO OBJECT ORIENTED MODELING

1.1 INTRODUCTION

Object is the basic unit of object oriented programming language. Object is the key to understand object-oriented technology. Look around right now and you will find many examples of real-world objects :

Object : Objects have states and behaviours. Example : A dog has states - color, name, breed as well as behaviours-wagging, barking, eating. An object is an instance of a class.

Class : A class can be defined as a template/blue print that describes the behaviours/states that object of its type support. Real-world objects share two characteristics : They all have state and behaviour.

State

Every object, at any given point of time would have to have a set of attributes defining its State.

Behaviour

Every object based on its state and optionally identity will have particular behaviour.

We live in a world of objects. These objects exist in nature, in man-made entities, in business, and in the products that we use. They can be categorized, described, organized, combined, manipulated and created. Therefore, an object-oriented view has come into picture for creation of computer software. An object-oriented approach to the development of software was proposed in late 1960s.

Object-Oriented development requires that object-oriented techniques be used during the analysis, and implementation of the system. This methodology asks the analyst to determine what the objects of the system are, how they behave over time or in response to events, and what responsibilities and relationships an object has to other objects. Object-oriented analysis has the analyst look at all the objects in a system, their commonalties, difference and how the system needs to manipulate the objects.

The complete OO (Object-Oriented) methodology revolves around the objects identified in the system. When observed closely, every object exhibits some characteristics and behaviour. The objects recognize and respond to certain events.

For example, considering a Window on the screen as an object, the size of the window gets changed when resize button of the window is clicked. Here the clicking of the button is an event to which the window responds by changing its state from the old size to the new size.

(1) Object Model

This model describes the objects in a system and their inter relationships. This model observes all the objects as static and does not pay any attention to their dynamic nature.

(2) Dynamic Model

This model depicts the dynamic aspects of the system. It portrays the changes occurring in the states of various objects with the events that might occur in the system.

Functional Model

This model basically describes the data transformations of the system. This describes the flow of data and the changes that occur to the data throughout the system.

While the Object Model is most important of all as it describes the basic element of the system, the objects, all the three models together describe the complete functional system. As compared to the conventional system development techniques, OO modeling provides many benefits. Among other benefits, there are all the benefits of using the Object Orientation. Some of these are :

(1) Reusability : The classes once defined can easily be used by other applications. This is achieved by defining classes and putting them into a library of classes where all the classes are maintained for future use. Whenever a new class is needed the programmer looks into the library of classes and if it is available, it can be picked up directly from there.

(2) Inheritance : The concept of inheritance helps the programmer use the existing code in another way, where making small additions to the existing classes can quickly create new classes. Programmer has to spend less time and effort and can concentrate on other aspects of the system due to the reusability feature of the methodology.

(3) Data Hiding : Encapsulation is a technique that allows the programmer to hide the internal functioning of the objects from the users of the objects. Encapsulation separates the internal functioning of the object from the external functioning thus providing the user flexibility to change the external behaviour of the object making the programmer code safe against the changes made by the user. The systems designed using this approach are closer to the real world as the real world functioning of the system is directly mapped into the system designed using this approach.

Why We Model

A model is an abstraction of the real thing. When you model a system, you abstract away any details that are irrelevant or potentially confusing. Your model is a simplification of the real system, so it allows the design and viability of a system to be understood, evaluated, and criticized quicker than if you had to dig through the actual system itself.

Modeling is a central part of all the activities that lead up to the deployment of good software.

- We build models to communicate the desired structure and behaviour of our system.
- We build models to visualize and control the system's architecture.
- We build models to better understand the system we are building, often exposing opportunities for simplification and reuse.
- We build models to manage risk.

1.2 THE IMPORTANCE OF MODELING

A model is a simplification of reality. We build models so that we can better understand the system we are developing. A model provides the blueprints of a system. Models may encompass detailed plans, as well as more general plans that give view of the system under consideration. A good model includes those elements that have broad effect and skip those minor elements that are not relevant to the given level of abstraction. Every system may be described from different aspects using different models and each model is therefore a semantically closed abstraction of the system. A model may be structural, emphasizing the organization of the system or it may be behavioural, emphasizing the dynamics of the system.

Through modeling, we achieve four aims :

1. Models help us to visualize a system as it is or as we want it to be.
2. Models permit us to specify the structure or behaviour of a system.
3. Models give us a template that guides us in constructing a system.
4. Models document the decisions we have made.

A model is a simplification of reality.

A model provides the blueprints of a system. Models may encompass detailed plans as well as more general plans. This is essentially the approach of "divide-and-conquer", a hard problem by dividing it into a series of smaller problems that you can solve.

1.3 PRINCIPLES OF MODELING

There are Four Basic Principles of Modeling

- The choice of what models to create has a profound influence on how a problem is attacked and how a solution is shaped.
- It means you have to choose your model correctly right model will illuminate problems and help you to gain the things which are not easily gain, wrong models will mislead you, causing you to focus on irrelevant issues.
- In software, the models you choose can greatly affect your world view. If you build a system through the eyes of a database developer, you will likely focus on entity-relationship models that push behaviour into triggers and stored procedures. If you build

a system through the eyes of a structured analyst, you will likely end up with models that are algorithmic-centric, with data flowing from process to process. If you build a system through the eyes of an object-oriented developer, you will end up with a system whose architecture is centered around a sea of classes and the patterns of interaction that direct how those classes work together. Any of these approaches might be right for a given application and development culture.

- Every model may be expressed at different levels of precision. The best kinds of models are those that let you choose your level of detail, depending on who is doing the viewing and why they need to view it.
- An analyst or an end user will want to focus on issues of what ; a developer will want to focus on issues of how. Both of these stakeholders will want to visualize a system at different levels of detail at different times.

  For example, Sometimes, a quick and simple executable model of the user interface is exactly what you need ; at other times, you have to get down and dirty with the bits, such as when you are specifying cross-system interfaces or wrestling with networking bottlenecks.
- The best models are connected to reality. It's best to have models that have a clear connection to reality, All models simplify reality; the trick is to be sure that your simplifications don't mask any important details.
- No single model is sufficient. Every nontrivial system is best approached through a small set of nearly independent models.
- If you are constructing a building, there is no single set of blueprints that reveal all its details. At the very least, you'll need floor plans, elevations, electrical plans, heating plans, and plumbing plans. The operative phrase here is "nearly independent." In this context, it means having models that can be built and studied separately but that are still interrelated.
- The same is true of object-oriented software systems. To understand the architecture of such a system, you need several complementary and interlocking views : a use case view (exposing the requirements of the system), a design view (capturing the vocabulary of the problem space and the solution space), a process view (modeling the distribution of the system's processes and threads), an implementation view (addressing the physical realization of the system) and a deployment view (focusing on system engineering issues).
- Each of these views may have structural as well as behavioural, aspects. Together, these views represent the blueprints of software.

1.4 OBJECT ORIENTED MODELING

In its very general sense, object oriented thinking is about objects reacting with each other and their environment. Interaction between objects is helped by message paths which provide hierarchies and precedence; allowing objects to communicate and send messages to one another. The power of this modular system is that it can be continually changed and extended to any degree of complexity and the final complexity does not have to be visualized from the beginning it can just grow or evolve. Also, unlike structural thinking, the complexity of the resultant outcome of an object oriented structure need not have to be understandable in its final stage; this allows the design of a structure to become so complex that it can exceed the capacity of even the designer to understand the final outcome. The object-oriented approach considers a system as a dynamic entity comprising components, which can really only be defined with respect to one another. What a system is and does can be described only in terms of its components and how they interact.

1.5 CONCEPTS OF OBJECT ORIENTATION

The principal concepts of object orientation are as follows :

- Object orientation is a technology for producing models that reflect a domain, such as a business domain or a machine domain, in a natural way, using the terminology of the domain.
- Object-oriented software development has five underlying concepts : objects, messages, classes, inheritance and polymorphism. Software objects have a state, a behaviour and an identity. The behaviour can depend upon the state and the state may be modified by the behaviour. Messages that provide the communication between the objects of a system and between systems themselves have five main categories : constructors, destructors, selectors, modifiers.
- Every object is a real-world "instance" of a class which is a type of template used to define the characteristics of an object. Each object has a name, attributes and operations. Classes are said to have an association if the objects they instantiate are linked or related.
- Object-oriented models, when constructed correctly are easy to communicate, change, expand, validate, and verify.
- When done correctly, systems built using object-oriented technology are flexible in response to change, have well-defined architectures and provide the opportunity to create and implement reusable components. The requirements of the system are traceable to the code of the system.
- Object-oriented models are conveniently implemented in software using object-oriented programming languages. Using programming languages that are not object-oriented to implement object-oriented systems is not recommended.

Object-oriented or object-orientation is a software engineering concept, in which concepts are represented as "objects". It can refer to:Object-oriented analysis and design

A software development methodology is a set of processes leads to the development of an application. The software processes describe how the work is to be carried out to achieve the original goal based on the system requirements. The software development process will continue to exist as long as the development system is in operation. Object-oriented systems development methods differ from traditional development techniques in that the traditional techniques view software as a collection of programs (or functions) and isolated data. "A software system is a set of mechanisms for performing certain action on certain data."

The main distinction between traditional system development methodologies and newer object-oriented methodologies depends on their primary focus

Traditional Approach
- Focuses on the functions of the system object-oriented systems development
- Centres on the object, which combines data and functionality.

In an object-oriented environment
- Software is a collection of discrete objects that encapsulate their data as well as the functionality to model real-world "objects."
- An object orientation yields important benefits to the practice of software construction.
- Each object has attributes (data) and methods (functions).
- Objects are grouped into classes; in object-oriented terms, we discover and describe the classes involved in the problem domain.
- Everything is an object and each object is responsible for itself.

Example

Consider the Windows application needs Windows objects. A Windows object is responsible for things like opening, sizing and closing itself. Frequently, when a window displays something, that something also is an object (a chart, for example). A chart object is responsible for things like maintaining its data and labels and even for drawing itself.

Object-oriented methods enable us to create sets of objects that works together synergistically to produce software that better model their problem domains than similar systems produced by traditional techniques. The systems are easier to adapt to changing requirements, easier to maintain, more robust promote greater de-sign and code reuse. Object-oriented development allows us to create modules of functionality. Once objects are defined, it can be taken for granted that they will perform their desired functions and you can seal them off in your mind like black boxes. Your attention as a programmer shifts to what they do rather than how they do it. Here are some reasons why object orientation works.

1.5.1 Importance of Object Orientation

Higher Level of Abstraction

The object-oriented approach supports abstraction at the object level. Since objects encapsulate both data (attributes) and functions (methods), they work at a higher level of abstraction. The development can proceed at the object level and ignore the rest of the system for as long as necessary. This makes designing, coding, testing, and maintaining the system much simpler.

Seamless Transition Among Different Phases of Software Development

The traditional approach to software development requires different styles and methodologies for each step of the process. Moving from one phase to another requires a complex transition of perspective between models that almost can be in different worlds. This transition not only can slow the development process but also increases the size of the project and the chance for errors introduced in moving from one language to another.

The object-oriented approach, on the other hand, essentially uses the same language to talk about analysis, design, programming and database design. This seamless approach reduces the level of complexity and redundancy and makes for clearer, more robust system development.

Encouragement of Good Programming Techniques

A class in an object-oriented system carefully delineates between its interfaces the routines and attributes within a class are held together tightly. In a properly designed system, the classes will be grouped into subsystems but remain independent therefore, changing one class has no impact on other classes and so the impact is minimized. However, the object-oriented approach is not a panacea; nothing is magical here that will promote perfect design or perfect code.

Promotion of Reusability

Objects are reusable because they are modeled directly out of a real-world problem domain. Each object stands by itself or within a small circle of peers (other objects). Within this framework, the class does not concern itself with the rest of the system or how it is going to be used within a particular system.

Benefits of Object Orientation

- Faster Development.
- Reduced Cost.
  - Reuse
- Higher quality systems.
- Improved architecture.
  - More adaptable.
  - More scalable.

1.6 OOP PRINCIPLES

An object has state, behaviour, and identity. The structure and behaviour of similar objects are defined in their common class. The terms instance and object are interchangeable. A class is a set of objects that share a common structure and a common behaviour. A single object is simply an instance of a class. All object-oriented programming languages provide mechanisms that help you implement the object-oriented model. They are encapsulation, inheritance and polymorphism.

Encapsulation

Encapsulation is the mechanism that binds together code and the data it manipulates and keeps both safe from outside interference and misuse. Abstraction and encapsulation are complementary concepts: abstraction focuses upon the observable behaviour of an object, whereas *encapsulation* focuses upon the implementation that gives rise to this behaviour.

Encapsulation is most often achieved through information biding, which is the process of hiding all the secrets of an object that do not contribute to its essential characteristics typically, the structure of an object is hidden as well as the, implementation of its methods.

In Java the basis of encapsulation is the class. When you create a class, you will specify the code and data (data members and member functions) that constitute that class. Collectively, these elements are called *members* of the class. Specifically, the data defined by the class are referred to as member variables or instance variables.

Since the purpose of a class is to encapsulate complexity, there are mechanisms for hiding the complexity of the implementation inside the class. Each method or variable in a class may be marked private or public.

Inheritance

Inheritance is the process by which one object acquires the properties of another object. This is important because it supports the concept of hierarchical classification. As mentioned earlier, most knowledge is made manageable by hierarchical (that is, top-down) classifications. For example, a Golden Retriever is part of the classification dog, which in turn is part of the mammal class, which is under the larger class animal. Inheritance interacts with encapsulation as well. If a given class encapsulates some attributes, then any subclass will have the same attributes *plus* any that it adds as part of its specialization This is a key concept that lets object-oriented programs grow in complexity linearly rather than geometrically. A new subclass inherits all of the attributes of all of its ancestors.

Polymorphisms

The concept of polymorphism is often expressed by the phrase "one interface, multiple methods." More precisely *Polymorphisms* means the ability to request that the same operations be performed by a wide range of different types of things.

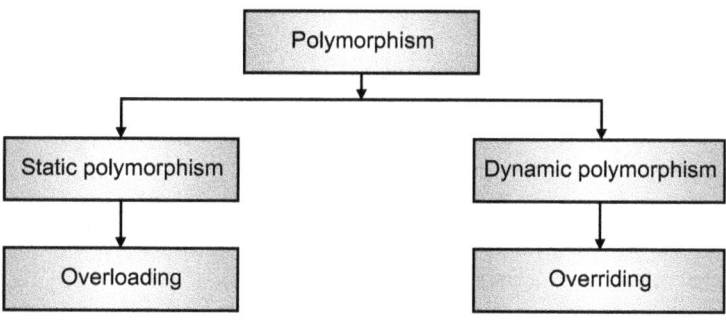

Fig. 1.1

Method Overloading

Method overloading is one of the ways that Java implements polymorphism.

In Java it is possible to define two or more methods within the same class that share the same name, as long as their parameter declarations are different.

When this is the case, the methods are said to be *overloaded*, and the process is referred to as *method overloading*.

```
// Demonstrate method overloading.
class OverloadDemo {
        void test()
        {
                System.out.println("No parameters");
        }
// Overload test for one integer parameter.
        void test(int a)
        {
           System.out.println("a: " + a);
        }
// Overload test for two integer parameters.
        void test(int a, int b)
        {
           System.out.println("a and b:" + a + " " + b);
        }
// overload test for a double parameter
        double test(double a)
```

```
        {
            System.out.println("double a: " + a);
            return a*a;
        }
    }
    class Overload {
        public static void main(String args[]) {
        OverloadDemo ob = new OverloadDemo();
        double result;

    // call all versions of test()
        ob.test();
        ob.test(10);
        ob.test(10, 20);
        result = ob.test(123.25);
        System.out.println("Result of ob.test(123.25):" + result);
        }
    }
```

This program generates the following output:
No parameters
a: 10
a and b: 10 20
double a: 123.25
Result of ob.test(123.25): 15190.5625

1.6.1 Method Overriding

In a class hierarchy, when a method in a subclass has the same name and type signature as a method in its superclass, then the method in the subclass is said to *override* the method in the superclass.

When an overridden method is called from within a subclass, it will always refer to the version of that method defined by the subclass. The version of the method defined by the superclass will be hidden. Consider the following:

```java
// Method overriding.
class A
{
  int i, j;
  A(int a, int b)
{
 i = a;
 j = b;
 }
// display i and j
  void show()
{
    System.out.println("i and j: " + i + " " + j);
    }
}
class B extends A
{
    int k;
    B(int a, int b, int c)
{
    super(a, b);
    k = c;
 }
// display k - this overrides show() in A
  void show()
{
    System.out.println("k: " + k);
    }
}
class Override
{
public static void main(String args[])
```

```
{
  B subOb = new B(1, 2, 3);
  subOb.show();
// this calls show() in B
  }
}
```
The output produced by this program is shown here:
k: 3

1.6.2 Object Oriented Methodology (OOM)

Object Oriented Methodology (OOM) is a system development approach encouraging and facilitating re-use of software components. With this methodology, a computer system can be developed on a component basis which enables the effective re-use of existing components and facilitates the sharing of its components by other systems.

An object-oriented methodology is defined as the system of principles and procedures applied to object-oriented software development.

1.6.3 Advantages of Object Oriented Methodology

Object Oriented Methodology closely represents the problem domain. Because of this, it is easier to produce and understand designs. The objects in the system are immune to requirement changes. Therefore, allows changes more easily. Object Oriented Methodology designs encourage more re-use. New applications can use the existing modules, thereby reduces the development cost and cycle time.

Object Oriented Methodology approach is more natural. It provides nice structures for thinking and abstracting and leads to modular design. While developing systems based on this approach, the analyst makes use of certain models to analyze and depict these objects. The methodology supports and uses three basic Models :

To deploy software that satisfies its intended purpose, you have to meet and engage users in a disciplined fashion, to expose the real requirements of your system. To develop software of lasting quality, you have to craft a solid architectural foundation that's resilient to change. To develop software rapidly, efficiently and effectively with a minimum of software scrap and rework, you have to have the right people, the right tools and the right focus.

To do all this consistently and predictably, with an appreciation for the lifetime costs of the system, you must have a sound development process that can adapt to the changing needs of your business and technology.

1.7 (4 + 1) VIEW ARCHITECURE

Visualizing, specifying, constructing and documenting a software-intensive system demands that the system be viewed from a number of perspectives. Different stakeholders- end users, analysts, developers, system integrators, testers, technical writers and project managers- each bring different agendas to a project and each looks that system in different ways at different times over the project's life. There are number of ways to break up your UML model diagrams into perspectives or views that capture a particular facet of your system.

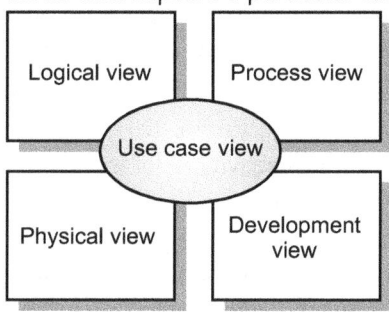

Fig. 1.2 : Philippe kruchten's 4+1 view model

Use Case View

- Describes the functionality of the system being modeled from the perspective of the outside world. This view is needed to describe what the system is supposed to do.
- The use-case view describes the functionality of the system that should deliver, as perceived by external actors. An actor interacts with the system; the actor can be a user or another system.
- Customers, designers, developers and testers use this view. It is described in use-case diagrams, sometimes with support from activity diagrams. The desired usage of the system is described as a number of use cases in the use-case view, where a use case is a generic description of a function requested.
- The use-case view is central, because its contents drive the development of the other views. The final goal of the system is to provide the functionality described in this view along with some nonfunctional properties. Hence, this view affects all the others. This view is also used to validate the system and finally to verify the functioning of the system by testing the use-case view with the customers (asking, "Is this what you want?") and against the finished system (asking, "Does the system work as specified?").

Logical View

- Describes the abstract descriptions of a system's parts. Used to model what a system is made up of and how the parts interact with each other. The types of UML diagrams that typically make up this view include class, object, state machine and interaction diagrams.

- The logical view describes how the system's functionality is provided. It is mainly for designers and developers. In contrast to the use-case view, the logical view looks inside the system.
- It describes both the static structure (classes, objects, and relationships) and the dynamic collaborations that occur when the objects send messages to each other to provide a given function. Properties such as persistence and concurrency are also defined, as well as the interfaces and the internal structure of classes.
- The static structure is described in class and object diagrams. The dynamic modeling is described in state machines, and interaction and activity diagrams.

Process View
- Describes the processes within the system. It is particularly helpful for visualizing the system. This view typically contains activity diagrams.
- The process view deals with the division of the system into processes and processors. This aspect, which is a nonfunctional property of the system, allows for efficient resource usage, parallel execution, and the handling of asynchronous events from the environment. Besides dividing the system into concurrently executing threads of control, this view must also deal with the communication and synchronization of these threads.
- The emphasis on a view that shows concurrency provides critical information for developers and integrators of the system.
- The view consists of dynamic diagrams (state machines, and interaction and activity diagrams) and implementation diagrams (interaction and deployment diagrams). A timing diagram provides a specialized tool for the process view. A timing diagram provides a way to show the current status of an object in terms of time. For example, this diagram can show how synchronized objects can queue to use a thread or process as a result of different strategies for implementing priority usage of resources.

Development View
- Describes how your system's parts are organized into modules and components. It is very useful to manage layers within your system's architecture. This view typically contains package and component diagrams.
- The implementation view describes the main modules and their dependencies.
- It is mainly for developers and consists of the main software artifacts. The artifacts include different types of code modules shown with their structure and dependencies. Additional information about the components, such as resource allocation (responsibility for a component) or other administrative information, such as a progress report for the development work, can also be added. The implementation view will likely require the use of extensions for a specific execution environment.

Physical View
- Describes how the system's design, as described in the three previous views, is brought to life as a set of real-world entities. The diagrams in this view show how the abstract parts map into the final deployed system. This view typically contains deployment diagrams.
- Finally, the deployment view shows the physical deployment of the system, such as the computers and devices (nodes) and how they connect to each other. The various execution environments within the processors can be specified as well. The deployment view is used by developers, integrators, and testers and is represented by the deployment diagram. This view also includes a mapping that shows how the artifacts are deployed in the physical architecture, for example, which programs or objects execute on each respective computer.

Architectural Approaches

The UML is largely process-independent, meaning that it is not tied to any particular software development life cycle. However, to get the most benefit from the UML, you should consider a process that is :
- Use case driven.
- Architecture-centric.
- Iterative and incremental.

Use case driven means that use cases are used as a primary artifact for establishing the desired behaviour of the system, for verifying and validating the system's architecture, for testing, and for communicating among the stakeholders of the project.

Architecture-centric means that a system's architecture is used as a primary artifact for conceptualizing, constructing, managing and evolving the system under development. An iterative process is one that involves managing a stream of executable releases. An is one that involves the continuous integration of the system's architecture to produce these releases, with each new release embodying incremental improvements over the other. Together, an iterative and incremental process is risk-driven, meaning that each new release is focused on attacking and reducing the most significant risks to the success of the project.

The Rational Unified Process is an iterative process. For simple systems, it would seem perfectly feasible to sequentially define the whole problem, design the entire solution, build the software and then test the end product. However, given the complexity and sophistication demanded of current systems, this linear approach to system development is unrealistic. An iterative approach advocates an increasing understanding of the problem through successive refinements and an incremental growth of an effective solution over multiple cycles. Built into the iterative approach is the flexibility to accommodate new requirements or tactical changes in business objectives. It also allows the project to identify and resolve risks sooner rather than later. The Rational Unified Process's activities emphasize the creation and maintenance of models rather than paper documents. Models especially those specified using the UML provide semantically rich representations of the software system under development. They can be viewed in multiple ways, and the information represented can be instantaneously captured and controlled electronically. The rationale behind the Rational Unified Process's focus on models rather than paper documents is to minimize the overhead associated with generating and maintaining documents and to maximize the relevant information content. Development under the Rational Unified Process is architecture-centric. The process focuses on the early development and baselining of a software architecture. Having a robust architecture in place facilitates parallel development, minimizes rework, and increases the probability of component reuse and eventual system maintainability. This architectural blueprint serves as a solid basis against which to plan and manage software component-based development.

Development activities under the Rational Unified Process are use case-driven. The Rational Unified Process places strong emphasis on building systems based on a thorough understanding of how the delivered system will be used. The notions of use cases and scenarios are used to align the process flow from requirements capture through testing and to provide traceable threads through development to the delivered system.

The Rational Unified Process supports object-oriented techniques. Rational Unified Process models supports the concepts of objects and classes and the relationships among them, and they use the UML as its common notation. The Rational Unified Process is a configurable process. Although no single process is suitable for all software development organizations, the Rational Unified Process is tailorable and can be scaled to fit the needs of projects ranging from small software development teams to large development organizations. The Rational Unified Process is founded on a simple and clear process architecture that provides commonality across a family of processes, and yet can be varied to accommodate various situations. Contained in the Rational Unified Process is guidance about how to configure the process to suit the needs of an organization. The Rational Unified Process encourages objective ongoing quality control and risk management. Quality assessment is built into the process, in all activities and involving all participants, using objective measurements and criteria. It is not treated as an afterthought or as a separate activity. Risk management is built into the process, so that risks to the success of the project are identified and attacked early in the development process, when there is time to react.

Iterative and Incremental

The Unified Process is an iterative and incremental development process. The Elaboration, Construction and Transition phases are divided into a series of timeboxed iterations. (The Inception phase may also be divided into iterations for a large project.) Each iteration results in an increment, which is a release of the system that contains added or improved functionality compared with the previous release. Although most iterations will include work in most of the process disciplines (e.g.Requirements, Design, Implementation, Testing) the relative effort and emphasis will change over the course of the project.

Architecture Centric

The Unified Process insists that architecture sit at the heart of the project team's efforts to shape the system. Since no single model is sufficient to cover all aspects of a system, the Unified Process supports multiple architectural models and views. One of the most important deliverables of the process is the executable architecture baseline which is created during the Elaboration phase. This partial implementation of the system serves to validate the architecture and act as a foundation for remaining development.

Risk Focused

The Unified Process requires the project team to focus on addressing the most critical risks early in the project life cycle. The deliverables of each iteration, especially in the Elaboration phase, must be selected in order to ensure that the greatest risks are addressed first.

1.8 RATIONAL UNIFIED PROCESS

Characteristics of the process :

- The Rational Unified Process is an iterative process.
- The Rational Unified Process activities emphasize the creation and maintenance of models rather than paper documents.
- Development under the Rational Unified Process is architecture-centric.
- Development activities under the Rational Unified Process are use case_ driven.
- The Rational Unified Process supports object-oriented techniques.
- The Rational Unified Process is a configurable process.
- The Rational Unified Process encourages objective ongoing quality control and risk management.

1.8.1 The Phases and Iterations of RUP

Iteration

- A project governed by a RUP process moves forward in increments called iterations.
- The goal of each iteration is to develop some working software that can be demonstrated to all the stakeholders to understand the software.
- Each phase in the Rational Unified Process can be further broken down into iterations. An iteration is a complete development loop resulting in a release of an executable product constituting a subset of the final product under development, which then is grown incrementally from iteration to iteration to become the final system or product.
- Each iteration goes through the various process workflows depending on the phase emphasis on each process workflow is different.

- During inception, the focus is on requirements capture. During elaboration, the focus turns towards analysis and design. In the construction, implementation is the central activity, and transition centers on deployment.

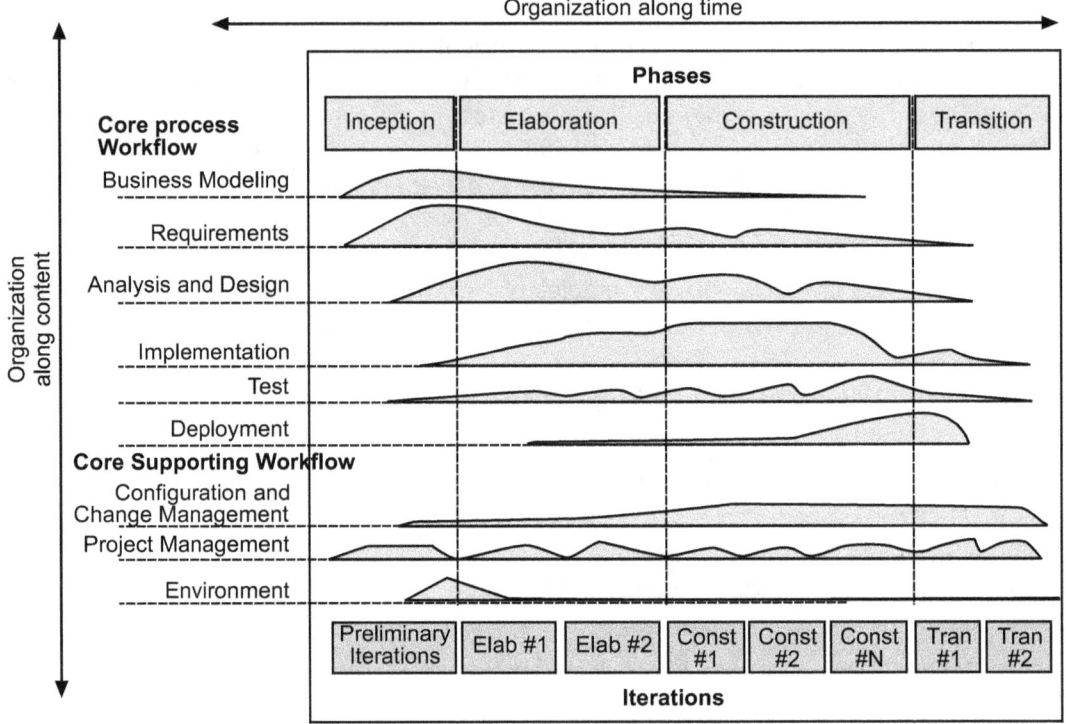

Fig. 1.3 : The phases and iterations of RUP

1.8.2 Inception

- Establish the business case for the system and delimit the project scope.
- The business case includes success criteria, risk assessment and estimates of the resources needed.
- Create an executable prototype that serves as a proof of concept.

The Outcomes of The Inception Phase are

- A vision document : a general vision of the core project's requirements, key features, and main constraints.
- An initial use-case model (10% -20%) complete.
- An initial project glossary (may optionally be partially expressed as a domain model).
- An initial business case, which includes business context, success criteria (revenue projection, market recognition, and so on) and financial forecast.

- An initial risk assessment.
- A project plan, showing phases and iterations.
- A business model, if necessary.
- One or several prototypes.

1.8.3 Elaboration

- Establish a firm understanding of the problem to be solved.
- Establish the architectural foundation of the software.
- Calibrate and support a detailed plan of subsequent iterations.
- Refine the process and set the team.
- Eliminate high risks.
- Analyze the problem domain, establish a sound architectural foundation, develop the project plan, and eliminate the highest risk elements of the project.
- To accomplish these objectives, you must have the "mile wide and inch deep" view of the system.
- Architectural decisions have to be made with an understanding of the whole system, its scope, major functionality and nonfunctional requirements such as performance requirements.
- An executable architecture prototype is built in one or more iterations, depending on the scope, size, risk, and novelty of the project.
- At the end of the elaboration phase, you examine the detailed system objectives and scope, the choice of architecture, and the resolution of major risks, and decide whether to proceed with construction.

The Outcomes of the Elaboration Phase are

- A use-case model (at least 80% complete) all use cases and actors have been identified, and most use case descriptions have been developed.
- Supplementary requirements capturing the non functional requirements and any requirements that are not associated with a specific use case.
- A Software Architecture Description.
- An executable architectural prototype.
- A revised risk list and a revised business case.
- A development plan for the overall project, including the coarse-grained project plan, showing iterations" and evaluation criteria for each iteration.
- An updated development case specifying the process to be used.
- A preliminary user manual (optional).

1.8.4 Construction

- During the construction phase, you iteratively and incrementally develop a complete product that is ready for transition to its user community. This implies describing the remaining requirements and acceptance criteria, fleshing out the design, and completing the implementation using programming languages like JAVA, C,C++ etc. and testing of the software.
- The iterations in the construction phase are not much different from the iterations of the Elaboration phase. Each iteration adds features to the software; features that the stakeholders care about and give feedback about.
- During this phase, one would expect the use case descriptions to stabilize to a certain extent; though in many project domains they will continue to change throughout the lifetime of the project.
- The construction phase is, in one sense, a manufacturing process where emphasis is placed on managing resources and controlling operations to optimize costs, schedules, and quality.
- At the end of the construction phase, you decide if the software, sites, and users are all ready to go operational.

Transition Phase

- During the transition phase, you deploy the software to the user or customer. Once the system has been put into the hands of its end users, issues often arise that require additional development in order to adjust the system, correct some undetected problems or finish some features that have been postponed.
- This phase typically starts with a beta release of the system, which is then replaced with the production system.
- At the end of the transition phase, you decide whether the life cycle objectives of the project have been met and determine if you should start another development cycle. This is also a point at which you wrap up the lessons learned on the project in order to improve your development process, which will be applied to the next project.

Advantages of RUP Software Development

1. This is a complete methodology in itself with an emphasis on accurate documentation.
2. It is proactively able to resolve the project risks associated with the client's evolving requirements requiring careful change request management
3. Less time is required for integration as the process of integration goes on throughout the software development life cycle.
4. The development time required is less due to reuse of components.
5. There is online training and tutorial available for this process.

Disadvantages of RUP Software Development

1. The team members need to be expert in their field to develop a software under this methodology.
2. The development process is too complex and disorganized.
3. On cutting edge projects which utilise new technology, the reuse of components will not be possible. Hence the time saving one could have made will be impossible to fulfill.
4. Integration throughout the process of software development, in theory sounds a good thing. But on particularly big projects with multiple development streams it will only add to the confusion and cause more issues during the stages of testing.

Process Workflows

The Rational Unified Process consists of nine process workflows.

1.	Business modeling	Describes the structure and dynamics of the organization
2.	Requirements	Describes the use case-based method for eliciting requirements
3.	Analysis and design	Describes the multiple architectural views.
4.	Implementation	Takes into account software development, unit text, and integration
5.	Test	Describes test cases, procedures, and defect-tracking metrics.
6.	Deployment	Covers the deliverable system configuration.
7.	Configuration management	Controls changes to and maintains the integrity of a project's artifacts
8.	Project management	Describes various strategies of working with an iterative process
9.	Environment	Covers the necessary infrastructures required to develop a system

An artifact (in the UML) is the specification of a physical piece of information that is used or produced by a software development process, or by deployment and operation of a system.

Examples of artifacts include model files, source files, scripts and binary executable files, a table in a database system, a development deliverable or a word-processing document, a mail message. Artifacts are the physical entities that are deployed on Nodes, Devices and Execution Environments. Other UML elements such as classes and components are first manifested into artifacts and instances of these artifacts are then deployed. Artifacts can also be composed of other artifacts.

For Example, Interface, Component etc.

Note : Artifacts : Each Rational Unified Process activity has associated artifacts either required as an input or generated as an output. Some artifacts are used to direct input to subsequent activities, kept as reference resources on the project, or generated in a format as contractual deliverables.

REVIEW QUESTIONS

1. Write on the following in brief :
   (a) Inception phase (w.r.t. RUP) its importance, scope.
   (b) Elaboration phase
   (c) Construction phase
   (d) Transition phase
2. Design view in 4 + 1 view of architecture.
3. Objective oriented feature: Encapsulation, Inheritance, Polymorphism, data hiding.
4. Explain in detail the logical view and process view of the 4 + 1 view model.
5. What activities do you carry out in the transition phase of rational unified process?
6. What are advantages of Object orientation?
7. Explain the importance of Modeling.
8. Describe OO principles.
9. Explain in detail artifact.

UNIT - II
INTRODUCTION TO UML

2.1 AN OVERVIEW OF THE UML : VISUALIZING, SPECIFYING, CONSTRUCTING, DOCUMENTING

The Unified Modeling Language (UML) is the standard modeling language for software and systems development. Systems being developed now are more complex than ever, and old software development methods simply do not efficiently scale up to the size of current systems. New paradigms are needed to keep up. Engineers in other disciplines have long used blueprints and models to design and construct complex systems. They are concise, precise and allow the viewer to understand at a glance what is going on. They also contain an enormous amount of information. The standards used for blueprinting buildings are the same, a door or window is always rendered the same way. In the past, this was not the case with software blueprints. Notational languages were language and method specific, so that a class in one language could look completely different in a different notation.

The Unified Modelling Language (UML) is a standard widely adopted graphical language that describes the artifacts of software systems with a focus on conceptual and physical representations. It provides a good bird's eye view as well as the minute details of the structural and behavioural aspects of a single system through the various views offered by UML. It is proprietary and language independent so that it may be used in any number of development environments.

The Object Management Group (OMG) is the body responsible for creating and maintaining the language specifications. They define UML as, "a graphical language for visualizing, specifying, constructing, and documenting the artifacts of a software intensive system". It is based on the UML Metamodel, which is a UML class diagram that specifies the syntactic and semantic characteristics of elements and relationships.

Current modelling trends involve models that can be translated into compilable and runable code. This is known as Model Driven Architecture (MDA) and is also being regulated by the OMG. As UML is the most widely used modelling language, it is very closely linked with MDA.

The relationship between the code and the model is not one-way. Forward engineering takes the model and generates source code from it. Reverse engineering takes the source code and creates a model. Code can be coupled with models so that modifying one automatically updates the other in a process known as roundtrip engineering, effectively keeping the model and source code synchronized. Tight integration of the code and the model results in the best of both worlds direct access to the code with all of the benefits of visual representations of that code.

Some of the biggest uses of UML include real-time embedded systems that deal with very complex problems and behaviours, business rules, game scenarios and grid computing, and patterns.

Definition : The UML is a language for visualizing, specifying, constructing and documenting the artifacts of a software-intensive system.

- The UML is appropriate for modeling systems ranging from enterprise information systems to distributed Web-based applications and even to hard real time embedded systems.
- It is a very expressive language, addressing all the views needed to develop and then deploy such systems.
- A language provides a vocabulary and the rules for combining words in that vocabulary for the purpose of communication.
- A modeling language is a language whose vocabulary and rules focus on the conceptual and physical representation of a system.
- UML is thus a standard language for software blueprints.
- The vocabulary and rules of a UML tell you how to create and read well formed models, but they don't tell you what models you should create and when you should create them.

Several factors contributed greatly to the widespread adoption of UML.

1. UML is language independent.

2. It does not advocate nor require a particular method.

3. It is readily accessible as UML specifications are free for download and any company may join the OMG.

Who uses UML?

Complex problems particularly require sufficient planning in order to avoid problems in development and more importantly in maintenance and update stages where changes are more arduous and costly. UML is one single language that allows people from different disciplines to work together to identify and solve these problems before they occur.

Developers and business analysts can map out requirements together in one language. There is no need to consider the underlying technology at this stage, which allows non-programmers to become more involved in the development process. Diagrams enhance the narrative and are stored electronically for simple archival.

UML is used in complex systems to not only capture object-oriented software information, but business rules information as well. From these business rules, a description of interfaces between systems and components can be generated. Often, this will require passing information between dissimilar languages and data formats, which makes language- and platform-independent UML a natural choice. The business models created form the framework for subsequent systems. Lots of developers still use a 'code only' approach. Any modelling done is informal and/or code-based (such as using packages) and is often captured on whiteboards and left undocumented. This can cause severe problems when the system is expanded or the original developers are no longer working on the project. With other people involved in the design process and a more efficient method of planning, developers are freed up for further architecting, analysis, design, and testing.

Applications of UML

The UML is intended primarily for software-intensive systems. It has been used effectively for domains such as :

- Enterprise information systems.
- Banking and financial services.
- Telecommunications.
- Transportation.
- Defense/aerospace.
- Retail.
- Medical electronics.
- Scientific.
- Distributed Web-based services.

The UML language is limited to software but also useful non software systems.

UML has Six Main Advantages

1. **It is a Formal Language**
   Every element is meaningful and strongly defined, while modelling the system it will not be misunderstood.
2. **It is Concise**
   The language is simple, easy to understand, and having straightforward notation.
3. **It is Comprehensive**
   It describes all important aspects of a system.
4. **It is Scalable**
   Where needed, the language is formal enough to handle massive system modeling projects, but it also scales down to small projects, avoiding overkill.
5. **It is Built on Lessons Learned**
   UML is the culmination of best practices in the object-oriented community during the past 15 years.
6. **It is the Standard**
   UML is controlled by an open standards group with active contributions from a worldwide group of vendors and academics, which fends off "vendor lock-in." The standard ensures UML's transformability and interoperability, which means you aren't tied to a particular product.

UML Goals

The UML has seven goals :

- To provide users with a ready-to-use, expressive visual modelling language for the development and exchange of meaningful models.
- To provide mechanisms for extensibility and specialisation in order to extend the central concepts.
- To be independent from specific programming languages and development processes.
- To provide a formal foundation for understanding the modelling language.
- To encourage further development in the OO tools market.
- To support higher-level development concepts including collaborations, frameworks, patterns, and components.
- To integrate best practices.

2.2 BACKGROUND, UML BASICS, INTRODUCING UML 2.0

- Object-oriented modeling languages appeared sometime between the mid 1970's.
- The number of identified modeling languages increased from less than 10 to more than 50 during the period between 1989 -1994.
- Darwinian forces in the marketplace led to three dominate methods, each having its own modeling language. Many users of these methods had trouble finding a modeling language that met their needs completely thus fueling the so-called method wars.
- Most notably Object-oriented Analysis & Design (OOAD) by Grady Booch Jacobson's OOSE (Object-Oriented Software Engineering) and Rumbaugh's OMT (Object Modeling Technique) are the prominent methods. Other important methods included Fusion, Shlaer-Mellor and Coad-Yourdon. Each of these was a complete method, although each was recognized as having strengths and weaknesses.
- Booch method was particularly expressive during the design and construction phases of projects. It support effective low-level design and its fine grain detail was even useful for documenting code. It was good at OO design, weaker at OO analysis.

2.2.1 Rumbaugh Method (OMT)

- OMT had a simpler modeling language. It was better at higher-level designs than Booch Method. It was good at OO analysis, weak at OO design.
- OOSE provided excellent support for use cases as a way to drive requirements capture, analysis and this made it good at very high-level design.
- By the mid 1990's, when Grady Booch (Rational Software Corporation), Ivar Jacobson Objectory) and James Rumbaugh (General Electric) began to adopt ideas from each other's methods, which collectively were becoming recognized as the leading object-oriented methods worldwide.

As the primary authors of the Booch, OOSE and OMT methods, we were motivated to create a unified modeling language for three reasons.
1. To model systems, from concept to executable artifact, using object-oriented techniques.
2. To address the issues of scale inherent in complex, mission-critical systems.
3. To create a modeling language usable by both humans and machines.

The UML effort started officially in October 1994, when Rumbaugh joined Booch at Rational.

The version 0.8 draft of the Unified Method (as it was then called) was released in October 1995.

Year	Versions of UML
October 1994-1995	When Rumbaugh joined Booch at Rational. The version 0.8 draft of the Unified Method
June 1996	Jacobson joined Rational incorporate OOSE resulted in the release of the UML version 0.9 documents.
November 14, 1997	UML 1.1 was adopted by the OMG
June 1998	OMG Revision Task Force (RTF) UML 1.2
In fall 1998	The RTF released UML 1.3
September 2001	UML 1.4
2002	UML 1.5 will be result of UML 1.4 with Action semantics
2002-2003	UML 2.0

As UML gone through several revisions, Version 2.0 is a substantial improvement of the architecture.

2.3 A CONCEPTUAL MODEL OF THE UML/BUILDING BLOCKS OF THE UML

To understand the UML, you need to form a conceptual model of the language, and this requires learning three major elements: the UML's basic building blocks, the rules that dictate how those building blocks may be put together and some common mechanisms that apply throughout the UML.

Building Blocks of the UML

The vocabulary of the UML encompasses three kinds of building blocks :
1. Things.
2. Relationships.
3. Diagrams.

- Things are the abstractions that are first-class citizens in a model.
- Relationships tie these things together.
- Diagrams group interesting collections of things.

2.3.1 Things in the UML

There are four kinds of things in the UML :
1. Structural things.
2. Behavioral things.
3. Grouping things.
4. Annotational things.

These things are the basic object-oriented building blocks of the UML.

We use them to write well formed models.

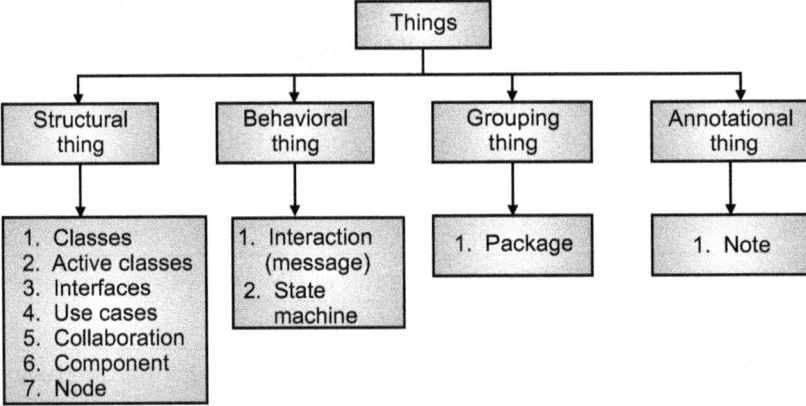

Fig. 2.1

2.3.1.1 Structural Things

Structural things are the nouns of UML models. These are the mostly static parts of a model, representing elements that are either conceptual or physical. There are seven kinds of structural things.

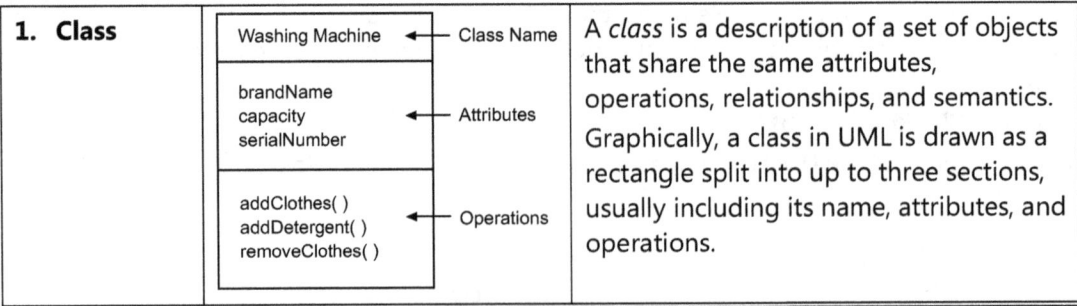

2. **Active Classes**	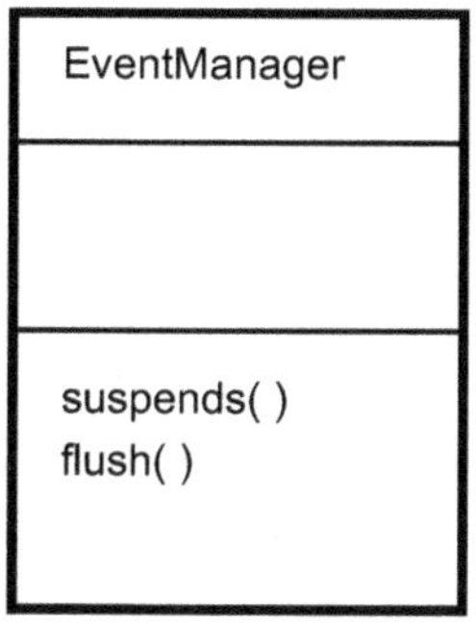 EventManager suspends( ) flush( )		An *active class* is a class whose objects own one or more processes or threads and therefore can initiate control activity. An active class is just like a class except that its objects represent elements whose behavior is concurrent with other elements. Graphically, an active class is rendered just like a class, but with heavy lines, usually including its name, attributes, and operations.
3. **Interface**	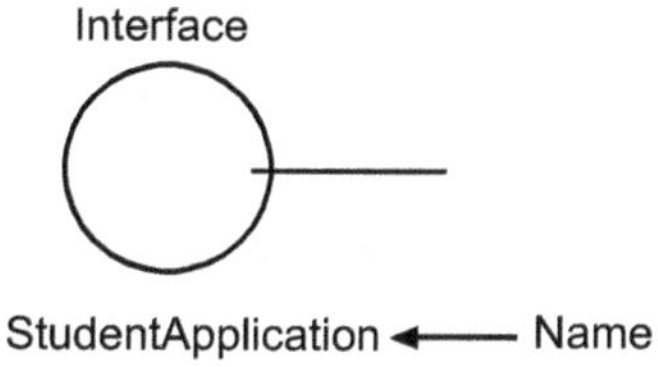 Interface ◯──── StudentApplication ◄──── Name		Interface is used to describe functionality without implementation. Interface is the just like a template where you define different functions not the implementation. When a class implements the interface it also implements the functionality as per the requirement. Interface is represented by a circle as shown below. It has a name which is generally written below the circle.
4. **Use Case**	 (Place order)		A *use case* is a description of set of sequence of actions that a system performs that yields an observable result of value to a particular actor. Graphically, a use case is rendered as an ellipse with solid lines, usually including only its name.
5. **Collabora-**	 (Chain of responsibility)		Collaboration represents responsibilities. Generally responsibilities are in a group. Collaboration defines interaction between elements. Collaboration is represented by a dotted eclipse as shown below. It has a name written inside the eclipse.

6. Component	<<component>> ConversionManagement	A *component* is a physical and replaceable part of a system that conforms to and provides the realization of a set of interfaces. For example, COM+ components or Java Beans, as well as components that are artifacts of the development process, such as source code files. Component is used to represent any part of a system for which UML diagrams are made.
7. Node	Node Server ← — Name	A node can be defined as a physical element that exists at run time, generally having at least some memory and often, processing capability. Node is used to represent physical part of a system like server, network etc. A node in UML is represented by a square box as shown below with a name. A node represents a physical component of the system.

2.3.1.2 Behavioral Things

A behavioral thing consists of the dynamic parts of UML models. These are the verbs of a model, representing behavior over time and space.

Following are the behavioral things :

1. Interaction	Interaction is defined as a behavior that consists of a group of messages exchanged among elements to accomplish a specific task.
2. State	State machine is useful when the state of an object in its life cycle is important. It defines the sequence of states an object goes through in response to events. Events are external factors responsible for state change.

2.3.1.3 Grouping Things

Grouping things are the organizational parts of UML models. It can be defined as a mechanism to group elements of a UML model together.

There is only one grouping thing available :

| Package | 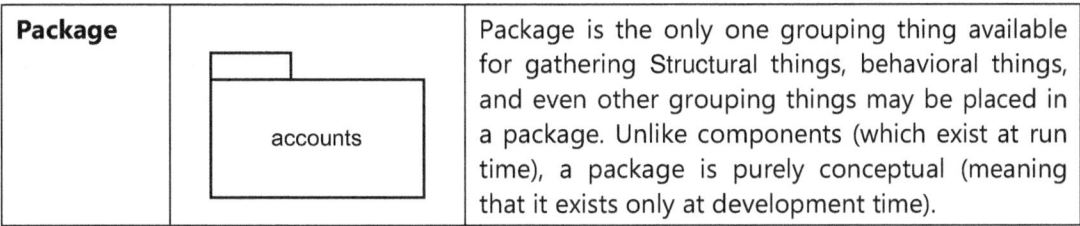 | Package is the only one grouping thing available for gathering Structural things, behavioral things, and even other grouping things may be placed in a package. Unlike components (which exist at run time), a package is purely conceptual (meaning that it exists only at development time). |

2.3.1.4 Annotational Things

Annotational things can be defined as a mechanism to capture remarks, descriptions, and comments of UML model elements.

Note : The only one Annotational thing available.

| Note | note | A note is used to render comments, constraints etc of an UML element. |

2.3.2 Relationship

Relationship is another most important building block of UML. It shows how elements are associated with each other and this association describes the functionality of an application. A model is not complete unless the relationships between elements are described properly. The Relationship gives a proper meaning to an UML model.

Following are the different types of relationships available in UML.

1. Dependency.
2. Association.
3. Generalization.
4. Realization.

(1) Dependency

A dependency is a semantic relationship between two things in which a change to one thing (the independent thing) may affect the semantics of the other thing (the dependent thing). Dependency is represented by a dotted arrow as shown below. The arrow head represents the independent element and the other end the dependent element.

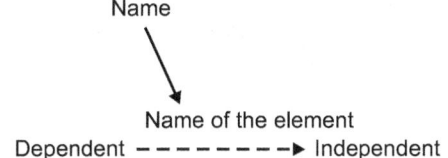

Name of the element
Dependent -- -- -- -- ▶ Independent

Dependency is used to represent dependency between two elements of a system.

(2) Association

An association is a structural relationship. An association is basically a set of links that connects elements of an UML model. It also describes how many objects are taking part in that relationship.

Association describes how the elements in an UML diagram are associated. Association is represented by a solid line with (without) arrows on both sides. The two ends represent two associated elements as shown below. The multiplicity is also mentioned at the ends (1, * etc) to show how many objects are associated. Association is used to represent the relationship between two elements of a system.

(3) Generalization

A generalization is a specialization/generalization relationship in which objects of the specialized element (the child) are substitutable for objects of the generalized element (the parent). Generalization is represented by an arrow with hollow arrow head as shown below. One end represents the parent element and the other end child element.

```
Child -----------▷ Parent
       Generalization
```

Generalization is used to describe parent-child relationship of two elements of a system.

(4) Realization

A realization is a semantic relationship between classifiers, wherein one classifier specifies a contract that another classifier guarantees to carry out.

You will encounter realization relationships in two places :

- Between interfaces and the classes or components that realize them, and
- Between use cases and the collaborations that realize them.

```
              Realization
Class -----------▷ Interface
```

2.3.3 UML Diagrams

UML diagrams are the ultimate output of the entire discussion. All the elements, relationships are used to make a complete UML diagram and the diagram represents a system. There are two broad categories of diagrams and then are again divided into sub-categories :

- Structural Diagrams.
- Behavioral Diagrams.
- Interaction diagrams.

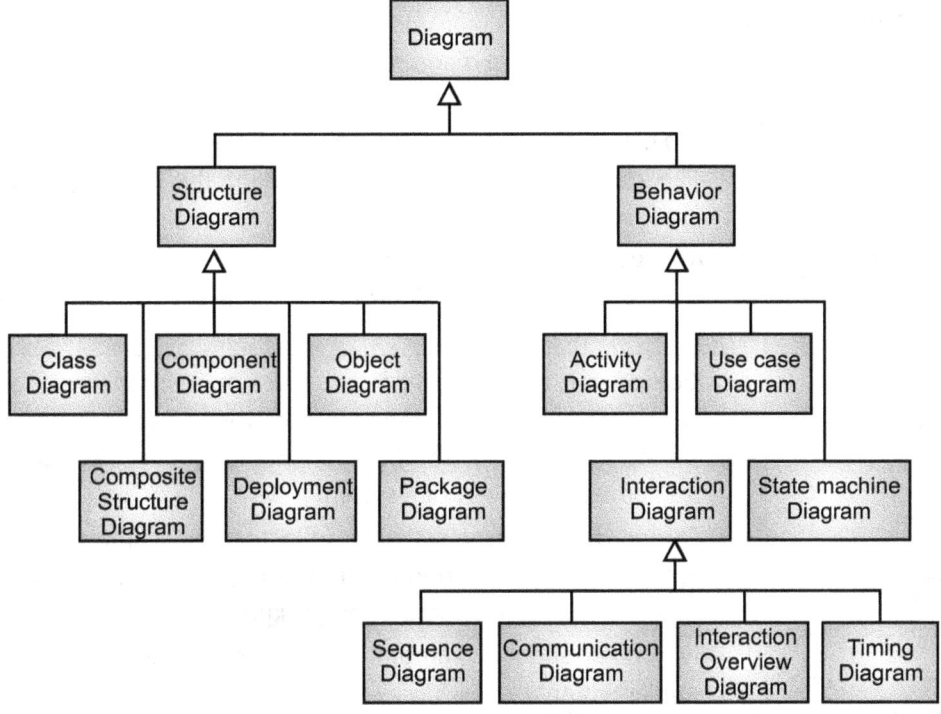

Fig. 2.2

2.3.3.1 Structural Diagrams

The structural diagrams represent the static aspect of the system. These static aspects represent those parts of a diagram which forms the main structure and therefore stable.

These static parts are represents by classes, interfaces, objects, components and nodes.

Class Diagram	<ul><li>Class diagrams are the most common diagrams used in UML.</li><li>Class diagram consists of classes, interfaces, associations and collaboration.</li><li>Class diagrams basically represent the object oriented view of a system which is static in nature.</li><li>Active class is used in a class diagram to represent the concurrency of the system.</li><li>Class diagram represents the object orientation of a system. So it is generally used for development purpose. This is the most widely used diagram at the time of system construction.</li></ul>

Object Diagram	• Object diagrams can be described as an instance of class diagram. So these diagrams are more close to real life scenarios where we implement a system. • Object diagrams are a set of objects and their relationships just like class diagrams and also represent the static view of the system. • The usage of object diagrams is similar to class diagrams but they are used to build prototype of a system from practical perspective.
Component Diagram	• Component diagrams represent a set of components and their relationships. These components consist of classes, interfaces or collaborations. So Component diagrams represent the implementation view of a system. • During design phase software artifacts (classes, interfaces etc) of a system are arranged in different groups depending upon their relationship. Now these groups are known as components. Finally, component diagrams are used to visualize the implementation.
Deployment Diagram	• Deployment diagrams are a set of nodes and their relationships. These nodes are physical entities where the components are deployed. • Deployment diagrams are used for visualizing deployment view of a system. This is generally used by the deployment team.
Composite Structure Diagram	• Depicts the internal structure of a classifier (such as a class, component, or use case), including the interaction points of the classifier to other parts of the system.
Package Diagram	• Shows how model elements are organized into packages as well as the dependencies between packages.

Note : If the above descriptions and usages are observed carefully then it is very clear that all the diagrams are having some relationship with one another. Component diagrams are dependent upon the classes, interfaces etc. which are part of class/object diagram. Again the deployment diagram is dependent upon the components which are used to make a component diagrams.

2.3.3.2 Behavioral Diagrams

Any system can have two aspects, static and dynamic. So a model is considered as complete when both the aspects are covered fully. Behavioral diagrams basically capture the dynamic aspect of a system. Dynamic aspect can be further described as the changing/moving parts of a system. UML has the following three types of behavioral diagrams :

Use Case Diagram	Use case diagrams are a set of use cases, actors and their relationships. They represent the use case view of a system. A use case represents a particular functionality of a system. So use case diagram is used to describe the relationships among the functionalities and their internal/external controllers. These controllers are known as actors.
State Machine Diagram	Any real time system is expected to be reacted by some kind of internal/external events. These events are responsible for state change of the system. State machine diagram is used to represent the event driven state change of a system. It basically describes the state change of a class, interface etc. State machine diagram is used to visualize the reaction of a system by internal/external factors.
Activity Diagram	Activity diagram describes the flow of control in a system. So it consists of activities and links. The flow can be sequential, concurrent or branched. Activities are nothing but the functions of a system. Numbers of activity diagrams are prepared to capture the entire flow in a system. Activity diagrams are used to visualize the flow of controls in a system. This is prepared to have an idea of how the system will work when executed.

2.3.3.3 Interaction Diagrams

A subset of behaviour diagrams which emphasize object interactions. There are four interaction diagrams as follows :

Sequence Diagram	A sequence diagram is an interaction diagram. From the name it is clear that the diagram deals with some sequences, which are the sequence of messages flowing from one object to another. Interaction among the components of a system is very important from implementation and execution perspective. So Sequence diagram is used to visualize the sequence of calls in a system to perform a specific functionality.

Communication Diagram	Communication diagram is another form of interaction diagram. It represents the structural organization of a system and the messages sent/received. Structural organization consists of objects and links. The purpose of Communication diagram is similar to sequence diagram. But the specific purpose of Communication diagram is to visualize the organization of objects and their interaction.
Timing Diagram	Depicts the change in state or condition of a classifier instance or role over time. Typically used to show the change in state of an object over time in response to external events.
Interaction Overview Diagram	A variant of an activity diagram which overviews the control flow within a system or business process. Each node/activity within the diagram can represent another interaction diagram.

Note : Dynamic nature of a system is very difficult to capture. So UML has provided features to capture the dynamics of a system from different angles. Sequence diagrams and collaboration diagrams are isomorphic so they can be converted from one another without losing any information. This is also true for state machine and activity diagram.

2.4 COMMON MECHANISMS IN THE UML : SPECIFICATIONS, ADORNMENTS, COMMON DIVISIONS

Specifications

- The UML is a graphical language. Rather, behind every part of its graphical notation there is a specification that provides a textual statement of the syntax and semantics of that building block.
- For example, behind a class icon is a specification that provides the full set of attributes, operations (including their full signatures), and behaviors that the class embodies; visually, that class icon might only show a small part of this specification. Furthermore, there might be another view of that class that presents a completely different set of parts yet is still consistent with the class's underlying specification.
- You use the UML's graphical notation to visualize a system; you use the UML's specification to state the system's details. Given this split, it's possible to build up a model incrementally by drawing diagrams and then adding semantics to the model's specifications, or directly by creating a specification, perhaps by reverse engineering an existing system, and then creating diagrams that are projections into those specifications.
- The UML's specifications provide a semantic backplane that contains all the parts of all the models of a system, each part related to one another in a consistent fashion. The

UML's diagrams are thus simply visual projections into that backplane, each diagram revealing a specific interesting aspect of the system.

Adornments

- Most elements in the UML have a unique and direct graphical notation that provides a visual representation of the most important aspects of the element.
- For example, the notation for a class is intentionally designed to be easy to draw, because classes are the most common element found in modeling object-oriented systems. The class notation also exposes the most important aspects of a class, namely its name, attributes, and operations.
- A class's specification may include other details, such as whether it is abstract or the visibility of its attributes and operations. Many of these details can be rendered as graphical or textual adornments to the class's basic rectangular notation.
- For example, Fig. 2.3 shows a class, adorned to indicate that it is an abstract class with two public, one protected, and one private operation.

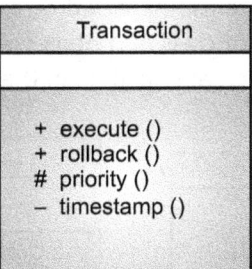

Fig. 2.3

- Every element in the UML's notation starts with a basic symbol, to which can be added a variety of adornments specific to that symbol.

Adornments are textual or graphical items that are added to an element's basic notation and are used to visualize details from the element's specification. For example, the basic notation for an association is a line, but this may be adorned with such details as the role and multiplicity of each end. In using the UML, the general rule to follow is this: Start with the basic notation for each element and then add other adornments only as they are necessary to convey specific information that is important to your model.

Most adornments are rendered by placing text near the element of interest or by adding a graphic symbol to the basic notation. However, sometimes you'll want to adorn an element with more detail than can be accommodated by simple text or graphics. In the case of such things as classes, components, and nodes, you can add an extra compartment below the usual compartments to provide this information, as Fig. 2.4 shows.

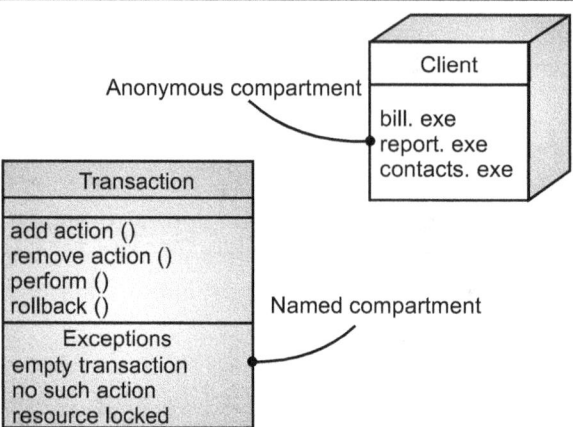

Fig. 2.4 : Extra compartments

Common Divisions

- In modeling object-oriented systems, the world often gets divided in at least a couple of ways. First, there is the division of class and object. A class is an abstraction; an object is one concrete manifestation of that abstraction. In the UML, you can model classes as well as objects, as shown in Fig. 2.5.

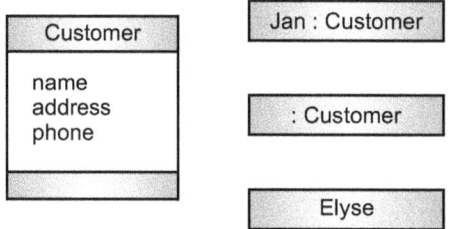

Fig. 2.5 : Class with object(s)

- In this figure, there is one class, named Customer, together with three objects: Jan (which is marked explicitly as being a Customer object), :Customer (an anonymous Customer object), and Elyse (which in its specification is marked as being a kind of Customer object, although it's not shown explicitly here).

2.5 EXTENSIBILITY MECHANISMS

The UML provides a standard language for writing software blueprints, but it is not possible for one closed language to ever be sufficient to express all possible nuances of all models across all domains. For this reason, the UML is open-ended, making it possible for you to extend the language in controlled ways.

The UML's extensibility mechanisms include :

1. Stereotypes

2. Tagged values
3. Constraints
4. Profiles

2.5.1 Stereotypes

- A stereotype extends the vocabulary of the UML, allowing you to create new kinds of building blocks that are derived from existing ones but that are specific to your problem.
- Stereotypes signify a special use or intent and can be applied to almost any element of UML notation, such as classes, use cases, components, associations, dependency relationships and so forth. Stereotypes modify the meaning of an element and describe the element's role within your model.
- The stereotype is shown using guillemots at either end of the stereotype name, as in «stereotype_name»

For Example : If you are working in a programming language, such as Java you will often want to model interfaces. Interfaces are just abstract classes, although they are treated in very special ways. Typically, you only want to show abstract view, nothing else. You can make interfaces first class citizens in your models meaning that they are treated like basic building blocks by marking them with an appropriate stereotype, as for the interface *sorting*.

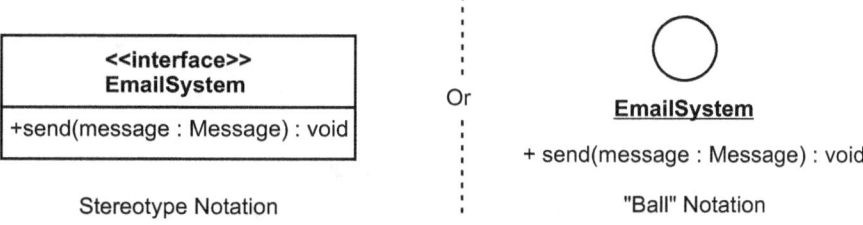

Fig. 2.6 : Shows representation of interface by sterotyping class thing

2.5.2 Tagged Value

Tagged values are properties attached to UML elements. A tagged value is an extra property that can be added to UML element, so that you can specify additional information that you normally could not. The information can be used both by human beings and machines. Human beings can use them to add administrative information about the models, such as author of a model, the time it was last modified, and so on. Machines can use them to process the models in a certain way.

For example, code generation might be parameterized by properties in the model to indicate what kind of code to generate. Note that properties are normally not present in the finished system. They contain information about the models and the elements in the models, not information that should be handled by the final system. A tagged value explicitly defines a property as a name-value pair. In a tagged value, the name is referred to as the tag. Each tag represents a particular kind of property applicable to one or more kinds of elements. Both the tag and the value are encoded as strings. The notation for a property is {tag = value} or {tag1 = value1, tag2 = value2...} or {tag}.

For example :

    {status = "under construction", system analyst = "Bob Smith"}

2.5.3 Constraint

A constraint is a semantic condition or restriction on elements. Constraints are applied to elements using an expression; one constraint applies to one kind of element. Thus, while a constraint can involve many elements, they must be of the same. The constraints are displayed in braces ({constraint}), either directly in the diagrams or separately (typically available through a constraint window in a development support tool). A constraint can be displayed directly in the diagram next to the view element it constrains. If many elements of the same kind are involved in a constraint, the constraint should be displayed near a dashed line that crosses all the elements involved in the constraint.

For example, you might need to show that a boss must have a higher salary than his or her assistant, and this could be shown as {person.boss.salary >= person.assistant.salary} next to the salary attribute. The UML specification uses OCL to express constraints on modeling elements.

2.5.4 Profiles

- UML specification is not broad and detailed enough to encompass all of the modeling aspects for every particular programming platform or modeling domain. To satisfy these needs, UML can be extended.
- The UML metamodel is extended with three basics stereotypes, tagged values, and constraints.
- When you group a set of these extensions to model a specific platform or domain, you create a profile. It can be thought of creating new language to the UML.
- Profiles can be built to model the peculiarities of various platforms (such as J2EE and .NET), vertical domains (such as the banking telecommunication, and aerospace), and modeling domains (such as system engineering, real-time analysis and design, and testing).
- In theory there are unlimited numbers of profiles. Modelers may create their own profiles, and modeling tools vendors may introduce profiles into their tools to model certain aspect of modeling.

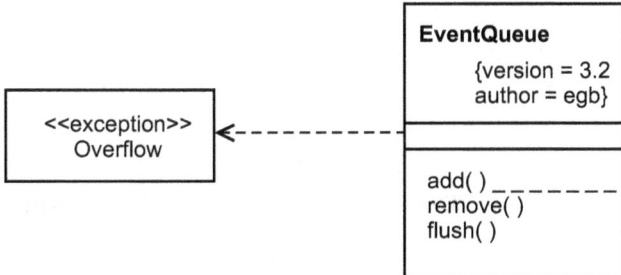

Fig. 2.7 : Shows tagged value and profiles

2.6 OBJECT CONSTRAINT LANGUAGE

OCL Basics, OCL Syntax, Advanced OCL Modeling

OCL is a language that allows to extra information to UML mode. It allows to do following things :

- Write queries to access model elements and their values.
- State constrints on model elements.
- Define query operation.

You can't specify the behaviour with OCL. It is not action language for UML. OCL does not alter the values of the model. OCL can't define the operation other query operation. OCL only execute the query operation that doesn't change the values. OCL can't be used to define the business rules at runtime.

There are several reasons why OCL is useful :

- OCL allows modelling tool to generate code based on OCL expressions such as preconditions and post conditions.
- OCL helps to make modelling more precise.
- OCL is a part OCUP(OMG Certified UML Professional).

There are reasons why OCL is not useful :

- Hard to understand due to odd shortcuts.
- Most of modelers are not familiar with OCL.
- Object constraint Language provides the semantics for declaring static requirements for attributes and operations.

If constraints are expressed in a standard and predictable way, then user and automated tools can understand the constraint. This allows automatic checking of constraints in your diagrams and in the code generated from the diagrams.

OCL developed at IBM for business modeling.

Building blocks of OCL expressions.

1. OCL has four built-in types: Boolean, Integer, Real and String.
2. OCL has the basic arithmetic, logic, and comparison operators. OCL also has more advanced functions such as returning the maximum of two values and concatenating Strings. OCL is a typed language, so the operator has to make sense for its values. For example, you can't take the sum of an Integer and a Boolean.

Group	Operators	Used with Types	Example OCL Expression
Arithmetic	+, -, *, /	Integer, Real	baseCost + tax
Additional Arithmetic	abs(), max(), min( )	Integer, Real	score1.max(score2)
Comparison	<, <=, >, >=	Integer, Real	rate > .75
Equality	=, <>	All	age = 65 title <> 'CEO'
Boolean	and, or, xor, not	Boolean	isMale and (age >= 65)
String	concat( ), size( ), substring( ), toInteger( ), toReal( )	String	title.substring(1,3)

Constraints

In UML diagrams, OCL is primarily used to write constraints in class diagrams and guard conditions in state and activity diagrams.

There are three types of constraint that can be applied to class members using OCL :

Invariants

Invariants are defined on class attributes. An invariant is a constraint that must always be true; otherwise the system is in an invalid state. For example, rating must be always greater than or equals to 0.

Preconditions

A precondition is a constraint that is defined on a method and is checked before the method executes. Preconditions are frequently used to validate input parameters to a method.

Postconditions

A postcondition is also defined on a method and is checked after the method executes. Postconditions are frequently used to describe how values were changed by a method. Constraints are specified using either the OCL statement in curly brackets next to the class member or in a separate note, as shown in Fig. 2.6.

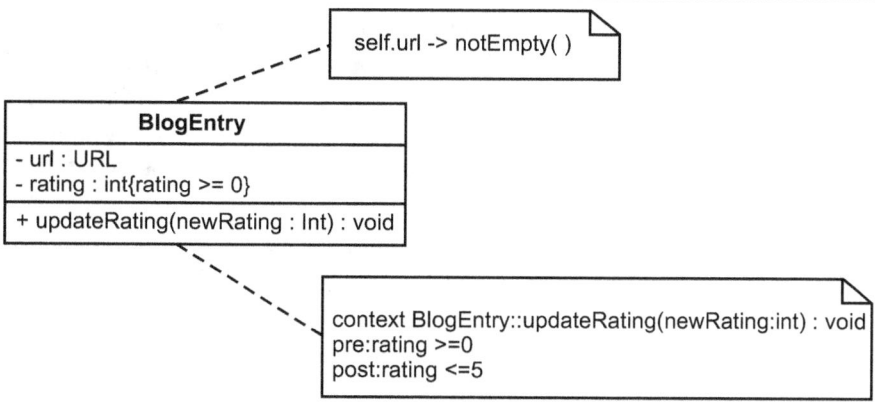

Fig. 2.8 : Shows contraint on classes

References

- Synergy Learning & Gentleware AG 2006.
- Unified Modeling Language User Guide by Grady Booch, James Rambaug, Ivar Jacobson, Publisher Addison Wesley
- UML in a Nutshell, O'Reilly publisher

REVIEW QUESTIONS

1. Describe relationships.
2. Define UML 2.0
3. Explain new features of UML 2.0.
4. Write short note on UML profile and OCL.
5. What do you understand by UML goals: executable UML, Extensibility?
6. Explain Basic building block of UML 2.0.
7. What was the need for standardization in context of UML?

Ans. : Large enterprise applications must be structured in a way that enables scalability, security, and robust execution under stressful conditions, and their structure and architecture must be defined clearly enough that maintenance programmers can quickly find and fix a bug that shows up long after the original authors have moved on to other projects. Modeling is an Essential Part of large software projects, and helpful to medium and even small projects as well.

The process of gathering and analyzing an application's requirements, and incorporating them into a program design, is a complex one and the industry currently supports many *methodologies* that define formal procedures specifying how to go about it. One characteristic of UML – is that it has wide spread industry support.

It is that it is *methodology-independent*. Regardless of the methodology that you use to perform your analysis and design, you can use UML to express the results. And, using XMI (XML Metadata Interchange, another OMG standard), you can transfer your UML model from one tool into a repository, or into another tool for refinement or the next step in your chosen development process. These are the benefits of standardization.

Developing UML standards is an important first step in achieving consistency and efficiency in an enterprise. Consistent modeling means consistent understanding between the modelers and their audience.

8. Give following four OCL concepts/notations with example of your own to explain the concepts represented by the notation.

(i) Let, (ii) Context, (iii) Reject, (iv) Set.

Ans. : The Object Constraint Language - the **OCL** is used to specify constraints on objects in the **UML.**

(i) let expression

To define a variable that can be used in the constraint. The scope is the OCL expression.

context Person **inv** :

let income : Integer = self.job.salary->sum() **in**

if isUnemployed **then**

income < 100

else

income >= 100

endif

(ii) Context

All classifiers (types, classes, interfaces, associations, datatypes, from an UML model are types in the OCL expressions that are attached to the model. Each OCL expression is written in the context of an instance of a specific type

context Person

...

(iii) Reject

Reject Operation on a Collection.

Obtains the subset of all elements of the collection for which a Boolean expression evaluates to False.

Alternative expressions for the reject operation.

collection->reject(Boolean-expression)

collection->reject(v | Boolean-expression-with-v)

collection->reject(v: Type | Boolean-expression-with-v)

The collection of employees of a company who have not at least 18 years old is empty

context Company inv:

self.employee->reject(age>=18)->isEmpty()

A reject expression can always be restated as a select with the negated expression

(**reject**): c->reject(v : T | b(v)):: Collection(T) = c->select(v:T | not(e(v))).

context *TypeName* **inv**:

(iv) Set

OCL includes a set of supplementary predefined types.

Collection: an abstract type with four concrete collection types.

Set: the mathematical set (without duplicate elements).

Set {1 , 2 , 5} Set {`apple', `orange', `strawberry'}

OrderedSet: a set in which the elements are ordered by their position.

OrderedSet {5, 4, 3, 2, 1}

Set Operations

S, S_1, S_2 are values of type Set(t), B is a value of type Bag(t), v is a value of type t.

	Signature	**Semantics**
union	Set(t) × Set(t) → Set(t)	$S_1 \cap S_2$
union	Set(t) × Bag(t) → Bag(t)	$S \cup B$
intersection	Set(t) × Set(t) → Set(t)	$S_1 \cap S_2$
intersection	Set(t) × Bag(g) → Set(t)	$S \cup B$
-	Set(t) × Set(t) → Set(t)	$S_1 \cap S_2$
aymmetricDifference	Set(t) × Set(t) → Set(t)	$(S_1 - S_2) \cup (S_2 - S_1)$
including	Set(t) × t → Set(t)	$S \cup \{v\}$
excluding	Set(t) × t → Set(t)	$S - \{v\}$
aaSet	Set(t) → Set(t)	
aaOrderSet	Set(t) → OrderSet(t)	
aaBag	Set(t) → Bag(t)	
aaSequence	Set(t) → Sequence(t)	

9. Write short notes on UML profiles (illustrate with examples from web development as a domain to extent UML).
10. Illustrate new UML 2.0 features; input and output PINS, manifest.
11. What do these terms mean OCL, OCL invariant, For all?
12. Limitations of UML 1.3 which were overcome in UML 2.0.
13. Need for modeling, planning software system before constructing them.
14. What changes have development diagrams undergone from UML 1.3 to UML 2.0?
15. How do UML profiles help customization of UML?
16. With own examples explain extensibility mechanisms of UML.

UNIT - III
CLASS DIAGRAM AND COMPOSITE STRUCTURE DIAGRAM

3.1 OBJECT DIAGRAM

Terms and Concepts

An object diagram describes a set of objects and their relationships at a particular point in time. Graphically, an object diagram is a collection of vertices and arcs.

Common Properties
- An object diagram is having common properties like all other diagrams.
- It is a special kind of diagram.
- It differentiates from others due to its contents.

Contents

Objects are at the heart of any object-oriented system at runtime. When the system you designed is actually in use, objects make-up its parts and bring all of your carefully designed classes to life. An object diagram shows a set of objects and their relationships at a specific point in time.

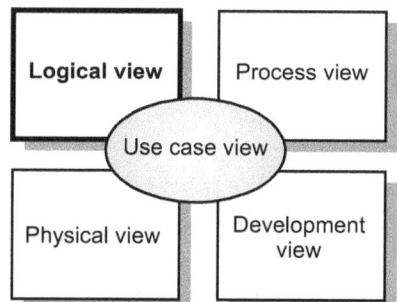

Fig. 3.1 : 4+1 Architectural view

To draw an object diagram, the first things you need to add are the actual objects themselves. Object notation is actually very simple if you are already familiar with class notation; an object is shown with a rectangle, just like a class, but to show that this is an instance of a class rather than the class itself, the title is underlined as shown in Fig. 3.2.

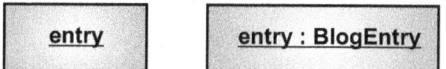

Fig. 3.2 : Representation of objects in UML

- An Object is a representation of an entity.
- Each object in a system has three characteristics : state, behavior, and identity.
- The State of an object is one of the possible conditions in which it may exist.

- The state of an object typically changes over time.

Anonymous Objects

Anonymous objects are typically useful when the name of the object is not important within the context that it is being used.

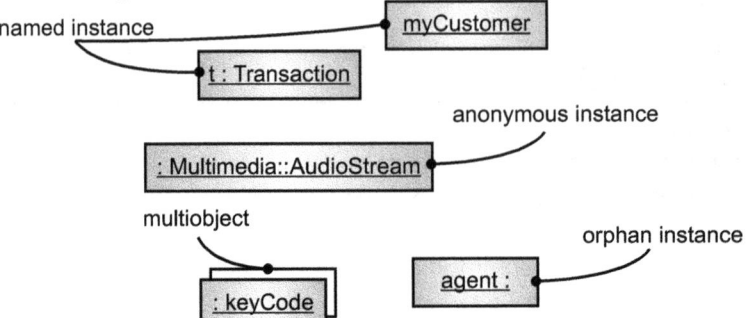

Fig. 3.3 : Representation of different types of objects

For example, it is a common programming idiom when you create an event handler in Java using an anonymous object because you do not care what the name of the object is, just that it is registered with the appropriate event source as shown in :

```
with a JButton
public void initialiseUI( ) {

  //... Other method implementation code ...

  JButton button = new Jbutton("Submit");
  button.addActionListener(new ActionListener{
    public void actionPerformed(ActionEvent e)
    {
      System.out.println("The button was pressed so it's time to do something ...");
    }
  });

  //... Other method implementation code ...

}
```

Links and Constraints

Objects on their own are not very interesting or helpful. To really show how your objects will work together in a particular runtime configuration, you need to tie those objects together using links, as shown in Fig. 3.4.

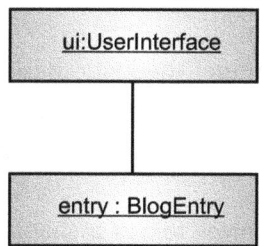

Fig. 3.4 : Links are shown using a line between the two objects that are being linked

Links between objects correspond to associations between the object's classes. This means that where constraint rules have been applied to an association, the link must keep to those rules.

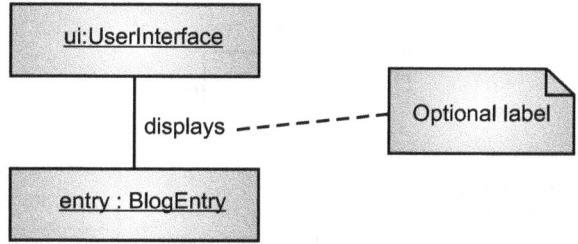

Fig. 3.5 : To play some tunes, a Blog Entry object is connected to a User Interface object

An object diagram is essentially an instance of a class diagram or the static part of an interaction diagram.

Examples of Object Diagram

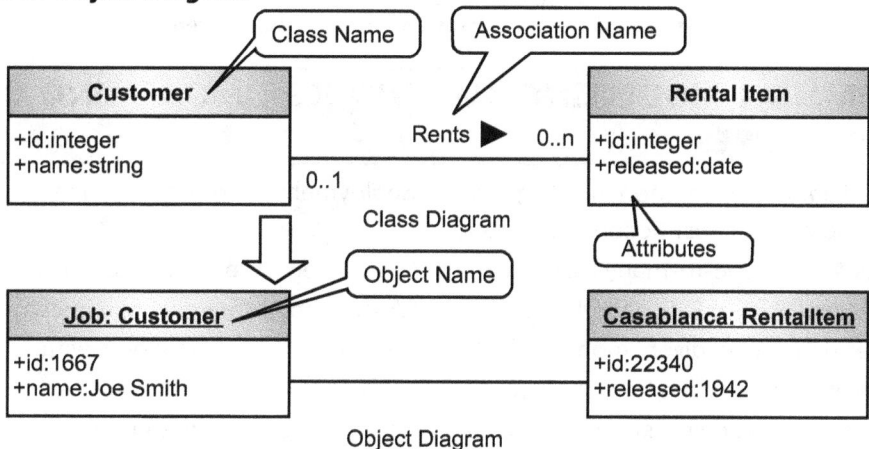

Fig. 3.6 : Shows how to convert class diagram into object diagram

Common Uses

- Object diagrams are used to model the static design view or static process view of a system.
- This view primarily supports the functional requirements of a system.
- To model object structures.
- Modelling object structures involves taking a snapshot of the objects in a system at a given moment in time.
- An object diagram represents one static frame in the dynamic storyboard represented by an interaction diagram.
- You use object diagrams to visualize, specify, construct and document the existence of certain instances in your system, together with their relationships to one another.

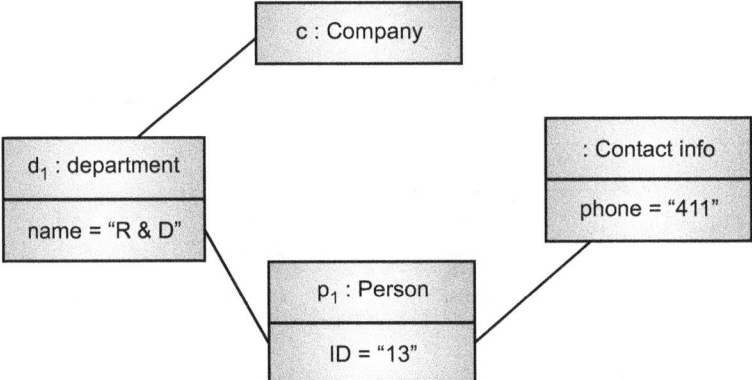

Fig. 3.7 : Object diagram for organization system

3.2 COMMON MODELLING TECHNIQUES : MODELLING OBJECT STRUCTURES

- Class diagram, a component diagram or deployment diagrams are really useful for capturing a set of abstractions as a group.
- If class A has a one-to-many association to class B, then for one instance of A there might be five instances of B; for another instance of A there might be only one instance of B.
- Furthermore, at a given moment in time, that instance of A, along with the related instances of B, will each have certain values for their attributes and state machines.
- If you freeze a running system or just imagine a moment of time in a modelled system, you will find a set of objects, each in a specific state, and each in a particular relationship to other objects.

- You can use object diagrams to visualize, specify, construct, and document the structure of these objects. Object diagrams are especially useful for modelling complex data structures.
- When you model your system's design view, a set of class diagrams can be used to completely specify the semantics of your abstractions and their relationships. With object diagrams, however, you cannot completely specify the object structure of your system. For an individual class, there may be a multitude of possible instances and for a set of classes in relationship to one another, there may be many times more possible configurations of these objects. Therefore, when you use object diagrams, you can only meaningfully expose interesting sets of concrete or prototypical objects. This is what it means to model an object structure
- An object diagram shows one set of objects in relation to one another at one moment in time.

To Model an Object Structure
- Identify the mechanism you'd like to model. A mechanism represents some function or behaviour of the part of the system you are modeling that results from the interaction of a society of classes, interfaces and other things.
- For each mechanism, identify the classes, interfaces and other elements that participate in this collaboration; identify the relationships among these things as well.
- Consider one scenario that walks through this mechanism. Freeze that scenario at a moment in time and render each object that participates in the mechanism.
- Expose the state and attribute values of each such object as necessary to understand the scenario.
- Similarly, expose the links among these objects, representing instances of associations among them.

3.3 CLASS DIAGRAM

Terms and Concepts

A class describes a set of classes, interfaces, and collaborations and their relationships. Graphically, a class diagram is a collection of vertices and arcs.

Common Properties

A class diagram is just a special kind of diagram and shares the same common properties as do all other diagrams. What distinguishes a class diagram from all other kinds of diagrams is its particular content.

Contents

Class diagrams commonly contain the following things :
- Classes.
- Interfaces.

- Collaborations.
- Dependency, generalization, and association relationships.

Like all other diagrams, class diagrams may contain notes and constraints.

Class diagrams may also contain packages or subsystems, both of which are used to group elements of your model into larger chunks. Sometimes, you will want to place instances in your class diagrams as well, especially when you want to visualize the (possibly dynamic) type of an instance.

- Classes are at the heart of any object-oriented system.
- A system's structure is made-up of a collection of pieces often referred to as *objects*.
- Class diagrams shows a set of classes, interfaces and collaborations and their relationships.
- Graphically, a class diagram is a collection of vertices and arcs.
- A class represents a group of things that have common state and behavior. You can think of a class as a blueprint for an object in an object-oriented system.
- In UML speak; a class is a kind of *classifier*. For example, Volkswagen, Toyota and Ford are all cars, so you can represent them using a class named Car.
- Each specific type of car is an *instance* of that class, or an *object*.

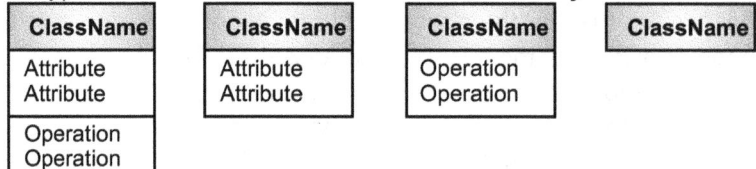

Fig. 3.8 : Various ways to represent class

You represent a class with a rectangular box divided into *compartments* (see Fig 3.8).

- The first compartment holds the name of the class.
- The second compartment holds attributes.
- The third compartment is used for operations/modules.

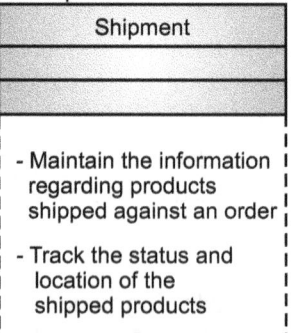

Fig. 3.9 : Class notation with responsibilities

There is Fourth Optional compartment, which used to show responsibilities (see Fig. 3.9). The responsibility compartment shown by dotted line. You can hide any compartment of the class if that increases the readability of your diagram, it does not mean it is empty. You may add compartments to a class to show additional information, such as exceptions or events, though this is outside of the typical notation.

Visibility

One of the most important details you can specify for a classifier's attributes and operations is its visibility. The visibility of a feature specifies whether it can be used by other classifiers. In the UML, you can specify any of four levels of visibility.

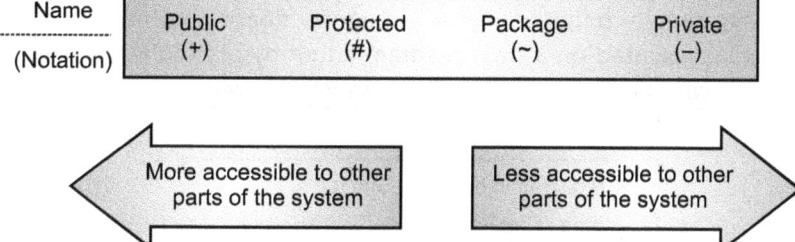

Fig. 3.10 : UML's four different visibility classifications

	Name	Notation Description
1.	Public	Any outside classifier with visibility to the given classifier can use the feature specified by rendering the symbol **+**.
2.	Protected	Any descendant of the classifier can use the feature; specified by rendering the symbol **#**.
3.	Private	Only the classifier itself can use the feature; specified by rendering the symbol **-**.
4.	Package	Any classifier in the same package, and its descendant can use the feature **~**.

The First Compartment : Class Name

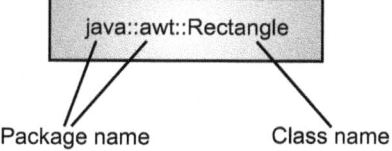

Fig. 3.11 : Class example

UML suggests that the class name :

- A class name may be text consisting of any number of letters, numbers, and certain punctuation marks (except for marks such as the double colon, which is used to separate a class name and the name of its enclosing package) and may continue over several lines.

In practice, class names are short nouns or noun phrases drawn from the vocabulary of the system you are modeling.
- Start with a capital letter.
- Be centered in the top compartment.
- Be written in a boldface font.
- Be written in italics if the class is *abstract*.

3.3.1 The Second Compartment Class State

Attributes

A class's attributes are the pieces of information that represent the state of an object. Attributes can be simple primitive types (integers, floating-point numbers etc.) These attributes can be represented on a class diagram either by placing them inside their section of the class box known as inline attributes or by association with another class.

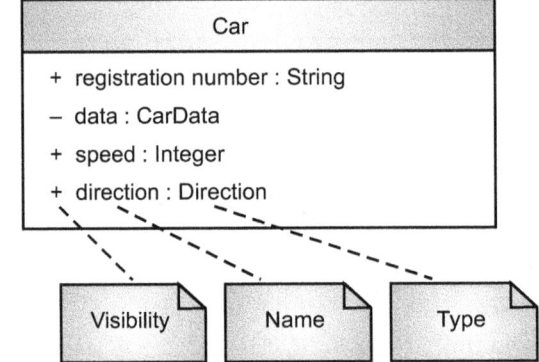

Fig. 3.12 : Class diagram which shows inline attribute

3.3.2 The Third Compartment Class Behavior : Operations

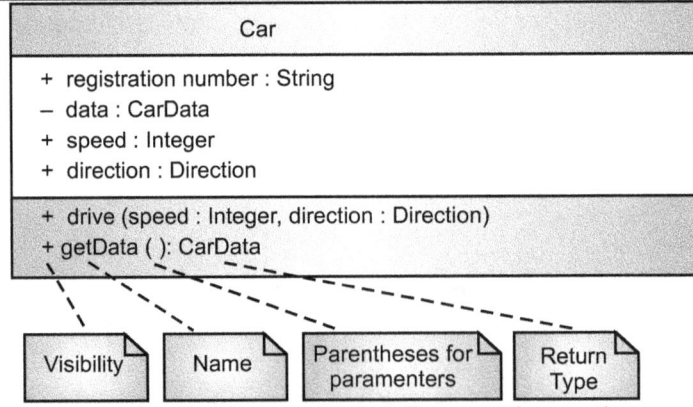

Fig. 3.13 : The class car has attributes and operations

Operations manipulate the attributes or perform other actions. Operations are normally called functions, but they are inside a class and can be applied only to objects of that class. An operation is described with a return-type, a name and zero or more parameters. Together, the visibility property, return-type, name and a pair of parentheses with zero or more than parameters are the signature of the operation. The signature describes everything needed for the operation.

The operations in a class describe what the class can do (not how), that is, what services it offers; thus they could be seen as the interface to the class. Just like an attribute, an operation can have visibility and scope.

The operation drive has two parameters, *speed* and *direction*. The operation getData has a return type, CarData.

Note : Forward engineering is the process of transforming a model into code through a mapping to an implementation language. Forward engineering results in a loss of information, because models written in the UML are semantically richer than any current object-oriented programming language. In fact, this is a major reason why you need models in addition to code. Structural features, such as collaborations, and behavioral features, such as interactions can be visualized clearly in the UML, but not so clearly from raw code.

If the Car class in Fig. 3.13 was going to be implemented as a Java class in software, then the source code would look something like that shown below on the next page :

```
public class Car
{
    // The four attributes from Fig. 3.13
    public String registration_number
    private CarData data;
    public int speed;
    public Direction direction;
    //Implementation of methods of class car
    public drive(int speed, Direction direction)
    {
    ....
    }
public Cardata getData()
    {
    ...
    }
}
```

3.3.3 Abstract, Root, Leaf and Polymorphic Classes

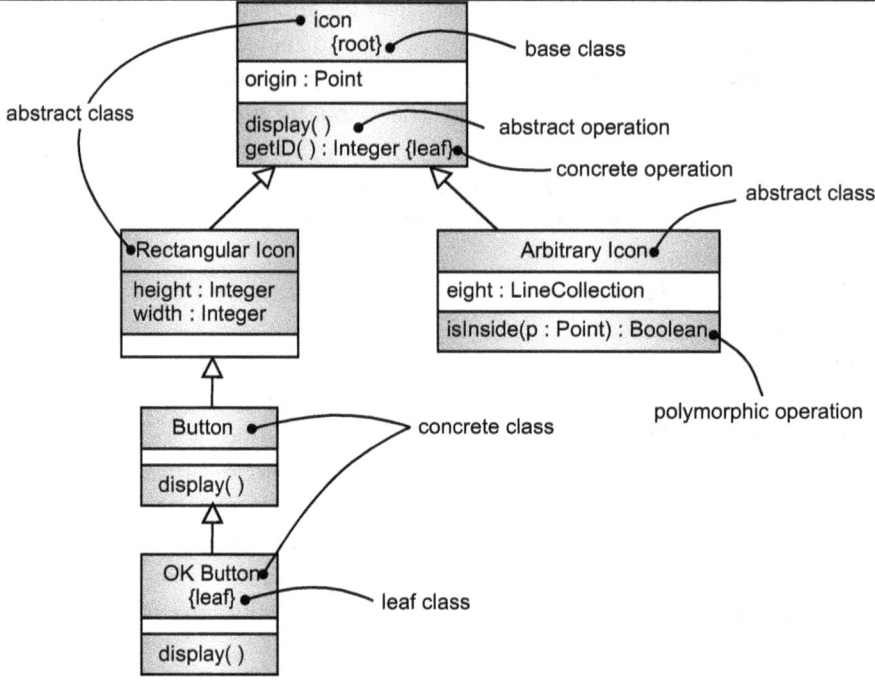

Fig. 3.14 : Abstract and concrete classes and operations

You use generalization relationships to model a lattice of classes, with more-generalized abstractions at the top of the hierarchy and more-specific ones at the bottom. Within these hierarchies, it's common to specify that certain classes are abstract meaning that they may not have any direct instances. In the UML, you specify that a class is abstract by writing its name in italics. For example, as Fig. 3.14 shows, *Icon, RectangularIcon,* and *ArbitraryIcon* are all abstract classes. By contrast a concrete class (such as Button and OK Button) is one that may have direct instances. Whenever you use a class, you will probably want to inherit features from other, more-general, classes and have other, more-specific, classes inherit features from it. These are the normal semantics you get from classes in the UML. However, you can also specify that a class may have no children. Such an element is called a leaf class and is specified in the UML by writing the property leaf below the class's name. For example, in the Fig. 3.14, OKButton is a leaf class, so it may have no children. Less common but still useful is the ability to specify that a class may have no parents. Such an element is called a root class and is specified in the UML by writing the property root below the class's name. For example, in the Fig. 3.14 Icon is a root class. Especially when you have multiple, independent inheritance lattices, it's useful to designate the head of each hierarchy in this manner.

3.4 RELATIONSHIPS

A relationship is a connection among things. In object-oriented modeling, the three most important relationships are dependencies, generalizations and associations.

Graphically, a relationship is rendered as a path, with different kinds of lines used to distinguish the kinds of relationships.

These relationships are the basic relational building blocks of the UML. You use them to write well-formed models.

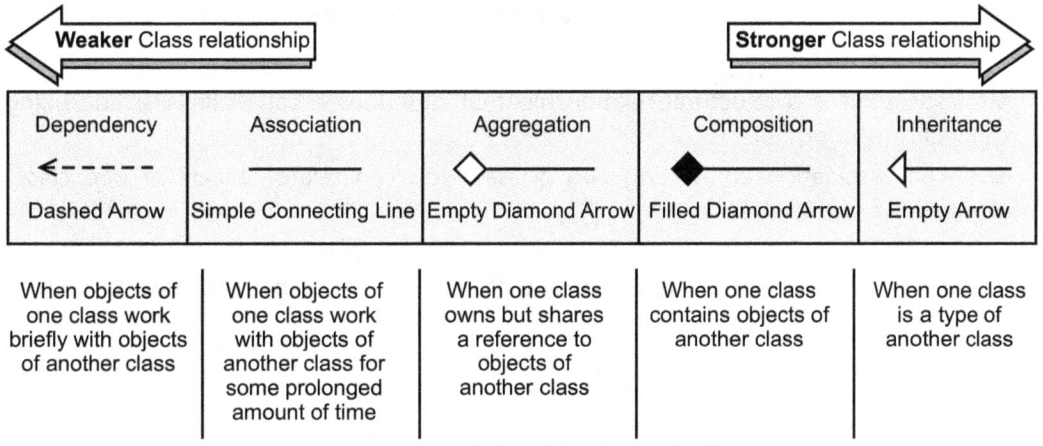

Fig. 3.15 : Relationships in nutshell

3.4.1 Dependency

- A *dependency* is a semantic relationship between two things in which a change to one thing (the independent thing) may affect the semantics of the other thing (the dependent thing).
- Most often, you will use dependencies between classes to show that one class uses operations from another class or it uses variables or arguments typed by the other class.
- Graphically, a dependency is rendered as a dashed line, possibly directed and occasionally including a label as shown below :

---------->

Dependency implies only that objects of a class can work together; therefore, it is considered to be the weakest direct relationship that can exist between two classes.

For Example

If the Person class of the Bank Management System needed to work with a Personal Information class's object then this dependency would be drawn using the dependency arrow as shown in Fig. 3.16.

The Fig. 3.16 depicts the method get Personal Info of class Person is dependent on the object of Personal Information class for required service.

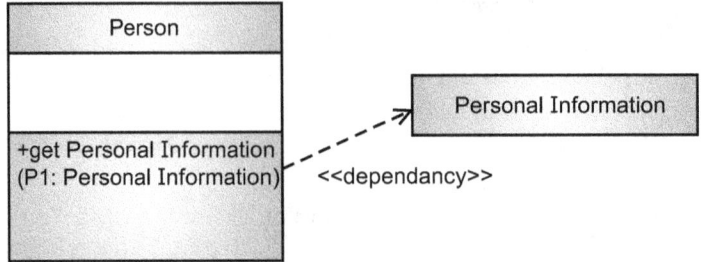

Fig. 3.16 : Dependency relationship between the classifier

3.4.2 Association

- An association is a structural relationship that describes a set of links, a link being a connection among objects.
- Given an association connecting two classes, you can relate objects of one class to objects of the other class.
- Graphically, an association is rendered as a solid line connecting two classes, possibly directed, occasionally including a label and often containing other adornments, such as
    (1) Multiplicity and
    (2) Role names as shown in Fig. 3.17.

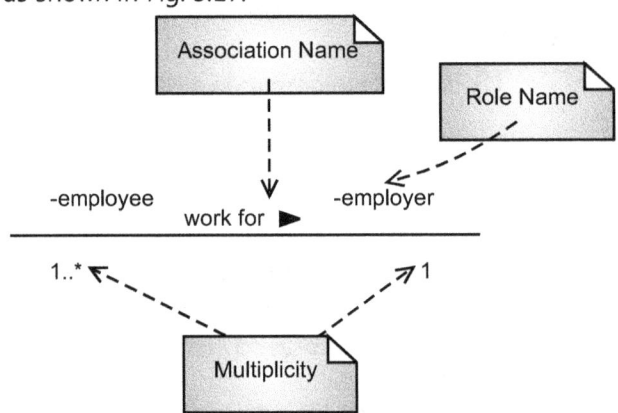

Fig. 3.17 : Associations relationship with its adornments

Role

When a class participates in an association, it has a specific role that it plays in that relationship.

A role is just the face the class at the near end of the association presents to the class at the other end of the association.

In Fig. 3.17 a person playing the role of employee is associated with a company playing the role of employer.

3.4.2.1 Multiplicity

An association represents a structural relationship among objects. In many modeling situations, it's important for you to state how many objects may be connected across an instance of an association. This "how many" is called the multiplicity of an association's role and is written as an expression that evaluates to a range of values or an explicit value as in Fig. 3.18. Although dependency simply allows one class to use objects of another class, association means that a class will actually contain a reference to an object, or objects, of the other class in the form of an attribute. If you find yourself saying that a class works with an object of another class, then the relationship between those classes is a great candidate for association rather than just a dependency (See Fig. 3.18).

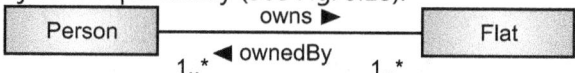

Fig. 3.18 : Association relationship

Converting above model in JAVA code (Forward Engineering) we obtain,

```
public class Person {
    public Flat owns;
    // ... Other Attributes and Methods declared here ...
}
public class Flat {
    public Person ownedBy;
    // ... Other Attributes and Methods declared here ...
}
```

3.4.2.2 Navigability

Navigability is often applied to an association relationship to describe which class contains the attribute that supports the relationship. You can explicitly forbid navigation from one class to another by placing a small X on the association line at the end of the class you can not navigate to. Thus if we want to say that "person owns zero or many flats," but we do not want to say anything explicitly about flat being 'owned by' persons. We can draw the following diagram.

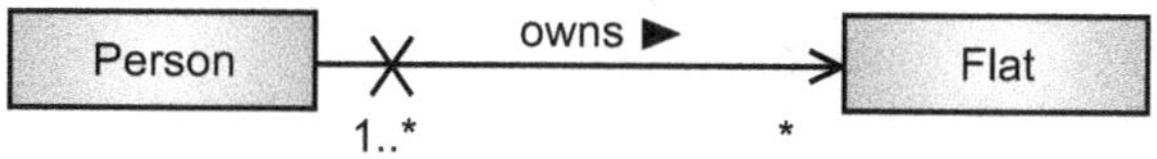

Fig. 3.19 : Association with navigability

Converting above model in JAVA code (Forward Engineering) we obtain,

```
public class Person {
    public Flat owns;
    // ... Other Attributes and Methods declared here ...
}
public class Flat {
```

// ... Other Attributes and Methods declared here ...
}

3.4.3 Aggregation

It is invariant of association relationship, which shows 'whole-part' relationship between two classifiers. Aggregation is really just a stronger version of association and is used to indicate that a class actually 'owns a' but may share objects of another class. Aggregation is shown by using an empty diamond arrowhead next to the owning class, as shown in Fig. 3.20. It shows that Team owns a player but players can also be part of another team like Mumbai Ranaji team, Maharashtra state team, IPL team etc. (see Fig. 3.20)

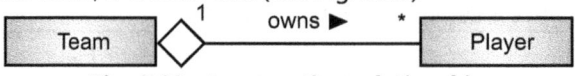

Fig. 3.20 : Aggregation relationship

3.4.4 Composition

Composition is an even stronger relationship than aggregation, although they work in very similar ways. Composition is shown using a closed or filled, diamond arrowhead as shown in Fig. 3.21.

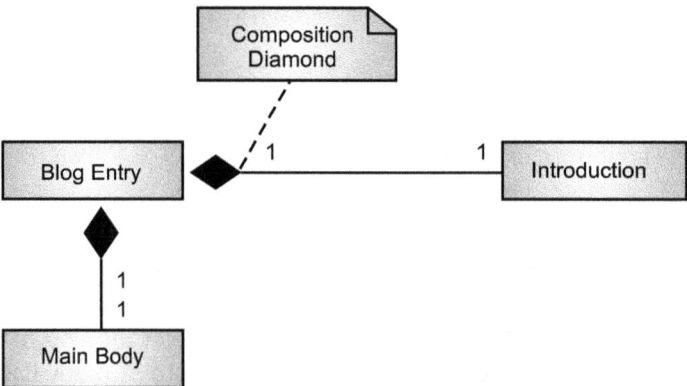

Fig. 3.21 : Composition relationship

In composition relationship parts cannot be shared by another system parts. If we delete 'part' then there will be no existence of 'whole'.

3.4.5 Generalization

- A generalization is a specialization/generalization relationship in which objects of the specialized element (the child) are substitutable for objects of the generalized element (the parent). It also known as Inheritance.
- In this way, the child shares the structure and the behavior of the parent. Graphically, a generalization relationship is rendered as a solid line with a hollow arrowhead pointing to the parent, as in Fig. 3.22.

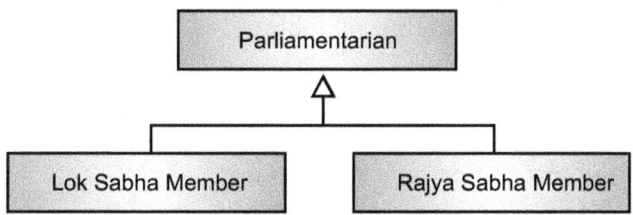

Fig. 3.22 : Specialization/generalization relationship

3.4.6 Realization

- A realization is a semantic relationship between classifiers, wherein one classifier specifies a contract that another classifier guarantees to carry out.
- You will encounter realization relationships in two places :
  (1) Between interfaces and the classes or components that realize them, and
  (2) Between use cases and the collaborations that realize them.
- Graphically, a realization relationship is rendered as a cross between a generalization and a dependency relationship.
- You show realization using a dashed line starting at the realizing classifier and leading to the interface, with a closed arrowhead at the end, as shown below.

----------▷

Instead, a class is said to *realize* an interface if it provides an implementation for the operations and properties. Fig. 3.23 shows a class Person realizes the *Sortable* interface.

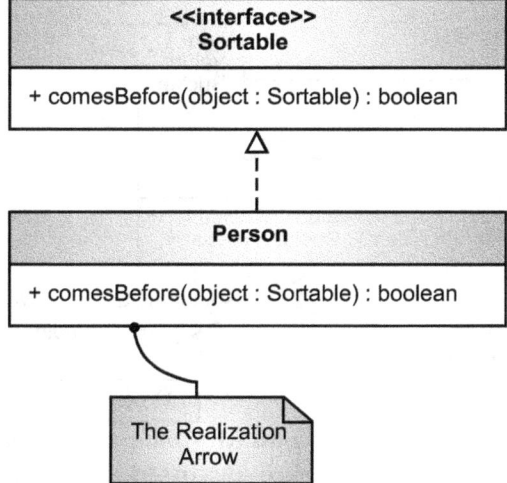

Fig. 3.23 : Shows a class Person realizes the sortable interface

Forward Engineering for above realization model ;

public interface Sortable
{

```
    public Boolean comesBefore(Sortable sortable);
}
public class Person implements Sortable
{
  public Boolean comesBefore(Sortable sortable)
  {
    //Implements the definition/logic of comesBefore for sorting..
  }

  // ... Implementations of the other operations ...
}
```

3.5 ADVANCED RELATIONSHIPS

When you model the things that form the vocabulary of your system, you must also model how those things stand in relationship to one another. Relationships can be complex, however. Visualizing, specifying, constructing and documenting webs of relationships require a number of advanced features.

3.5.1 Stereotypes on Dependency

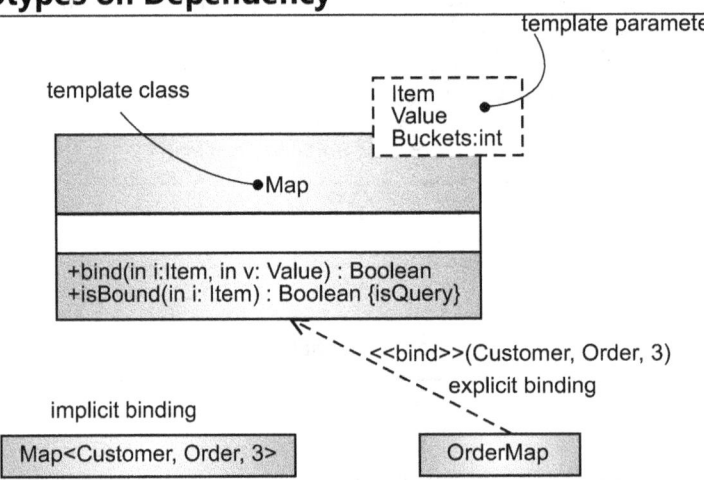

Fig. 3.24 : Template class with 'bind' relationship

The basic properties of dependencies are discussed in previous Section 3.4.1 plain, unadorned dependency relationship is sufficient for most of the using relationships you will encounter. However, if you want to specify a shade of meaning, the UML defines a number of stereotypes that may be applied to dependency relationships. There are 17 such stereotypes, all of which can be organized into six groups.

1. First, there are eight stereotypes that apply to dependency relationships among classes and objects in class diagrams.

1. bind	Specifies that the source instantiates the target template using the given actual parameters.

You will use bind when you want to model the details of template classes. For example, the relationship between a template container class and an instantiation of that class would be modeled as a bind dependency. Bind includes a list of actual arguments that map to the formal arguments of the template (See Fig. 3.24).

2. derive	Specifies that the source may be computed from the target.

You will use derive when you want to model the relationship between two attributes or two associations, one of which is concrete and the other is conceptual. For example, a Person class might have the attribute BirthDate (which is concrete), as well as the attribute Age (which can be derived from BirthDate, so is not separately manifest in the class). You would show the relationship between Age and BirthDate by using a derive dependency, showing Age derived from BirthDate.

3. permit/ friend	Specifies that the source is given special visibility into the target.

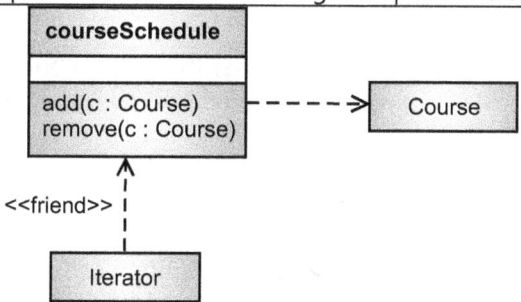

Fig. 3.25 : Shows a set of classes with <<friend>> relationship

For example, Fig. 3.25 shows a set of classes drawn from a system that manages the assignment of students and instructors to courses in a university. This Fig. 3.25 shows a dependency from CourseS chedule to Course, because Course is used in both the 'add' and 'remove' operations of Course Schedule.

4. instance Of	Specifies that the source object is an instance of the target classifier.
5. instantiate	Specifies that the source creates instances of the target.

These last two stereotypes let you model class/object relationships explicitly. You will use instance of when you want to model the relationship between a class and an object in the same diagram or between a class and its metaclass. You will use instantiate when you want to specify which element creates objects of another.

6. power type	Specifies that the target is a powertype of the source; a powertype is a classifier whose objects are all the children of a given parent.

| 7. refine | Specifies that the source is at a finer degree of abstraction than the target. |

You will use refine when you want to model classes that are essentially the same but at different levels of abstraction. For example, during analysis, you might encounter a Customer class which, during design, you refine into a more detailed Customer class, complete with its implementation.

| 8. use | Specifies that the semantics of the source element depends on the semantics of the public part of the target |

You will apply use when you want to explicitly mark a dependency as a using relationship, in contrast to the shades of dependencies other stereotypes provide. Continuing, there are two stereotypes that apply to dependency relationships among packages.

For more Relationship in Package as following :

| 1. access | Specifies that the source package is granted the right to reference the elements of the target package. |
| 2. import | A kind of access that specifies that the public contents of the target package enter the flat namespace of the source, as if they had been declared in the source. |

Two stereotypes apply to dependency relationships among use cases :

| 1. extend | Specifies that the target use case extends the behavior of the source. |
| 2. include | Specifies that the source use case explicitly incorporates the behavior of another use case at a location specified by the source. |

You will encounter three stereotypes when modeling interactions among objects.

| 1. become | Specifies that the target is the same object as the source but at a later point in time and with possibly different values, state or roles. |
| 2. call | Specifies that the source operation invokes the target operation. |

| 3. copy | Specifies that the target object is an exact, but independent, copy of the source. |

You will use become and copy when you want to show the role, state or attribute value of one object at different points in time or space. You will use call when you want to model the calling dependencies among operations. One stereotype you will encounter in the context of state machines is

| 1. send | Specifies that the source operation sends the target event |

You will use send when you want to model an operation (such as found in the action associated with a state transition) dispatching a given event to a target object (which in turn might have an associated state machine). The send dependency in effect lets you tie independent state machines together.

Finally, one stereotype that you will encounter in the context of organizing the elements of your system into subsystems and models is.

| 1. trace | Specifies that the target is an historical ancestor of the source. |

Use trace when you want to model the relationships among elements in different models. For example, in the context of a system's architecture, a use case in a use case model (representing a functional requirement) might trace to a package in the corresponding design model (representing the artifacts that realize that use case).

3.5.2 Stereotype and Constrains on Generalization

A plain, unadorned generalization relationship is sufficient for most of the inheritance relationships. However, if you want to specify a shade of meaning, the UML defines one stereotype and four constraints that may be applied to generalization relationships.

First, there is the one stereotype.

| 1. implementation | Specifies that the child inherits the implementation of the parent but does not make public nor support its interfaces, thereby violating substitutability. |

Use implementation when you want to model private inheritance, such as found in C++.

Next, there are four standard constraints that apply to generalization relationships.

| 1. complete | Specifies that all children in the generalization have been specified in the model (although some may be elided in the diagram) and that no additional children are permitted. |
| 2. incomplete | Specifies that not all children in the generalization have been specified (even if some are elided) and that additional children are permitted. |

Unless otherwise stated, you can assume that any diagram shows only a partial view of an inheritance lattice and so is elided. However, elision is different from the completeness of a model. Specifically, use the complete constraint when you want to show explicitly that you have fully specified a hierarchy in the model (although no one diagram may show that hierarchy) ; You will use incomplete to show explicitly that you have not stated the full specification of the hierarchy in the model (although one diagram may show everything in the model).

3. disjoint	Specifies that objects of the parent may have no more than one of the children as a type.
4. overlapping	Specifies that objects of the parent may have more than one of the children as a type.

These two constraints apply only in the context of multiple inheritances. You will use disjoint and overlapping when you want to distinguish between static classification (disjoint) and dynamic classification (overlapping).

3.5.3 Constraints on Association

An association is a structural relationship, specifying that objects of one thing are connected to objects of another.

There are four basic adornments that apply to an association :

(1) A name,
(2) The role at each end of the association,
(3) The multiplicity at each end of the association and
(4) Aggregation.

For advanced uses, there are a number of other properties you can use to model subtle details, such as :

1. Navigation,
2. Qualification, and
3. Various flavors of aggregation.

(1) Navigation

Refer Section 3.4.2.2 of Navigability.

(2) Qualification

In the context of an association, one of the most common modeling idioms you will encounter is the problem of lookup. Given an object at one end of an association, how do you identify an object or set of objects at the other end? For example, consider the problem of modeling a work desk at a manufacturing site at which returned items are processed to be fixed. As Fig. 3.26 shows, you would model an association between two classes, WorkDesk and ReturnedItem. In the context of the WorkDesk, you would have a jobId that would identify a particular ReturnedItem. In that sense, jobId is an attribute of the association. It's not a feature of ReturnedItem because items really have no knowledge of things like repairs or jobs. Then, given an object of WorkDesk and given a particular value for jobId, you can navigate to zero or one objects of ReturnedItem. In the UML, you would model this idiom using a qualifier, which is an association attribute whose values partition the set of objects related to an object across an association. You render a qualifier as a small rectangle attached to the end of an association, placing the attributes in the rectangle, as the Fig. 3.26 shows. The source object, together with the values of the qualifier's attributes, yield a target object (if the target multiplicity is at most one) or a set of objects (if the target multiplicity is many).

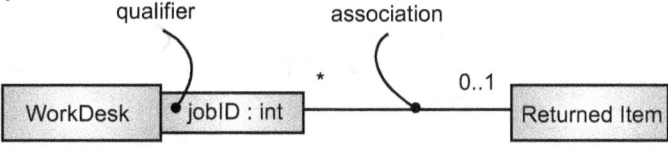

Fig. 3.26 : Qualification

3.5.4 Interface Specifier

An interface is a collection of operations that are used to specify a service of a class or a component; every class may realize many interfaces. Collectively, the interfaces realized by a class represent a complete specification of the behavior of that class. However, in the context of an association with another target class, a source class may choose to present only part of its face to the world.

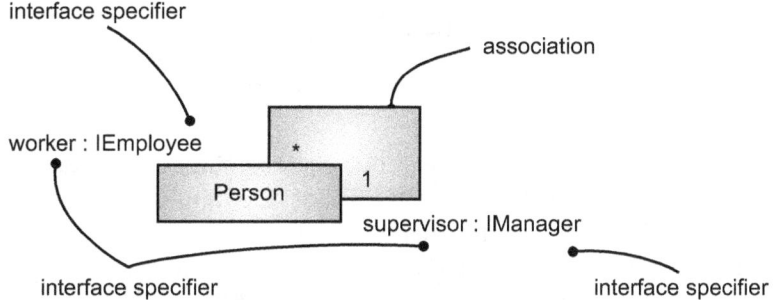

Fig. 3.27 : Interface specifiers

For example, in the vocabulary of a human resources system, a Person class may realize many interfaces: IManager, IEmployee, IOfficer, and so on. As Fig. 3.27 shows, you can model the relationship between a supervisor and her workers with a one-to-many association, explicitly labeling the roles of this association as supervisor and worker.

In the context of this association, a Person in the role of supervisor presents only the IManager face to the worker; a Person in the role of worker presents only the IEmployee face to the supervisor.

As the Fig. 3.27 shows, you can explicitly show the type of role using the syntax rolename : iname, where iname is some interface of the other classifier.

3.5.5 Association Classes

In an association between two classes, the association itself might have properties. For example, in an employer/employee relationship between a Company and a Person, there is a Job that represents the properties of that relationship that apply to exactly one pairing of the Person and Company. It would not be appropriate to model this situation with a Company to Job association together with a Job to Person association. That would not tie a specific instance of the Job to the specific pairing of Company and Person. In the UML, you would model this as an association class, which is a modeling element that has both association and class properties. An association class can be seen as an association that also has class properties, or as a class that also has association properties. You render an association class as a class symbol attached by a dashed line to an association as in Fig. 3.28.

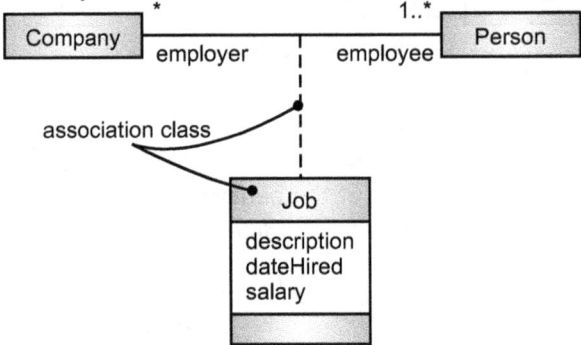

Fig. 3.28 : Association class

3.5.6 Interfaces

Interface is used to describe functionality without implementation. Interface is the just like a template where you define different functions not the implementation. When a class implements the interface it also implements the functionality as per the requirement. Interface is represented by a circle as shown below. It has a name which is generally written below the circle.

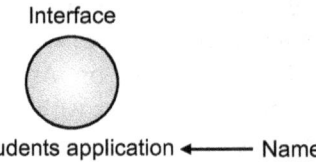

3.5.7 Template Classes

A template is a parameterized element. In such languages as C++ and Ada, you can write template classes each of which defines a family of classes (you can also write template functions, each of which defines a family of functions). A template includes slots for classes, objects, values and these slots serve as the template's parameters. You can not use a template directly; you have to instantiate it first. Instantiation involves binding these formal template parameters to actual ones. For a template class, the result is a concrete class that can be used just like any ordinary class.

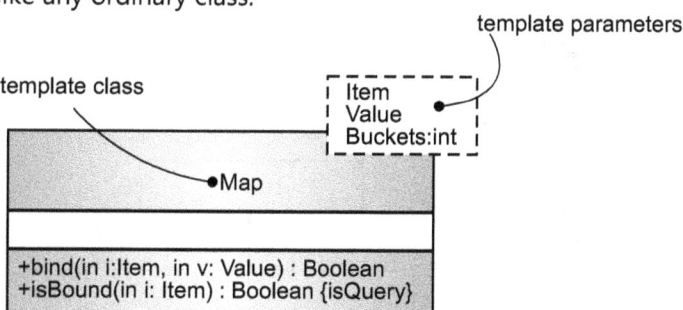

Fig. 3.29 : Template class

The most common use of template classes is to specify containers that can be instantiated for specific elements, making them type-safe. For example, the following C++ code fragment declares a parameterized Map class.

```
template<class Item, class Value, int Buckets>
class Map {
    public:
        virtual Boolean bind(const Item&, const Value&);
        virtual Boolean isBound(const Item&) const;
        ...
};
//You might then instantiate this template to map Customer objects to Order objects.
        m : Map<Customer, Order, 3>;
```

3.6 COMMON MODELING TECHNIQUES

3.6.1 Modeling Simple Collaborations

- Every class works in collaboration to perform certain tasks greater than individual. None of the class works alone.
- Class diagram is useful for visualizing, specifying, constructing and documenting the every aspect of your system.
- When you create a class diagram, you just model a part of the things and relationships that make up your system's design view. For this reason, each class diagram should focus on one collaboration at a time.

To Model a Collaboration

- Discover the mechanism to model that consists of some function or behaviour of the part of the system.

- For each mechanism, identify the elements such as classes, interfaces and other collaborations that participate in this collaboration. Identify the relationships among these things, as well.

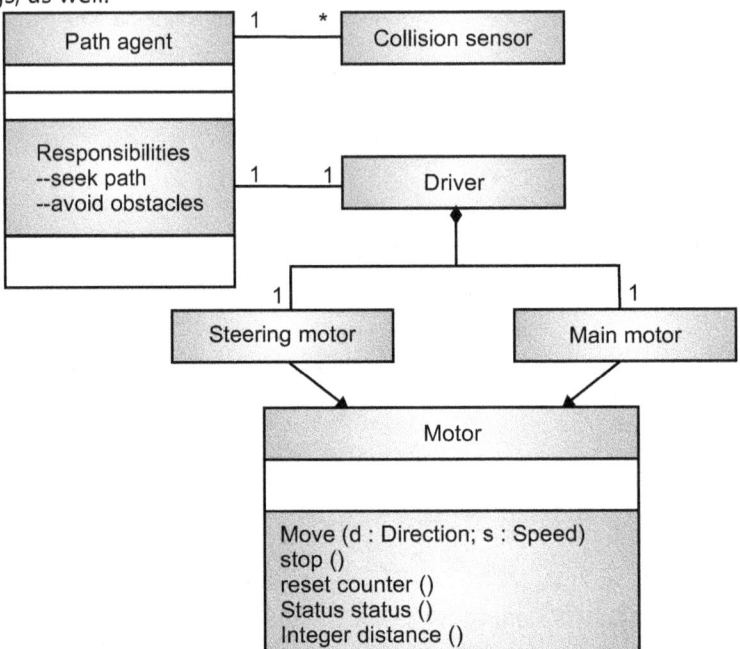

Fig. 3.30 : Simple collaboration

3.6.2 Modeling a Logical Database Schema

- The most of the systems are having persistent objects, which mean that they can be stored in a database for later retrieval. Most often, you will use a relational database, an object oriented database or a hybrid relational database for persistent storage.
- The UML is useful for modelling the logical database schemas as well as physical databases.
- The class diagrams go step further by permitting the modelling of behaviour whereas Entity-Relationship (E-R) diagrams focus only on data.

To Model a Schema
- Identify persistent classes in your model.
- Use tagged value to mark the persistent classes.
- Specify the structural details of the classes. The cardinalities and association have to be modelled carefully.
- Identify and design the common patterns that complicate physical database design, such as cyclic associations, one-to-one associations and n-ary associations.

- Model important data members who deal with the data access and data integrity.
- Use tools to transform your logical design into a physical design.

3.6.3 Forward and Reverse Engineering

Forward engineering results in a loss of information, because models written in the UML are semantically richer than any current object-oriented programming language. In fact, this is a major reason why you need models in addition to code. Structural features, such as collaborations and behavioral features, such as interactions can be visualized clearly in the UML, but not so clearly from raw code.

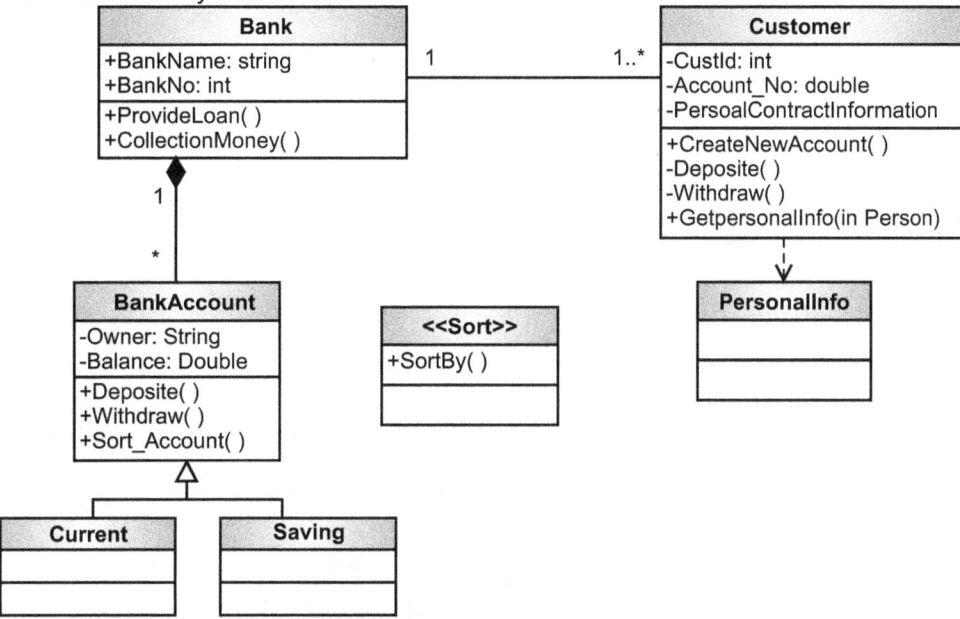

Fig. 3.31 : Class diagram

3.6.3.1 To Forward Engineer a Class Diagram

- Identify the rules for mapping to your implementation language or languages of choice. This is something you will want to do for your project or your organization as a whole.
- Depending on the semantics of the languages you choose, you may have to constrain your use of certain UML features.
- For example, the UML permits you to model multiple inheritance, but Smalltalk permits only single inheritance.
- You can either choose to prohibit developers from modeling with multiple inheritances (which makes your models language-dependent) or develop idioms that transform these richer features into the implementation language (which makes the mapping more complex).

- Use tagged values to specify your target language. You can do this at the level of individual classes if you need precise control. You can also do so at a higher level, such as with collaborations or packages.
- Use tools to forward engineer your models.

Forward Engineering of class diagram in to Java code

```
Class Bank
{
Customer cust=new Customer();        //Association Relationship
                                     between class bank & class
customer
public String Bankname;
public int Bankno;
public void collectionMoney()
{
………\\Method Body
}
public void provideLoan()
{
………\\Method Body

}
}
Class Customer
{
Bank b1=new Bank();                  //Association Relationship
    between class customer and
    class bank
int custId;
double AccountNo;
public void CreateNewaccount()
{
………\\Method Body
}
private int doposite()
{
………\\Method Body
```

```
}
private int withraw()
{
………….\\Method Body
}
public getPersonalInfo(Person p)
{
………….\\Method Body
}
public interface sort
{
public void softBy( );
}
Class BankAccount
{
String Owner;
Double balance;
Private double deposite()
{
………….\\Method Body
}
Private double withraw()
{
………….\\Method Body
}
public void sortBy( )
{
………….\\Method Body
}
Class CurrentAccount extends BankAccount
{
}
Class SavingAccount extends BankAccount
{
}
```

3.6.3.2 To Reverse Engineer a Class Diagram

- Identify the rules for mapping from your implementation language or languages of choice. This is something you will want to do for your project or your organization as a whole.
- Using a tool, point to the code you had like to reverse engineer. Use your tool to generate a new model or modify an existing one that was previously forward engineered.
- Using your tool, create a class diagram by querying the model. For example, you might start with one or more classes and then expand the diagram by following specific relationships or other neighboring classes. Expose or hide details of the contents of this class diagram as necessary to communicate your intent.

3.7 COMPOSITE STRUCTURES DIAGRAM

Composite structures provide a view of your system's parts and form part of the logical view of your system's model.

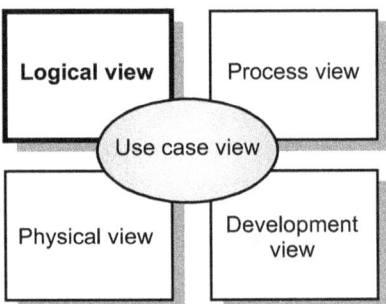

Fig. 3.32 : The logical view captures the abstract descriptions of a system's parts, including composite structures

3.7.1 Need of Composite Structure Diagram

- As a system becomes more complex, it is often helpful to decompose it in terms of functionality. To realize a piece of functionality, different elements of a system often work together and communicate information.
- UML 2.0 formalizes the concept of complex relationships between elements into the idea of composite structures.
- A Composite structure diagram models the parts of a class, component or collaboration, including the interaction points (ports) used to access features of the structure.
- Composite structures show how objects create a big picture. They model how objects work together inside a class or how objects achieve a goal.
- Composite structures are fairly advanced, but they are good to have in your bag of tricks because they are perfectly suited for specific modeling situations, such as following :

Internal Structures

Show the parts contained by a class and the relationships between the parts; this allows you to show context-sensitive relationships or relationships that hold in the context of a containing class.

Ports

Show how a class is used on your system with ports.

Collaborations

Show design patterns in your software and more generally, objects cooperating to achieve a goal.

3.7.2 Composite Structures

A structure is a set of interconnected elements that exist at runtime to collectively provide some piece of functionality.

For example, you can use a structure to represent the internal make-up of a classifier such as a subsystem (what objects are related to each other, who is communicating with whom etc.). UML calls such structures *internal structures*.

UML defines several symbols to capture the relationships and communications between elements in an internal structure.

3.7.3 Parts of a Class

When showing the internal structure of a class, you draw its parts or items contained by composition, inside the containing class.

Parts are specified by the role they play in the containing class.

It is written as <roleName> : <type>.

In Fig. 3.33, the part of type Introduction has the role blogIntro and the part of type MainBody has the role blogMain.

The *multiplicity*, or number of instances of that part, is written in the upper right-hand corner of the part.

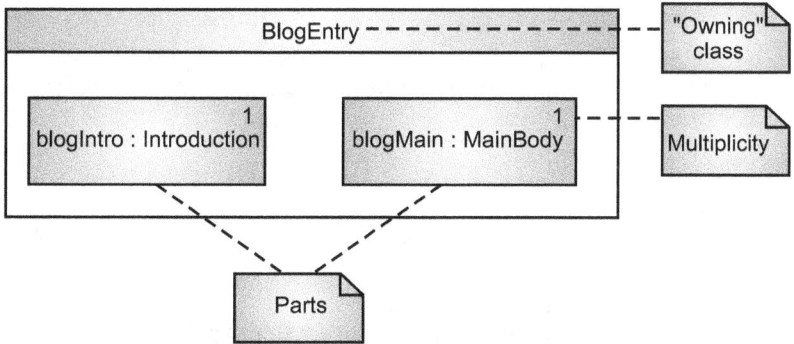

Fig. 3.33 : The internal structure of the blog entry class

3.7.4 Connectors

Connectors represent communication links between instances of classes participating in an internal structure. They can be runtime instances of associations or they can represent dynamic communication set-up at runtime. A connector is a link that enables communication between parts. A connector simply means that runtime instances of the parts can communicate. A connector can be a runtime instance of an association or a dynamic link established at runtime, such as an instance passed in as a parameter. You show a connector as a solid line between two instances (see Fig. 3.34).

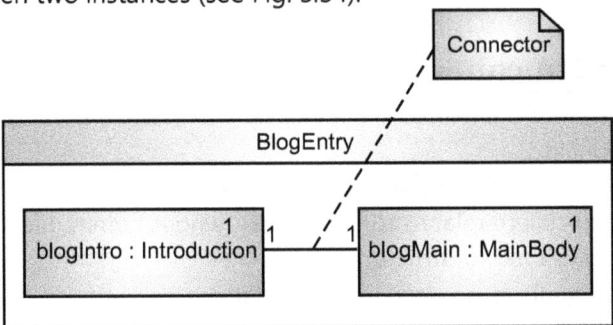

Fig. 3.34 : Using connectors to link parts in the internal structure of a class

3.7.5 Ports

A port is a way to offer functionality from a composite structure without exposing the internal details of how that functionality is realized. You show a port as a small square. You typically draw the name and multiplicity of the port near the square, though both may be hidden. If you draw the port on the edge of a classifier, the port is public and is available to the environment. If you draw the port inside a classifier, the port is protected and available only to the composite structure. Fig. 3.35 shows an example of port. For example, you may have a subsystem that can perform credit card payment verification.

The actual implementation of this functionality may be spread over several classes working in conjunction. The organization of these classes can be represented as an internal structure within the subsystem and the overall functionality or credit card verification, can be exposed using a port. Exposing the functionality through a port allows the subsystem to be used by any other classifier that conforms to the port's specifications.

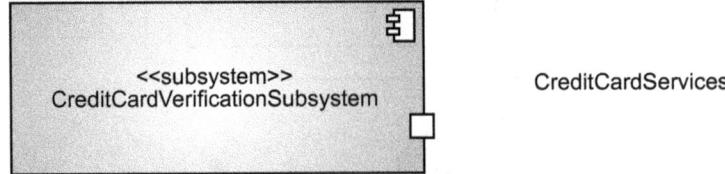

Fig. 3.35 : The credit Card verification subsystem with a single public port, credit card services

Required and Provided Interfaces

Ports are associated with required and provided interfaces :

(1) Required interfaces show what the owning classifier may ask of its environment through a given port.

(2) Provided interfaces show what functionality a classifier exposes to the environment.

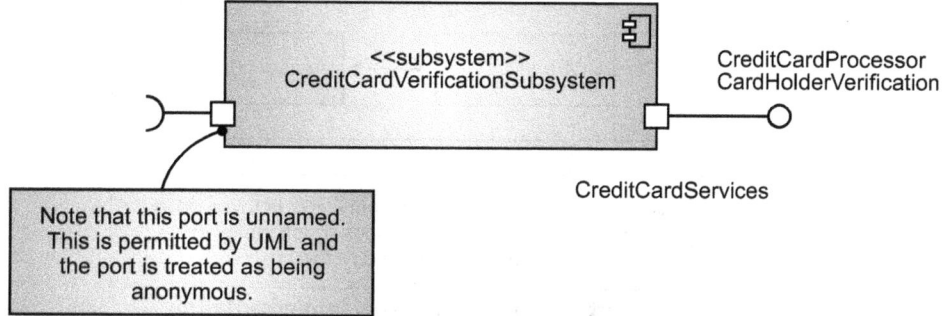

Fig. 3.36 : The credit card verification subsystem providing two interfaces (credit card processor and card holder verification) and requiring one (account services)

For example, our credit card payment system may provide an interface to verify credit cards, CreditCardProcessor, while requiring access to an account verification system, AccountServices, offered by the credit card company. If you use ports in your diagrams, the required and provided interfaces capture all the interaction the system may have with a given classifier.

Provided and required interfaces are typically shown using the ball and socket (lollipop) notation, (see Fig. 3.36) though you may explicitly type a port.

3.7.5.1 Realizing Port Implementations

Ports are wired to an internal implementation using connectors. If the classifier owning the port provides the implementation of the functionality itself, the port is considered a behavioral port.

In this case, the connector links to a state inside the classifier. This state is used to explain the behavior of the classifier when the port is used.

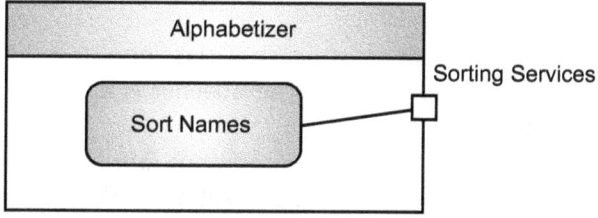

Fig. 3.37 : A behavioral port

On the other hand, if the functionality is realized by internal elements, you link the connector to internal classifiers that provide the implementation.

This is typically used for composite structures such as components and subsystems. Fig. 3.38 shows such a port.

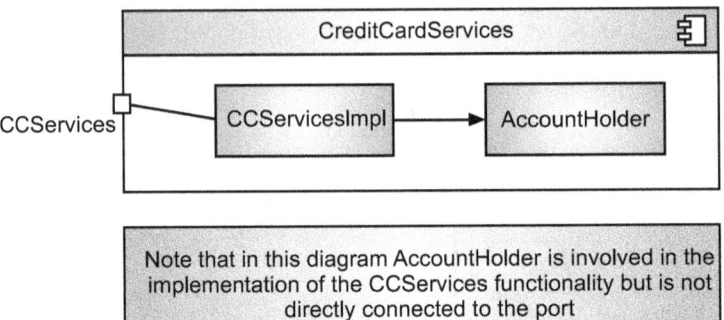

Fig. 3.38 : A port linked to an internal implementation

REVIEW QUESTIONS

1. What is the need of composite structure diagram?
2. Explain with examples different types of relationships in UML.
3. Explain Object diagram with example.
4. Explain Class diagram with example.
5. Describe advance relationships of class diagram.
6. Explain difference between association and link.
7. Explain forward and reverse engineering for class diagram, object diagram, and composite structure diagram.
9. What is the purpose and need and typical uses for class diagrams, state diagrams, explain.
10. Draw a class diagram for a typical compiler. Make suitable assumptions about scope and working of your compiler (write down the scope too).
11. What is a qualified ASSOCIATION relation in a class diagram, given approximate example and give notation in UML.

Ans. : Qualified association: association in which a class objects is identified from another class through a sort a "foreign key". The qualifier is an *attribute* of the *association* between two classes.

Qualifier : A property may have other properties (attributes) that serve as qualifiers. A qualifier is a property which defines a partition of the set of associated instances with respect to an instance at the qualified end. A qualifier is shown as a small rectangle attached to the qualified classifier also called the source. This qualifier rectangle is part of the association, not part of the classifier. UML does not allow qualifier to be suppressed. One or several attributes of the qualifier are drawn within the qualifier box, one to a line. Qualifier attributes have the same notation as classifier attributes, except that initial values are not used in this case. UML allows having a qualifier on each end of a single association.

For Example : If we wish to state (in the model) that the attribute *id* has to be unique across all student objects then we could use the idea of a *qualified association* between university and student. In this case *id* is an *attribute* of the association between *University* and *Student*. The University is responsible for allocating unique student numbers so the qualifier goes on it. For example,

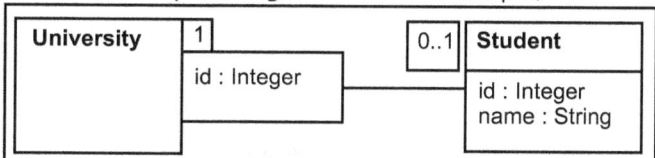

Fig. 3.39

Every student at the University has a unique student number. An id number may be associated with 0 or 1 student (0 is needed as an id may not have been assigned to a student yet e.g. printout of id numbers in advance of being used). A student is enrolled at one university. A one to many relationship is implied with qualified associations for example, a university can have many students each with their own unique id number.

12. Write short notes on templates (give example from C++ too).
13. What is a TYPE and how to model it in class diagram?

Ans. : The «type» stereotype indicates that the class is an interface. This means that it has no member variables, and that all of its member functions are pure virtual.

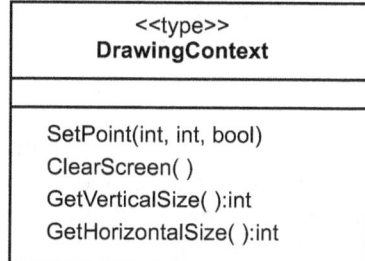

Fig. 3.40 : Type class

14. Show how composite structure can best represents cAR and its internal parts like door, transmission system, illustrate.

Ans. : In UML models, a composite structure diagram depicts the internal structure of structured classifiers by using parts, ports, and connectors. The composite structure diagram shows the internal details of a classifier and to describe the objects and roles that work together to perform the behavior of the containing classifier.

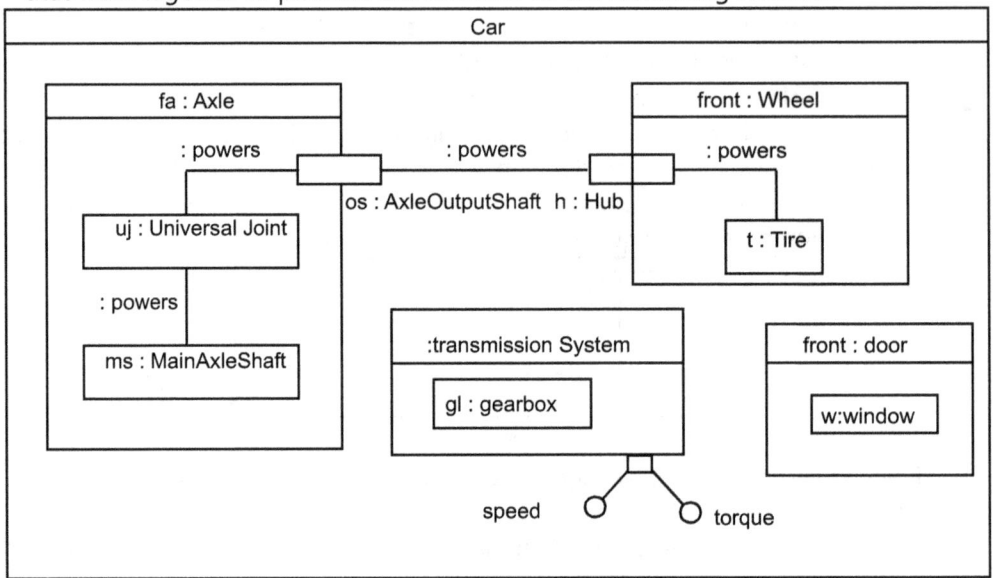

Fig. 3.41

15. Explain in detail Entity object and boundary object.

Ans. : Entity : This object type represents a domain entity in the area the system handles. It is typically passive in that it doesn't initiate interactions on its own. In information systems, entity objects are normally persistent and stored in a database. Entity objects typically participate in many use cases.

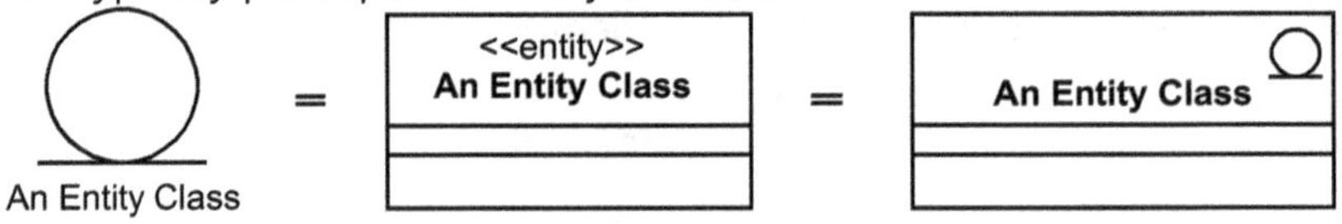

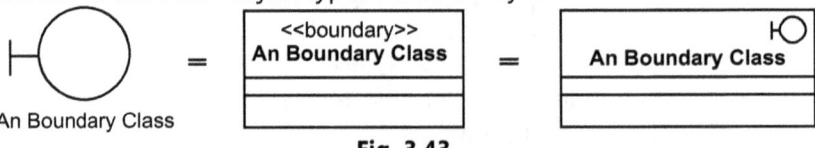

Fig. 3.42

Boundary : This object type lies close to the boundary of the system (though still within it). It interacts with the actors outside the system and passes messages to and from them to the other object types inside the system.

Fig. 3.43

16. (a) How do you show an exception in a class diagram? Give an approximate example and give notation in UML.

Ans. : **Exceptions :** Exceptions are thrown if any kind of unusual condition occurs that can be caught. Sometimes it also happens that the exception could not be caught and the program may get terminated.

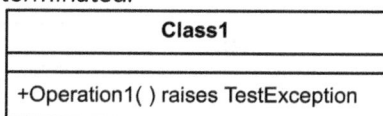

Fig. 3.44

(b) How do you implement an association relationship in C++?

17. (a) What is a derived attribute, class scope variable and how to model them in class diagram?

(b) Describe a technique for identifying classes/objects in a system.

Ans. : Good classes reflect the problem domain and have real names, not confusing or fake names from literature or sports. Believe it or not, we have seen a few projects that don't follow this simple rule, making the model hard to read. When you are looking for classes, a good use-case model helps tremendously. Rely on the use-case model and requirements specification in the search for classes. Pose the following types of questions :

Do I have information that should be stored or analyzed? If there is any information that has to be stored, transformed, analyzed, or handled in some other way, then it is a possible candidate for a class. The information might include concepts that must always be registered in the system or events or transactions that occur at a specific moment.

Do I have external systems? If so, they are normally of interest when you model. The external system might be seen as classes that your system contains or should interact with. Do I have any reusable patterns, class libraries, or components? If you have patterns, class libraries, or components from earlier projects, colleagues, or manufacturers, they normally contain class candidates. Are there devices that the system must handle? Any technical devices connected to the system turn into class candidates that handle these devices.

Do I have organizational parts? Representing an organization can be one with classes, especially in business models. Which roles do the actors in the business play? These roles can be seen as classes, such as user, system operator, customer, and so on.

18. Draw a class diagram for system descried here. Make suitable assumptions about the scope. An editor has to be implemented in C++ or java. The documents to be edited will be organized as sentences and words forming the sentence. For each word we would like to keep information on font, color. There has to be a class that helps apply

the editing changes and style (font, color) changes to the text. The user can interact with the editor in a small GUI window to give a search term which the editor has to locate in the text and highlight. And draw classes, attributes, operations and relationships between classes. Show which classes are entity, controller, GUI classes.

Ans. :

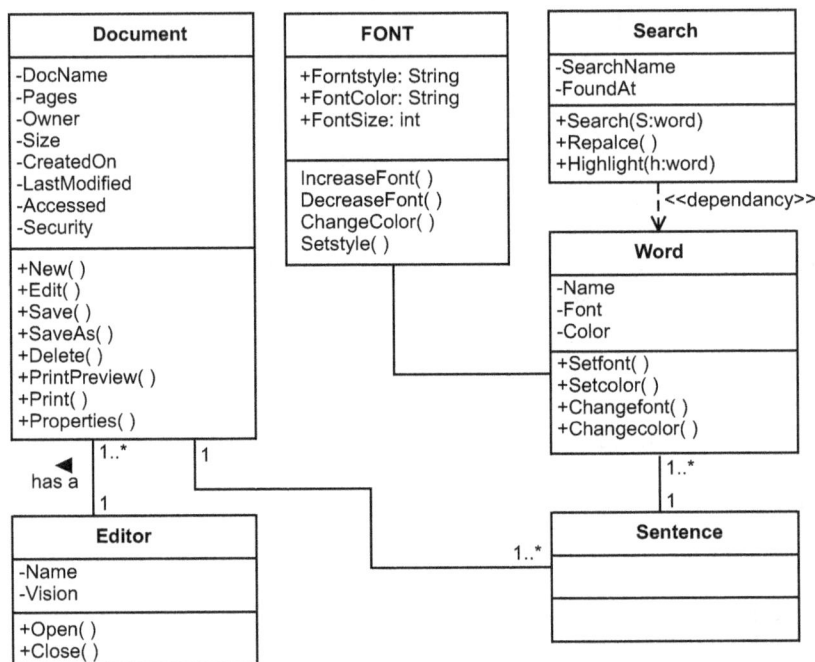

Fig. 3.45

19. Draw a class diagram for system described here. The system is for a hospital. Hospital has admitted patients and out-patients. Patients register themselves; maintain their past medical history and take appointments of doctors. Doctors prescribe treatment and if required recommend an admission into the hospital. Make suitable assumptions about the scope and draw classes, attributes, operations and relationship between classes.

Ans. : Refer Fig. 3.46.

20. How does one forward engineer an object diagram, Illustrate.

21. Draw a class diagram for a Garage system. Make suitable assumptions about scope and working of your Garage (write down the scope too). The garage is for different types of four wheelers. The advanced booking/appointment is done on phone. On the day of appointment as soon as a customer arrives, a job card is created to not all the problems, requirements for the vehicle. An engineer is assigned based on

availability to service a vehicle. On completion of the repair/maintenance/service the engineer prepares a report based on which a bill is created. The payment is accepted in cash against the bill. Your class diagram must show relevant attributes, methods, relationships.

Ans. : Refer Fig. 3.47.

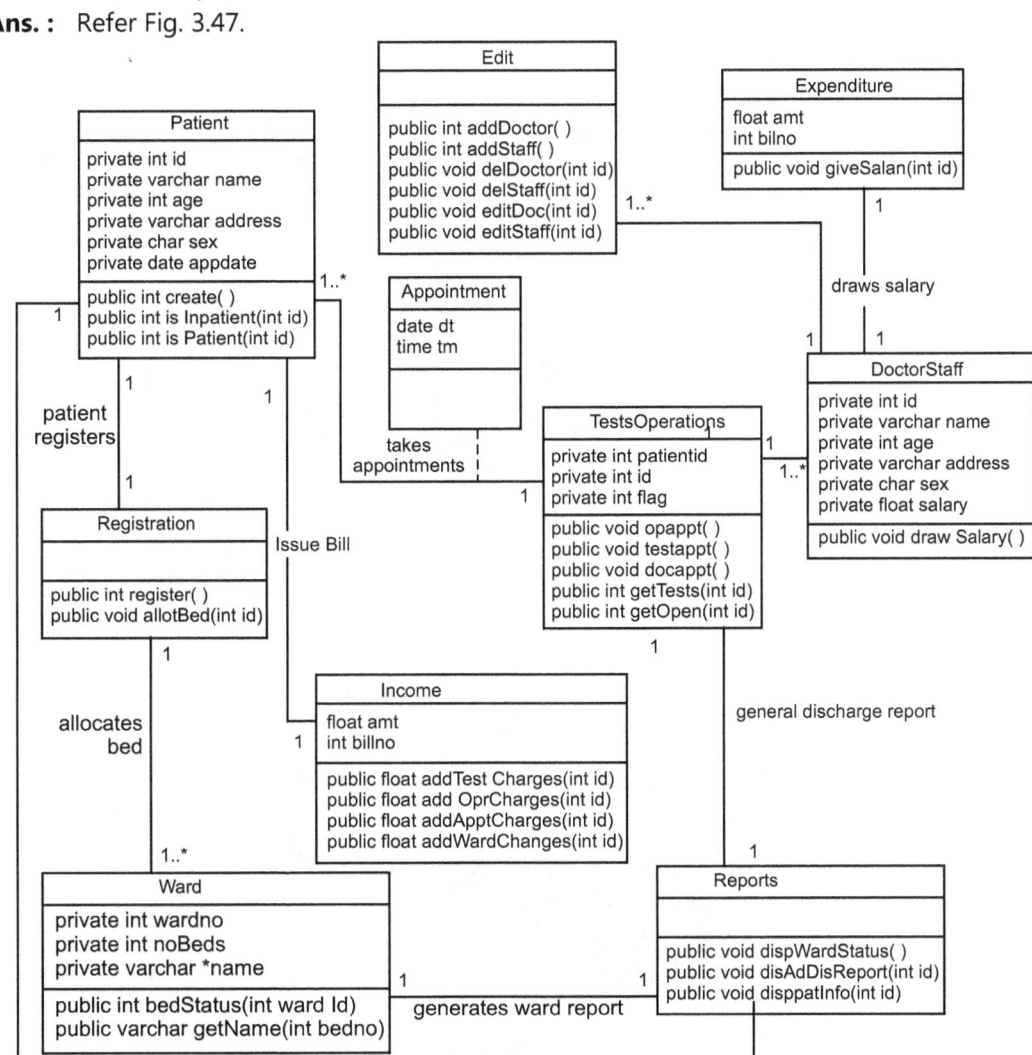

Fig. 3.46

Ans. :

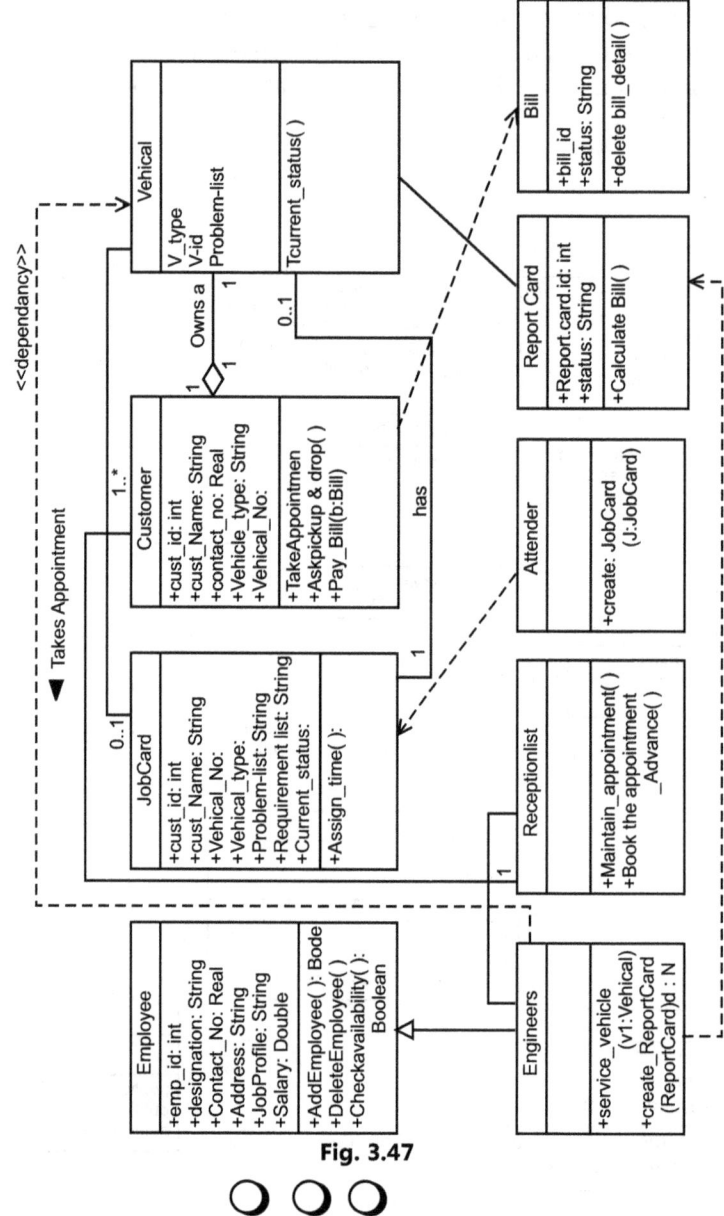

Fig. 3.47

UNIT - IV

BEHAVIORAL DIAGRAMS

4.1 USE CASE DIAGRAM

4.1.1 Introduction

Imagine that one fine day your requirements folks have just popped in for a coffee and to leave you the 200-page requirements document they have been working on for the past six months and they want that you and your team start designing. The requirements are still a little fuzzy, and they are all written in the language of the user confusing and ambiguous natural language rather than in a language that your system stakeholders can easily understand. What is the next step; you take this huge set of loosely defined requirements and still it into a format for your designers without losing important detail. To achieve this we have UML Use case diagram. The use-case model represents the use-case view of the system. This view is very important, as it affects all other views of the system. Both the logical and physical architecture are influenced by the use cases, because the functions specified in the use-case model are implemented in those architectures.

4.1.2 Purpose

- A use case is a case (or situation) where your system is used to fulfill one or more of your user's requirements.
- A use case captures a piece of functionality that the system provides.
- Use cases are at the heart of your model.
- It is an excellent starting point for of object-oriented system for development, design, testing and documentation.
- They describe a system's requirements strictly from the outside looking in.
- It is the first serious output from your model after a project is started.

Note : Use cases specify only what your system is supposed to do i.e., the system's functional requirements. They do not specify what the system shall not do, i.e., the system's non-functional requirements. Non-functional requirements often include performance targets and programming languages etc.

4.1.3 Notations

1. Use case	(Create a new Blog Account)	A use case captures the intended behavior of the system (or subsystem, class, or interface) you are developing, without having to specify how that behavior is implemented. Use case is something that provides some measurable result to the user or an external system.

2. Actor	![Actor stick figure labeled Administrator, and a box labeled <<actor>> Administrator]	Someone must initiate a use case, who is something outside the scope of the use case is called Actor. Represents anyone or any thing that must interact with the system. **An Actor may** Only input information to the system. Only receive information from the system.
3. Communication Lines	———————	A communication line connects an actor and a use case to show the actor participating in the use case
4. System Boundaries	[Administrator stick figure connected to an oval inside a box labeled ATM System]	There is an implicit separation between actors (external to your system) and use cases (internal to your system) that marks your system's boundary. Draw a box around all of the use cases but keep the actors outside of the box, with the name of the system at the top.

4.1.4 Use Case Relationships

(1) Actor and Use Case Generalization

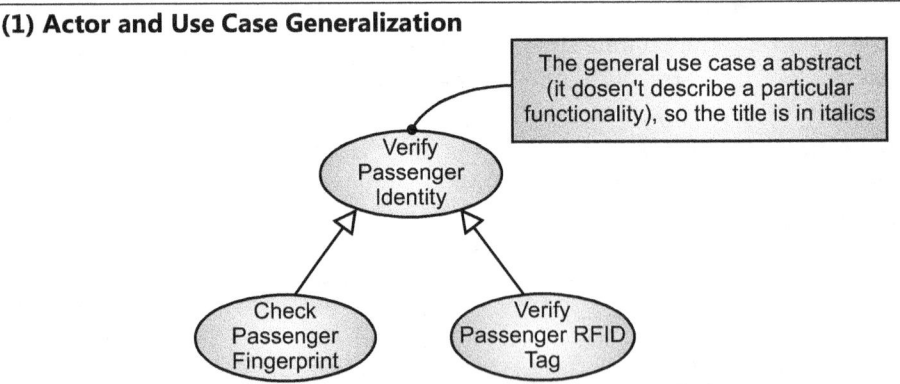

Fig. 4.1 : Shows use case generalization

Generalization among use cases is just like generalization among classes. Here it means that the child use case inherits the behavior and meaning of the parent use case. The child may add to or override the behavior of its parent; and the child may be substituted any place the parent appears (both the parent and the child may have concrete instances). When several actors, as part of their roles, also play a more generalized role, it is described as a generalization. This occurs when the behavior of the general role is described in an actor superclass. The specialized actors inherit the behavior of the superclass and then extend that behavior in some way. Generalization between actors is shown as a line with a hollow triangle at the end of the more general superclass, as shown in Fig. 4.2

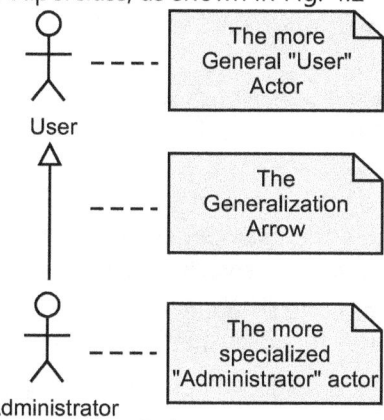

Fig. 4.2 : Showing that an administrator is a special kind of user

(2) The <<include>> Relationship

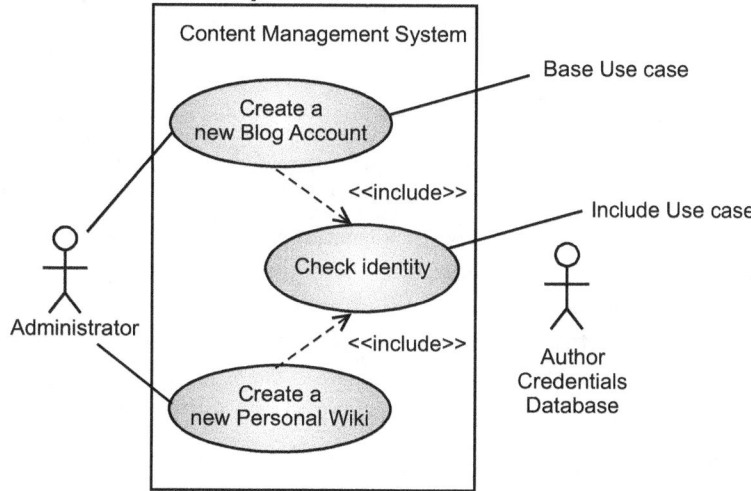

Fig. 4.3 : Showing <<include>> relationship

Include is a directed relationship between two use cases, implying that the behavior of the included use case is inserted into the behavior of the base use case. The base use case depends on the externally observable behavior of the included use case.

The use case that is included is always required in order for the base use case to execute. You can factor out common functionality from several use cases by creating a shared, included use case. The repetitive behavior shared between two use cases is best separated and captured within a totally new use case. The number of use case in your model can then reuse this new use case by using <<include>> relationship.

For Example

To create a new blog account and create a new Personal Wiki use cases we need common use case is checking identity using the <<include>> relationship as shown in Fig. 4.3.

(3) The <<Extend>> Relationship

This relationship specifies that the behavior of a use case may be improved by an additional use case. UML provides the ability to plug in additional functionality to a base use case if specified conditions are met.

For example, if you are modeling a banking application, you can have a use case named open account that specifies how the user can create a new account with the bank. You can offer a joint account that allowed a user to add other people to his account. The joint account functionality can be captured with a different, use case named Add Joint Member. In this case the specified condition for the extension is more than one member on the bank application. (see Fig. 4.4).

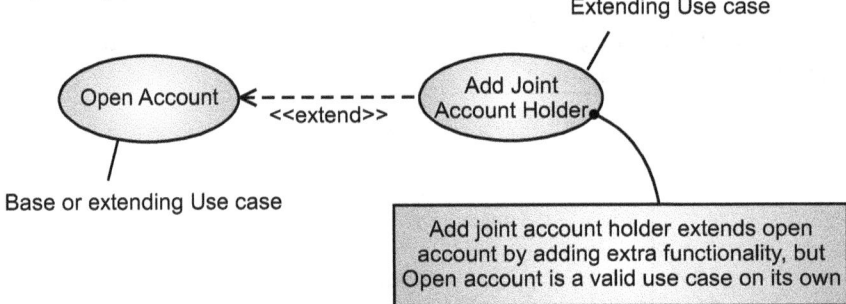

Fig. 4.4 : Showing <<extend>> relationship between use cases

The extension takes place at one or more specific extension points defined in the extended use case.

Note : However, that the extended use case is defined independently of the extending use case. Use case extension is intended to be used when there is some additional behavior that should be added, conditionally to the behavior defined in another use case.

4.1.5 Creating Use Case Diagram

Enough theory for now; let's take a look at a simple example. Suppose we are defining requirements for online shopping. Web customer uses some web site to make purchases online. Customer can view Items, make purchase and client can Register for website. View items use case is extended by several optional use cases like.

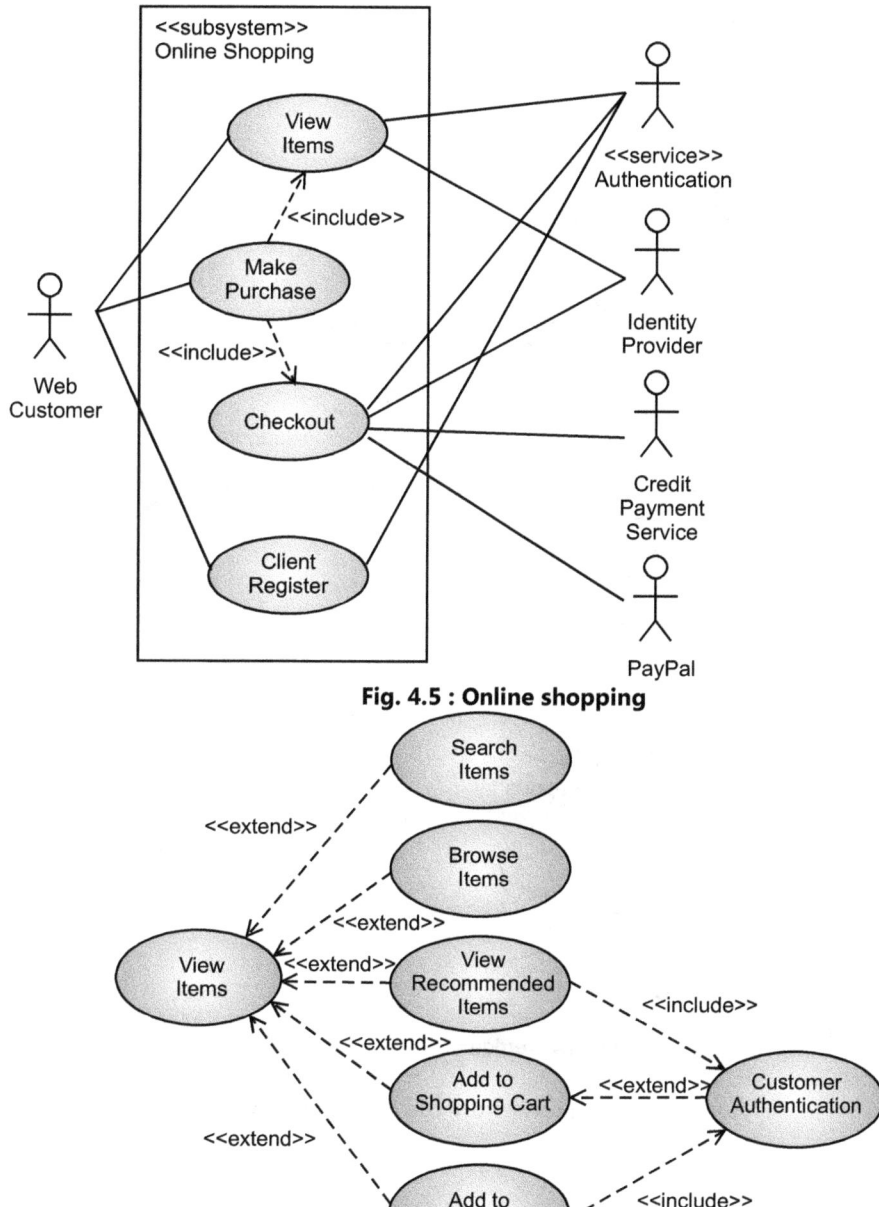

Fig. 4.5 : Online shopping

Fig. 4.6 : Online shopping

Examples :

Use Case diagram for Video Rental Store

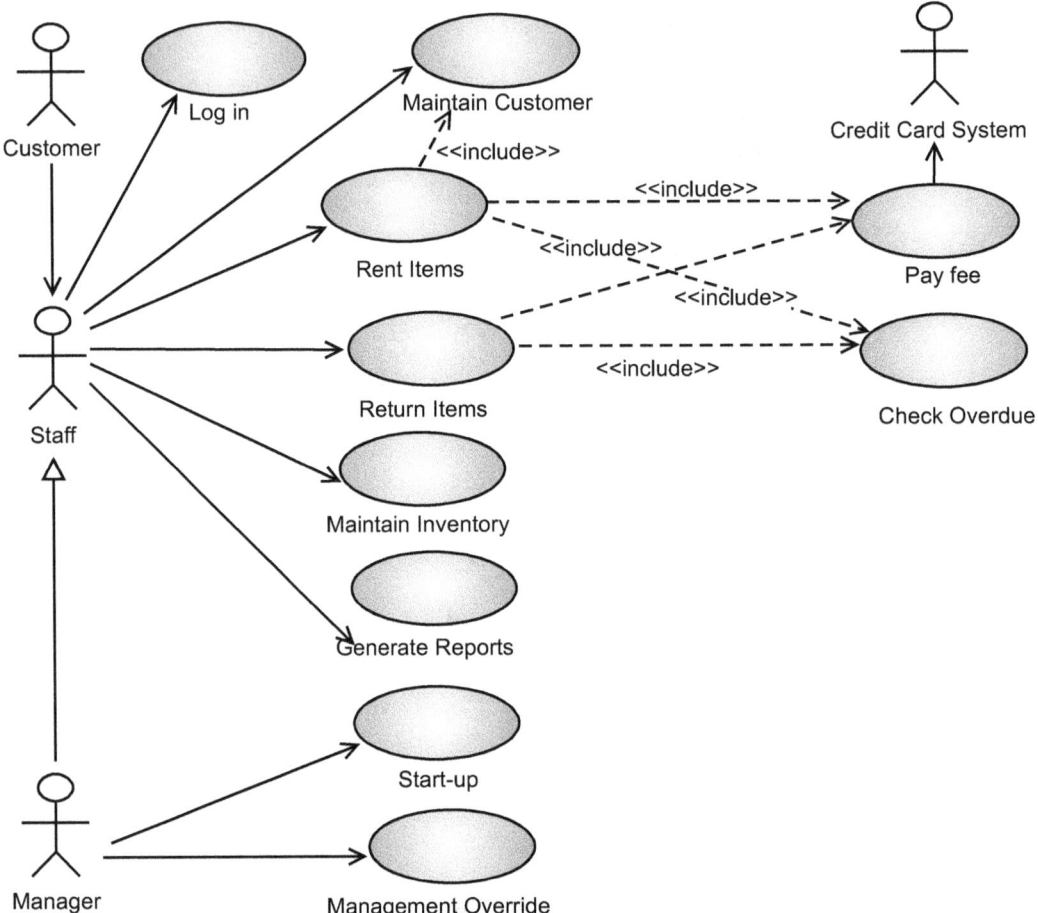

Fig. 4.7 : Video rental store use case diagram

(1) Use case diagram for Courseware Management System

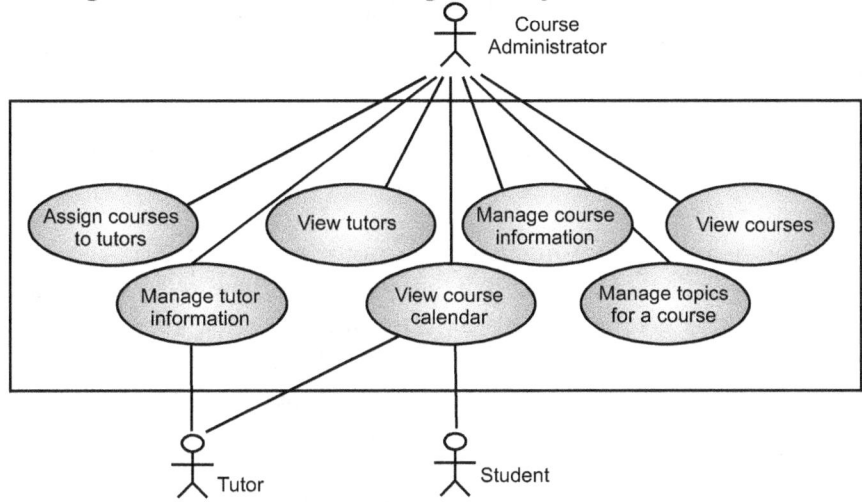

Fig. 4.8 : Courseware management system

(2) Use case diagram for Inventory system

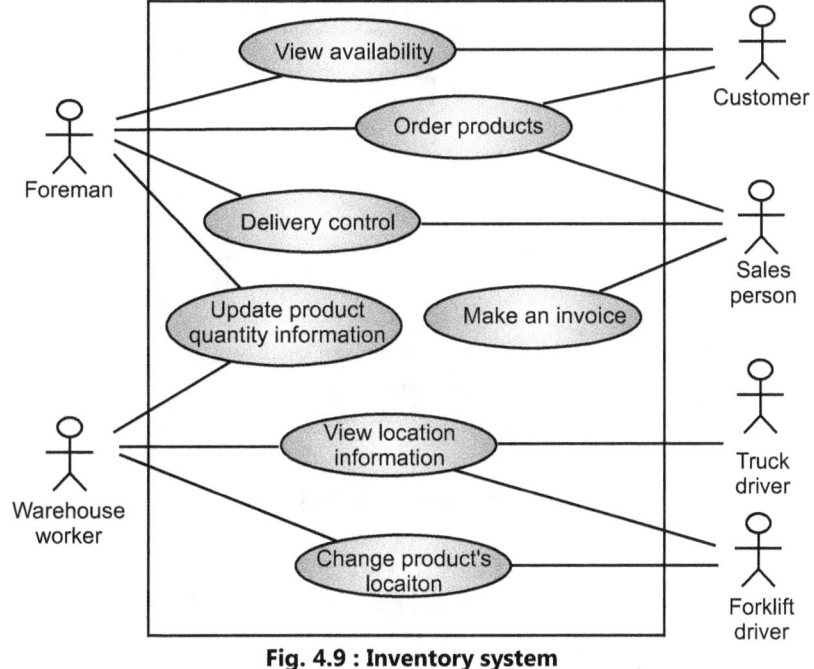

Fig. 4.9 : Inventory system

4.2 INTERACTION DIAGRAMS

From the name Interaction it is clear that the diagram is used to describe some type of interactions among the different elements in the model. So this interaction is a part of dynamic behaviour of the system.

This interactive behaviour is represented in UML by two diagrams known as Sequence diagram and Collaboration/communication diagram. The basic purposes of both the diagrams are similar.

Sequence diagram emphasizes on time sequence of messages and collaboration diagram emphasizes on the structural organization of the objects that send and receive messages.

- Interaction diagrams are defined by UML to emphasize the communication between objects, not the data manipulation associated with that communication.
- Interaction diagrams focus on specific messages between objects and how these messages come together to realize functionality.
- While composite structures show what objects fit together to fulfill a particular requirement, interaction diagrams show exactly how those objects will realize it. (not required)
- Sequence diagrams are an important member of the group known as interaction diagrams. Interaction diagrams model important runtime interactions between the parts that make-up your system and form part of the logical view of your model.

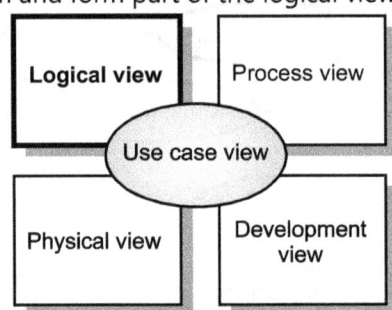

Fig. 4.10 : 4+1 Architectural view shown by interaction diagram

UML provides four types of interaction diagrams :

(1) The main diagram is the sequence diagram, which shows objects interacting along lifelines that represent general order.

(2) The communication diagram shows the messages passed between objects, focusing on the internal structure of the objects.

(3) The interaction overview diagram treats a sequence diagrams as the unit for a modified activity diagram that does not show any of the interaction details.

(4) The timing diagram shows interactions with a precise time axis.

4.3 SEQUENCE DIAGRAM

The sequence diagram is used primarily to show the interactions between objects in the sequential order that those interactions occur. Much like the class diagram, developers typically think sequence diagrams were meant exclusively for them. However, an organization's business staff can find sequence diagrams useful to communicate how the business currently works by showing how various business objects interact.

Besides documenting an organization's current affairs, a business-level sequence diagram can be used as a requirements document to communicate requirements for a future system implementation. During the requirements phase of a project, analysts can take use cases to the next level by providing a more formal level of refinement. When that occurs, use cases are often refined into one or more sequence diagrams.

An organization's technical staff can find sequence diagrams useful in documenting how a future system should behave. During the design phase, architects and developers can use the diagram to force out the system's object interactions, thus fleshing out overall system design.

One of the primary uses of sequence diagrams is in the transition from requirements expressed as use cases to the next and more formal level of refinement. Use cases are often refined into one or more sequence diagrams. In addition to their use in designing new systems, sequence diagrams can be used to document how objects in an existing (call it "legacy") system currently interact. This documentation is very useful when transitioning a system to another person or organization.

- Sequence diagrams illustrate how objects interact with each other.
- They focus on message sequences, that is, how messages are sent and received between a numbers of (not required) objects.
- Sequence diagrams are all about capturing the order of interactions between parts of your system. Using a sequence diagram, you can describe which interactions will be triggered when a particular use case is executed and in what order those interactions will occur.
- The main purpose of sequence diagrams is to show the order of events between the parts of your system that are involved in a particular interaction.

4.3.1 Generic and Instance Form

Sequence diagrams can be used in two forms : the generic form and the instance form.

1. The instance form describes a specific scenario in detail; it documents one possible interaction. The instance form does not have any conditions, branches or loops; it shows the interaction for just the chosen scenario.
2. The generic form describes all possible alternatives in a scenario; therefore branches, conditions and loops may be included.

4.3.2 Notations of Sequence Diagram

(1) Participants

The basic element of sequence diagram is collection of participants i.e. the parts of your system that interact with each other during the sequence (can be removed). The participants are always arranged horizontally with no two participants overlapping each other. Each participant has a corresponding lifeline running down the page. A participant's lifeline simply states that the part exists at that point in the sequence and is only really interesting when a part is created and/or deleted during a sequence (see Fig. 4.2).

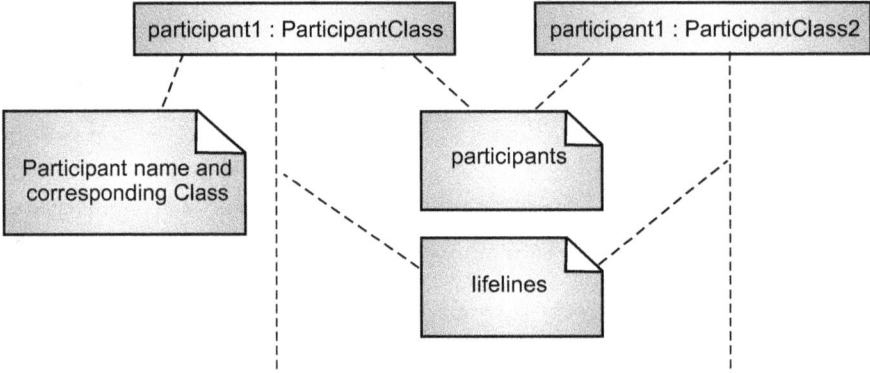

Fig. 4.11 : Participant with its lifeline

(2) Lifelines

When drawing a sequence diagram, lifeline notation elements are placed across the top of the diagram. Lifelines represent either roles or object instances that participate in the sequence being modeled. [**Note :** In fully modeled systems the objects (instances of classes) will also be modeled on a system's class diagram.] Lifelines are drawn as a box with a dashed line descending from the center of the bottom edge (Fig. 4.12). The lifeline's name is placed inside the box.

(3) Time

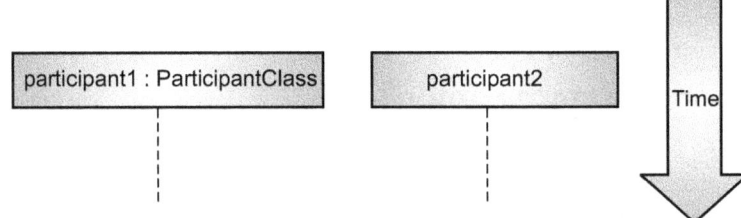

Fig. 4.12 : Time runs down the page on a sequence diagram in keeping with the participant lifeline

A sequence diagram describes the order in which the interactions take place, so time is an important factor. The lifeline represents the existence of an object at a particular time; it is drawn as an object icon with a dashed line extending down to the point at which the object stops existing. Time on a sequence diagram is all about ordering not duration. Sequence diagrams are first about the ordering of the interactions between participants; more detailed timing information is better shown on timing diagrams.

4.3.3 Events, Signals and Messages

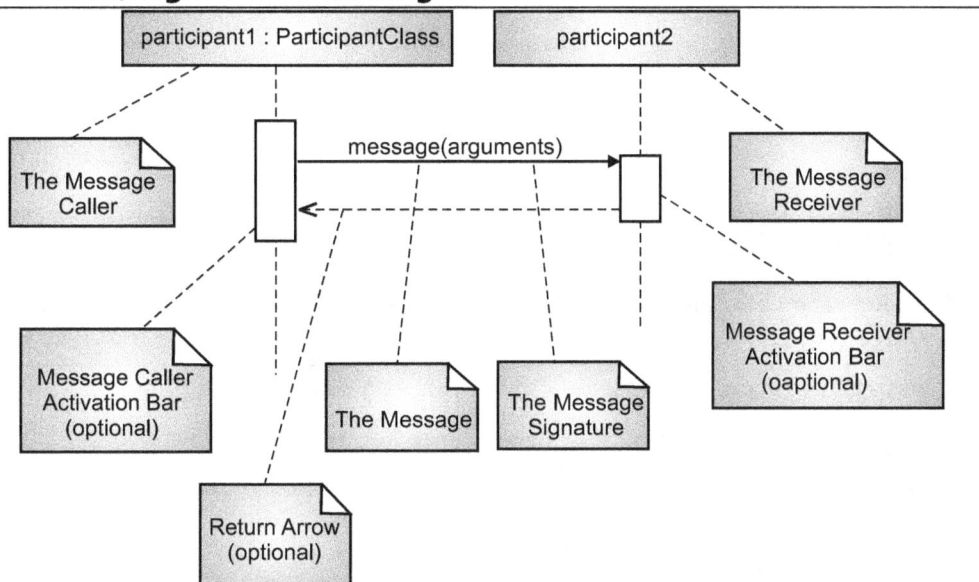

Fig. 4.13 : Interactions on a sequence diagram are as shown as messages between participants

A message is a communication between objects that conveys information with the expectation that action will be taken. An event is any point in an interaction where something occurs. Messages can be signals, operation invocations or something similar (For example, remote procedure calls [RPCs] in C++ or Remote Method Invocation [RMI] in Java). Messages can flow in whatever direction makes sense for the required interaction from left to right, right to left or even back to the message caller itself. Think of a message as an event that is passed from a message caller to get the message receiver to do something.

4.3.4 Message Signatures

Message arrow comes with a description, or signature. The format for a message signature is : Attribute = signal_or_message_name (arguments) : return_type.

You can specify any number of different arguments on a message, each separated using a comma. The format of an argument is : <name>:<class>

4.3.5 Activation Bars

When a message is passed to a participant it triggers or invokes, the receiving participant into doing something; at this point, the receiving participant is said to be active. To show that a participant is active, i.e., doing something, you can use an activation bar. It indicates that the sending participant is busy while it sends the message and the receiving participant is busy after the message has been received.

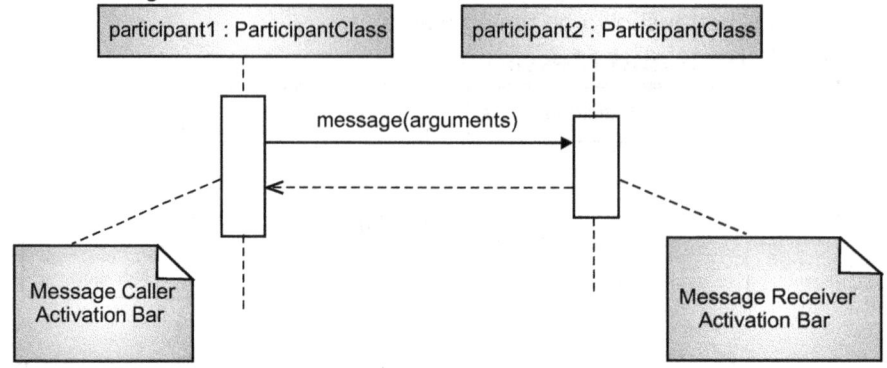

Fig. 4.14 : Activation bars show that a participant is busy doing something for a period of time

4.3.6 Message Arrows

There are five main types of message arrow for use on sequence diagram and each has its own meaning.

Synchronous Messages :
⎯⎯⎯⎯⎯⎯⎯→ A Synchronous Message

Asynchronous Message :
⎯⎯⎯⎯⎯⎯⎯▷ An Asynchronous Message

Return Message :
◀- - - - - - - - - - - - - A Return Message

A Participant Creation Messages and A Participant Destruction Messages

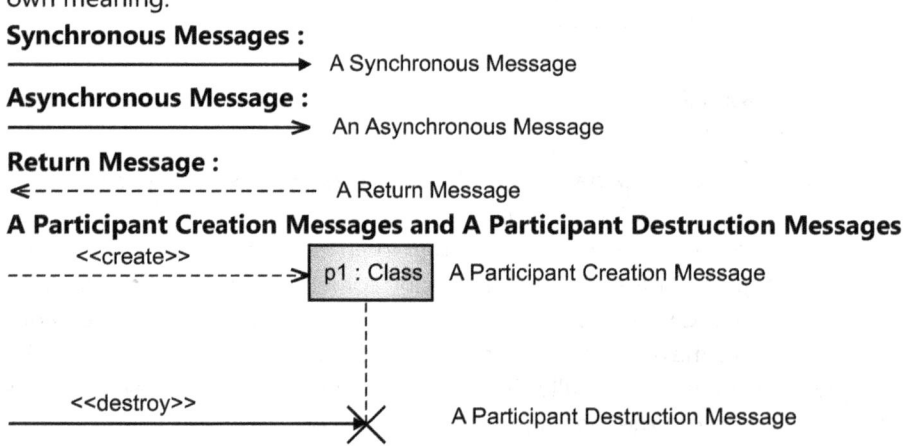

Fig. 4.15 : Create & Destruct Message

4.3.7 Synchronous Messages

A synchronous message is invoked when the Message Caller waits for the Message Receiver to return from the message invocation. Message Caller send message and suspend execution while waiting for response. Synchronous call messages are shown with filled arrow head. In following Fig. 4.16, the message Caller participant makes a single synchronous message invocation on the message Receiver participant.

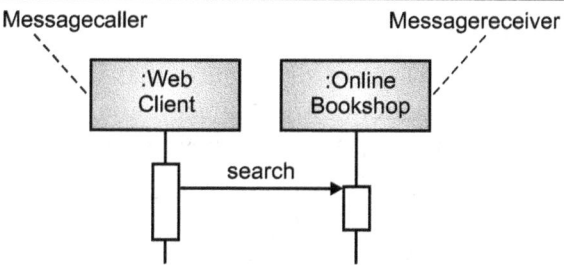

Fig. 4.16 : Web client searches online bookshop and waits for results

JAVA implementation code for message :

```
public class OnlineBookshop {      //messageReceiver class
  public void search( )   {
                           // Do something inside search;
  }
}
public class WebClient {           //messageCaller class
  private OnlineBookshop ob1;

                           // Other Methods and Attributes of the class are
                           declared here
                           // The messageRecevier attribute is initialized
                           elsewhere in the class.
  public doSomething(String[] args)   {
                           // The MessageCaller invokes the search( ) method
    this.ob1.search( );    // then waits for the method to return
                           // before carrying on here with the rest of its work
}
```

4.3.8 Asynchronous Messages

An asynchronous message is invoked by a Message Caller on a Message Receiver, but the Message Caller does not wait for the message invocation to return before carrying on with the rest of the interaction's steps. Asynchronous call send message and proceed immediately without waiting for return value. Asynchronous messages have an open arrow head.

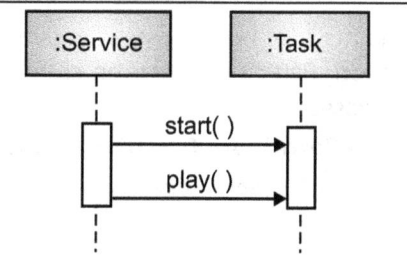

Fig. 4.17 : Service starts task and proceeds in parallel without waiting

4.3.9 The Return Message

The return message is an optional piece of notation that you can use at the end of an activation bar to show that the control flow of the activation returns to the participant that passed the original message. In code, a return arrow is similar to reaching the end of a method or explicitly calling a return statement.

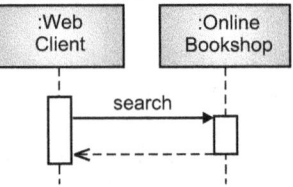

Fig. 4.18 : Web client searches online bookshop and waits for results to be returned

4.3.10 Participant Creation and Destruction Messages

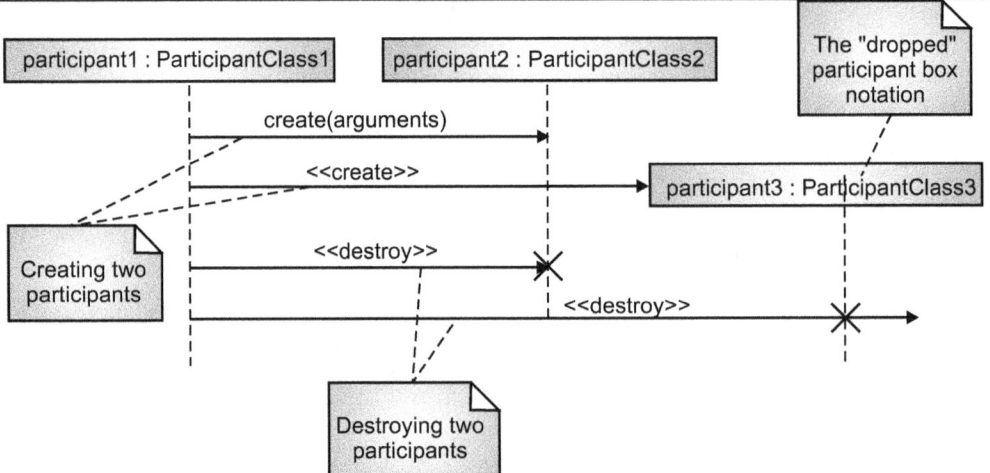

Fig. 4.19 : Both participant2 and participant3 are created throughout the course of this sequence diagram

Participants do not necessarily live for the entire duration of a sequence diagram's interaction. Participants can be created and destroyed according to the messages that are being passed.

Software Participant Creation in Java

```
public class MessageReceiver {

  // Attributes and Methods of the MessageReceiver class
}
```

```
public class MessageCaller {
  // Other Methods and Attributes of the class are declared here
  public void doSomething ( ) {

    // The MessageReceiver object is created

    MessageReceiver messageReceiver = new MessageReceiver ( );
  }
}
```

4.3.11 Nested Messages

When a message from one participant trigger receiving participant which result in (not required) one or more messages being sent by the receiving participant, those resulting messages are said to be nested messages.

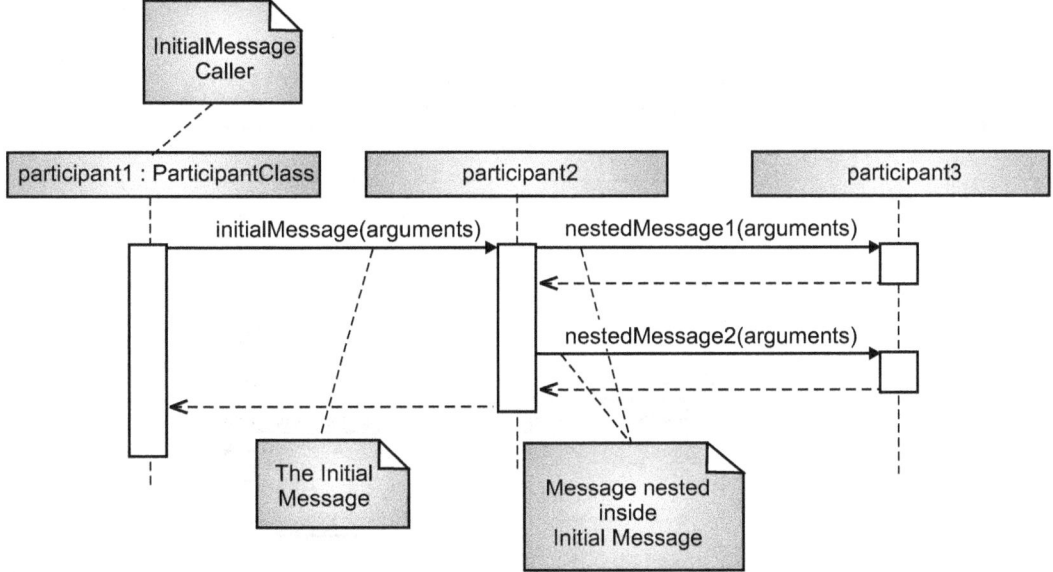

Fig. 4.20 : Shows two nested messages, when participant 2 receive initial message

Example of Sequence Diagram

Requirement

The content management system shall allow an administrator to create a new blog account, provided the personal details of the new blogger are verified using the author credentials database.

A Top-Level Sequence Diagram

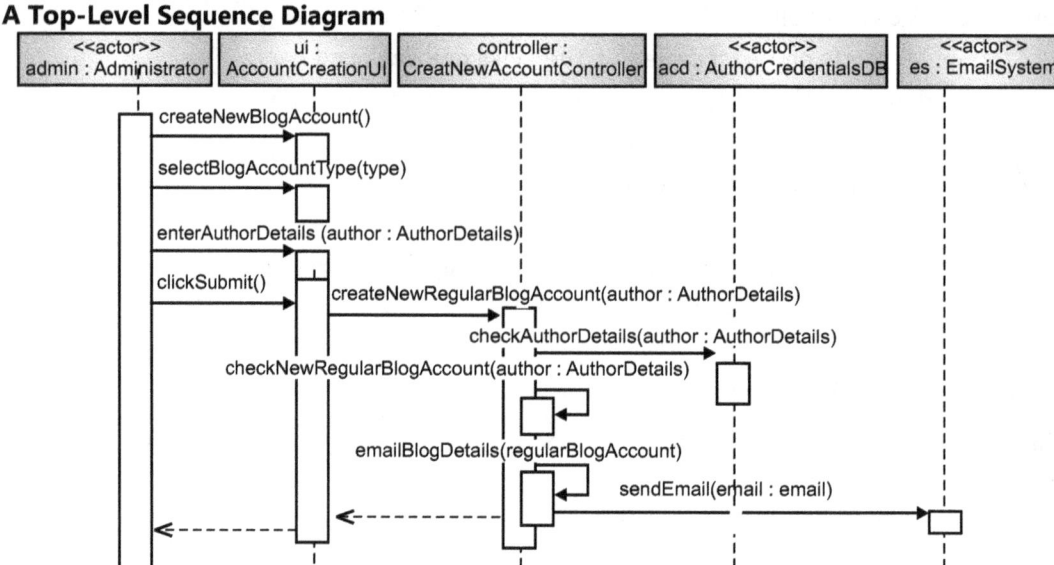

Fig. 4.21 : Sequence diagram for content management system

Adding and Deleting Participant in Middle of Sequence Diagram

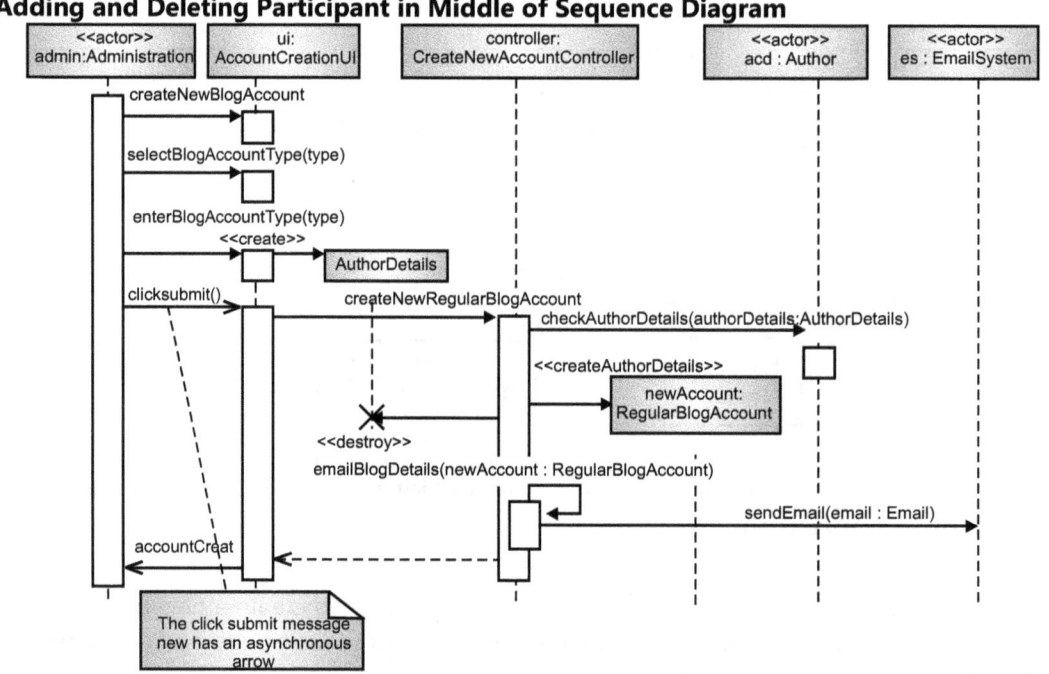

Fig. 4.22 : Sequence diagram for content management system

4.3.12 Sequence Fragments

A sequence fragment is used to represent complex interactions such as loops and alternate flows. It is represented as a box that encloses a portion of the interactions within a sequence diagram.

A sequence fragment's box overlaps the region of the sequence diagram where the fragment's interactions take place. A fragment box can contain any number of interactions and for large complex interactions, further nested fragments as well. The top left corner of the fragment box contains an operator. The fragment operator indicates which type of fragment this is.

4.3.13 A Brief Overview of UML 2.0's Fragment Types

UML 2.0 contains a broad set of different fragment types that you can apply to your sequence diagrams to make them more expressive,

Type	Parameters	Why is it useful?
ref	None	Represents an interaction that is defined elsewhere in the model. Helps you manage a large diagram by splitting and potentially reusing, a collection of interactions. Similar to the reuse modeled when the <<include>> use case relationship is applied.
assert	None	Specifies that the interactions contained within the fragment box must occur exactly as they are indicated; otherwise the fragment is declared invalid and an exception should be raised. Works in a similar fashion to the **assert** statement in Java. Useful when specifying that every step in an interaction must occur successfully, i.e., when modeling a transaction.
loop	min times, max times, [guard_condition]	Loops through the interactions contained within the fragment a specified number of times until the guard condition is evaluated to false. Very similar to the Java and C# for(..) loop. Useful when you are trying to execute a set of interactions for a specific number of times.
break	None	If the interactions contained within the break fragment occur, then any enclosing interaction, most commonly a loop fragment should be exited. Similar to the break statement in Java and C#.

alt	[guard_condition1] ... [guard_condition2] ... [else]	Depending on which guard condition evaluates to true first, the corresponding sub-collection of interactions will be executed. Helps you specify that a set of interactions will be executed only under certain conditions. Similar to an if(..) else statement in code.
opt	[guard_condition]	The interactions contained within this fragment will execute only if the guard condition evaluates to true. Similar to a simple if(..) statement in code with no corresponding else. Especially useful when showing steps that have been reused from another use case's sequence diagrams, where <<extend>> is the use case relationship.
neg	None	Declares that the interactions inside this fragment are not to be executed, ever. Helpful if you are just trying to mark a collection of interactions as not executed until you are sure that those interactions can be removed. Most useful if you happen to be lucky enough to be using an Executable UML tool where your sequence diagrams are actually being run. Also can be helpful to show that something cannot be done, for example, when you want to show that a participant cannot call read( ) on a socket after close( ). Works in a similar fashion to commenting out some method calls in code.
par	None	Specifies that interactions within this fragment can happily be executed in parallel. This is similar to saying that there is no need for any thread-safe locking required within a set of interactions.
region	None	Interactions within this type of fragment are said to be part of a critical region. A critical region is typically an area where a shared participant is updated. Combined with parallel interactions, specified using the par fragment type, you can model where interactions are not required to be thread or process-safe (par fragment) and where locks are required to prevent parallel interactions interleaving (region fragment). Has similarities synchronized blocks and object locks in Java.

Example of Sequence Diagram using a Sequence Fragments
(1) ref : reference

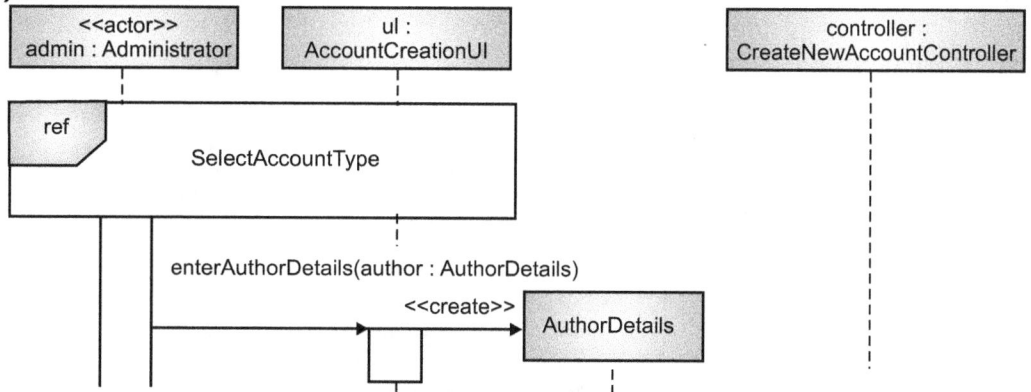

Fig. 4.23 : Sequence diagram for reference fragment

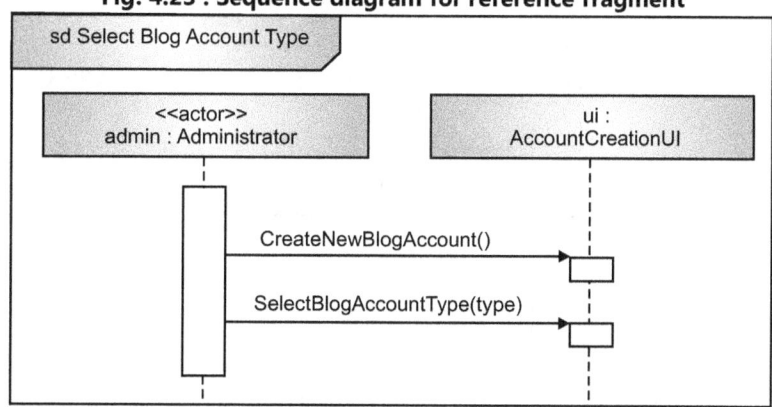

Fig. 4.24 : Sequence diagram for select blog account type

(2) assert : Assertion

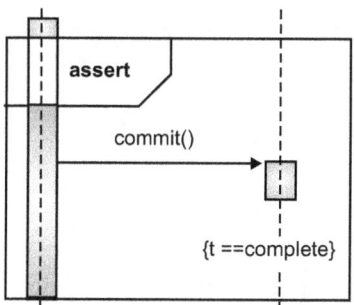

Fig. 4.25 : Commit( ) message should occur at this point, following with evaluation of state invariant

(3) loop(minval,maxval) : Loop

Following Fig. 4.26 shows the loop is expected to execute minimum 5 times and no more than 10 times. If guard condition [size<0] becomes false loop terminates regardless of the minimum number of iterations specified.

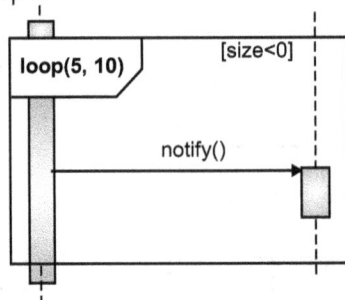

Fig. 4.26 : Loop fragment

(4) break

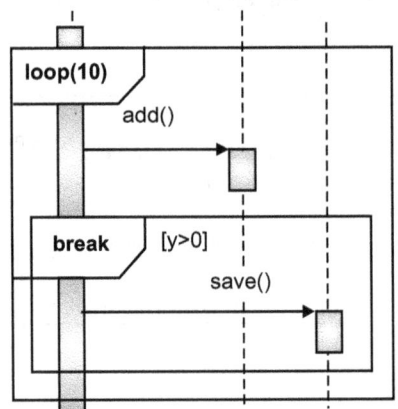

Fig. 4.27 : Break enclosing loop if y>0

(5) alt : Alternatives

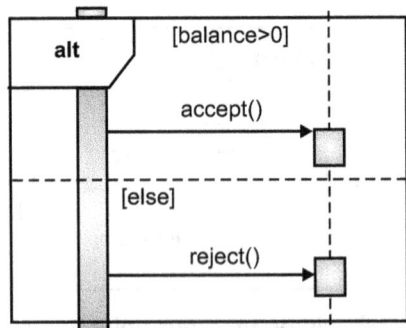

Fig. 4.28 : Call accept() if balance>0, call reject( ) otherwise

(6) opt : Option

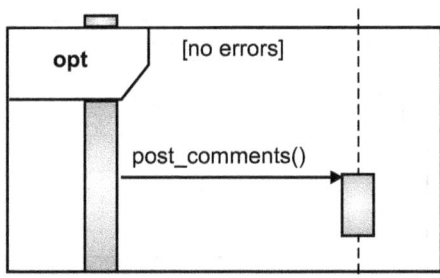

Fig. 4.29 : Post comments if there were no errors

(7) neg : Negative

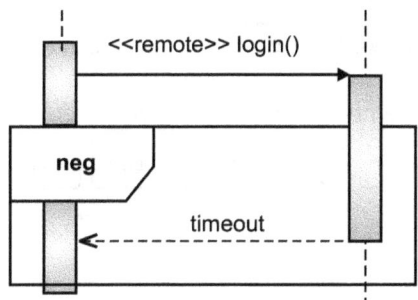

Fig. 4.30 : Should we receive back timeout message, it means the system has failed

(8) par : Parallel

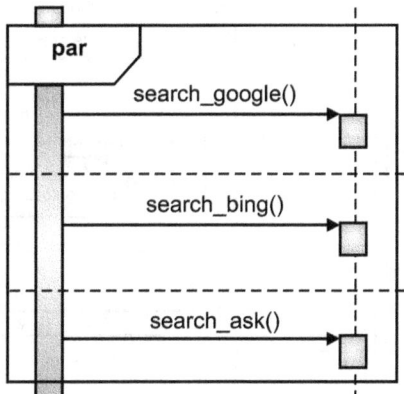

Fig. 4.31 : Search google, bing and ask in any order, possibly parallel

(9) region : Critical Region

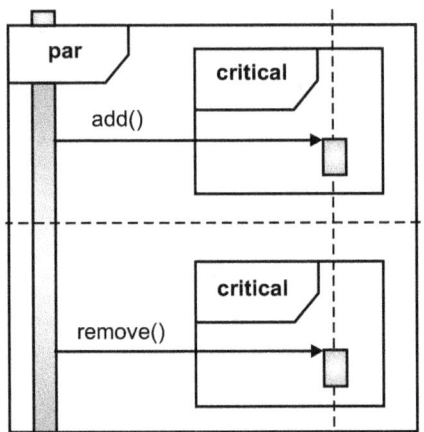

Fig. 4.32 : Add() or remove() could be called in parallel, but each one should run as a critical region

Following Fig. 4.33 shows refinement of Fig. 4.13 applying conditional fragment type.

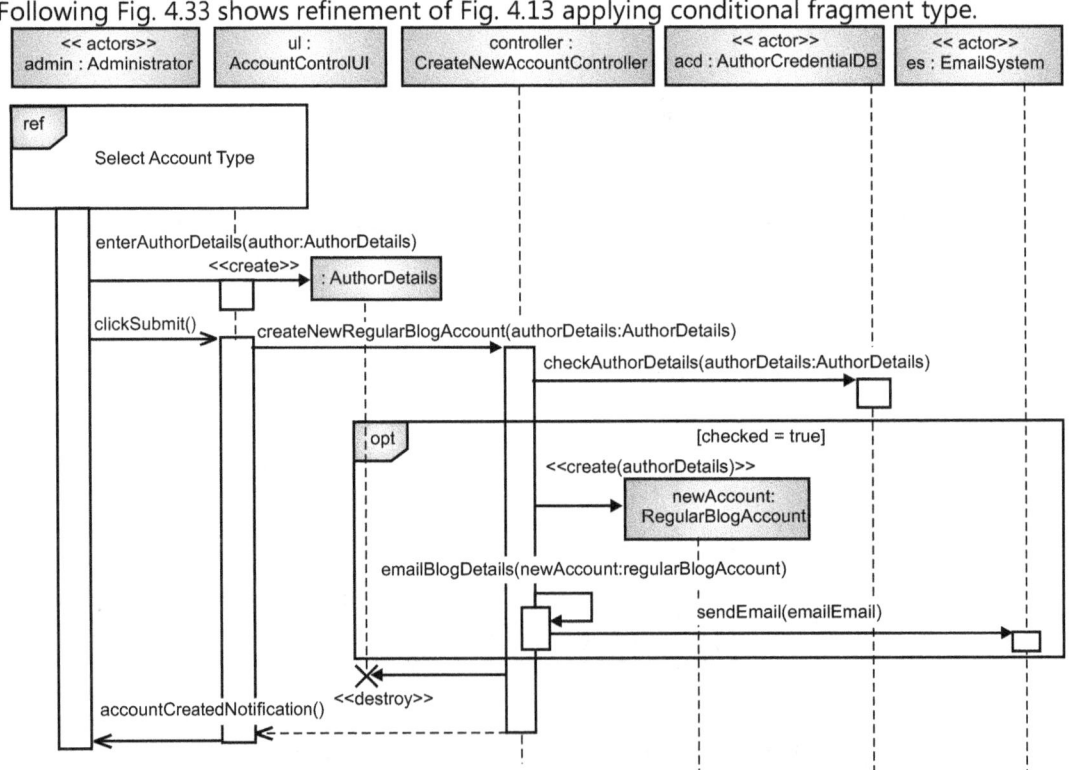

Fig. 4.33 : Example shows use of ref and opt fragment types

A referenced sequence diagram that contains the new account selection interactions

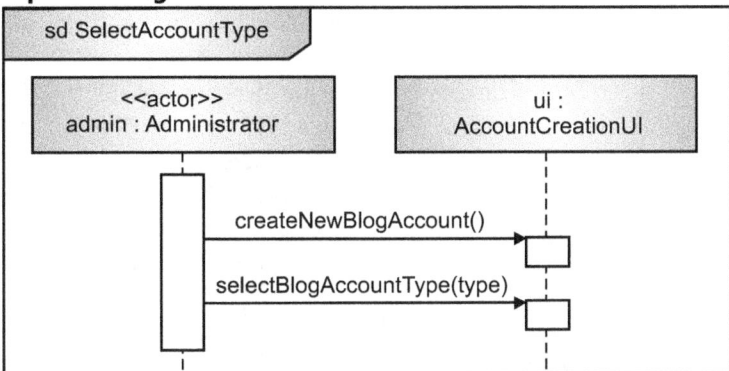

Fig. 4.34 : Sequence diagram for Select Account Type

4.4 COMMUNICATION/COLLABORATION DIAGRAM

- Communication diagrams add another perspective to an interaction by focusing on the links between the participants. Communication diagrams focus both on the interactions and the links among a set of collaborating objects. While the sequence diagram focuses roughly on time, the communication diagram variant focuses on space.
- Communication diagrams show objects and how messages are sent between the linked objects and thereby imply their relations.
- Communication diagrams are especially good at showing which links are needed between participants to pass an interaction's messages. With a quick glance at a communication diagram, you can tell which participants need to be connected for an interaction can take place. It is especially good to model the dynamic behavior of the use case.

You can use communication diagrams to explore how objects in a system or application work together. Communication diagrams can identify the following aspects of an interaction or task :

- Objects that participate in the interaction.
- Interfaces that the participating classes require.
- Structural changes that an interaction requires.
- Data that is passed between the objects in an interaction.

4.4.1 Lifeline and Message

Lifeline

- Lifeline is a specialization of Named Element which represents an individual participant in the Interaction. While Parts and Structural Features may have multiplicity greater than 1, Lifelines represent only one interacting entity. A Lifeline is shown as a rectangle (corresponding to "head" in sequence diagrams). Lifeline in sequence diagrams does have "tail" representing the line of life whereas "lifeline" in communication diagram has no line, just "head".

- Participants on a communication diagram are represented by a rectangle. The participant's name and class are then placed in the middle of the rectangle. A participant's name is formatted as <name> : <class>, similar to participants on a sequence diagram. A communication link is shown with a single line that connects two participants. A link's purpose is to allow messages to be passed between the different participants; without a link, the two participants cannot interact with each other.

Fig. 4.35 : Lifeline "data" of class Stock

Message :

- Message in communication diagram is shown as a line with sequence expression and arrow above the line. The arrow indicates direction of the communication.
- A message on a communication diagram is shown using a filled arrow from the message sender to the message receiver.

Examples :

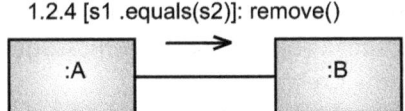

Fig. 4.36 : Instance of class A sends remove( ) message to instance of B if s1 is equal to s2

Fig. 4.37 : Two messages are passed along the link between participant1 and participant2

4.4.2 Nested Message

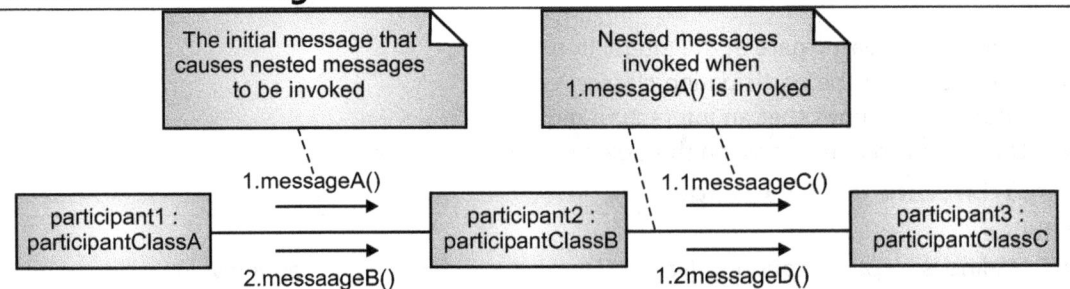

Fig. 4.38 : MessageA( ) directly leads to nested 1.1 messageC( ), followed by nested messageD( ), before message 2 is invoked

4.4.3 Messages Occurring at the Same Time

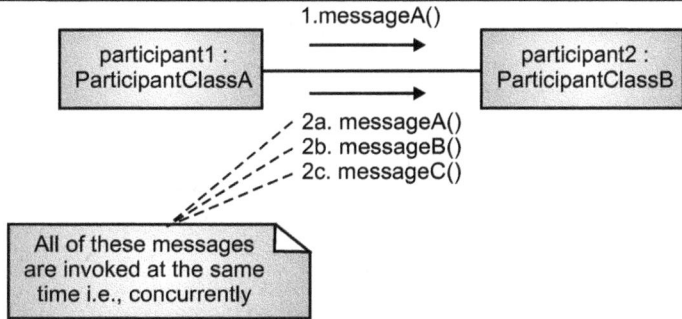

Fig. 4.39 : Messages 2a. messageB( ), 2b. messageB( ),

and 2c. messageC() are all invoked at the same time after 1.

messageA( ) has been invoked

4.4.4 Invoking a Message Multiple Times

The diagram shows that a message is invoked a number of times similar to for(..) loop.

*[i = 0 .. 9]

4.4.5 Sending a Message Based on a Condition

A guard condition is made up of a logical Boolean statement. When the guard condition evaluates to true, the associated message will be invoked otherwise, the message is skipped.

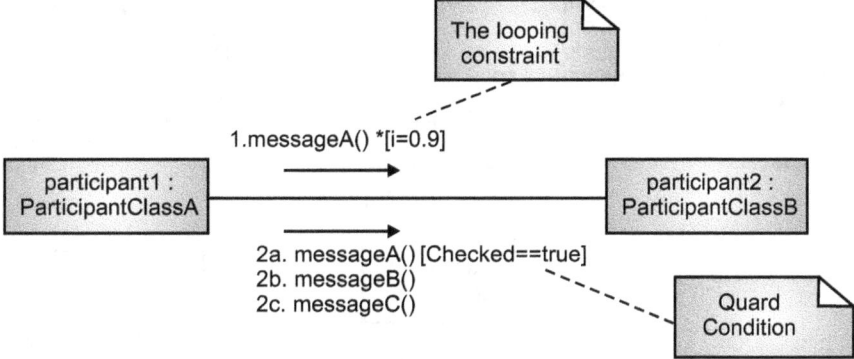

Fig. 4.40 : The addition of a new looping constraint to 1. messageA( ) means that the message

will be invoked 10 times before the next set of messages2a, 2b,

and 2c can be invoked and the 2a.messageA

( ) will get invoked if [check==true] returns true

4.4.6 Message to Itself

A participant talking to itself. Object invokes its own method.

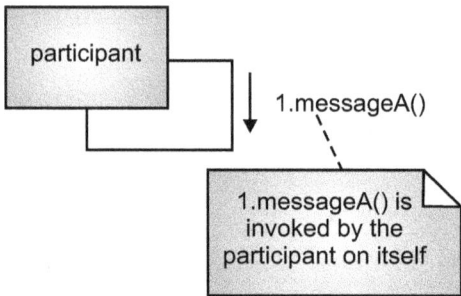

Fig. 4.41 : The participant can invoke 1. messageA( ) on itself because it has a communication line to itself

4.4.7 Examples of Communication Diagram

(1) Draw communication diagram for student-Seminar system

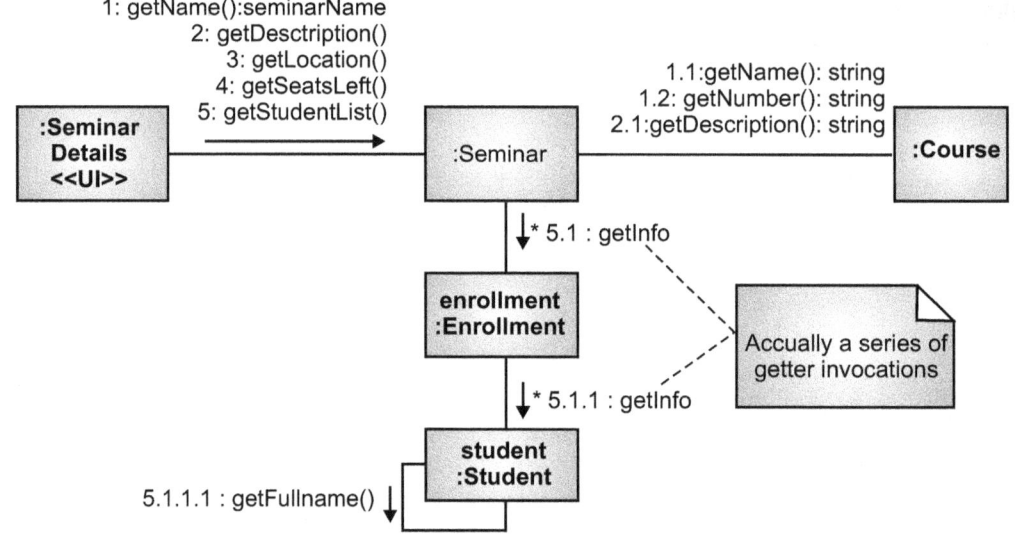

Fig. 4.42 : Student Seminar System

(2) Draw communication diagram for Content Management System

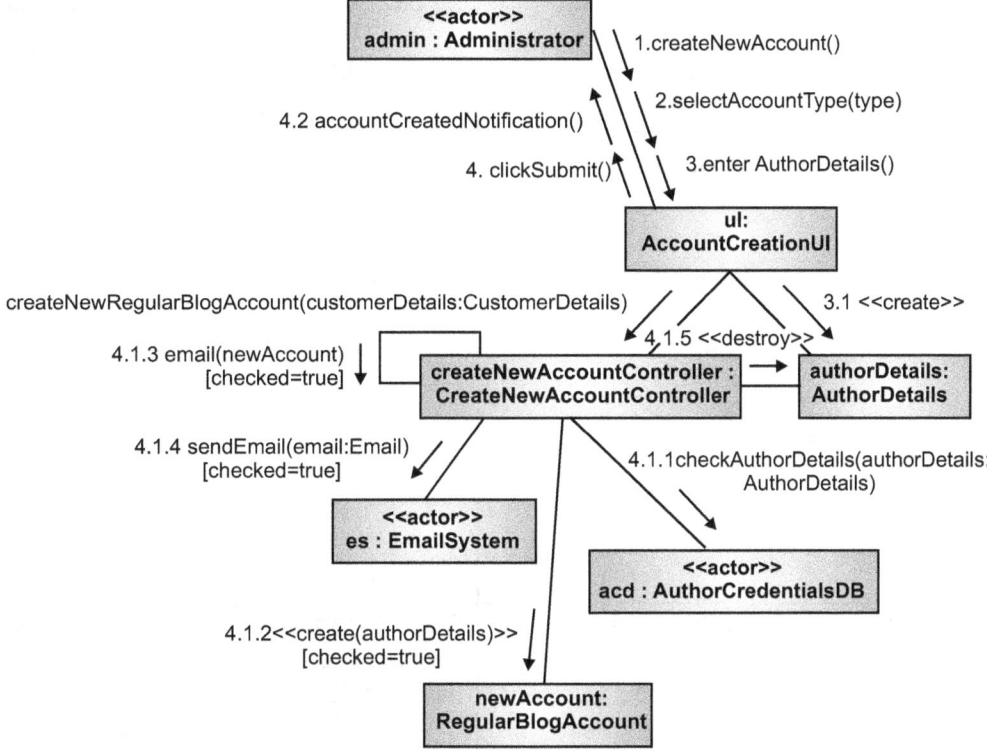

Fig. 4.43 : Content management system

(3) Draw Communication Diagram for Online Bookshop

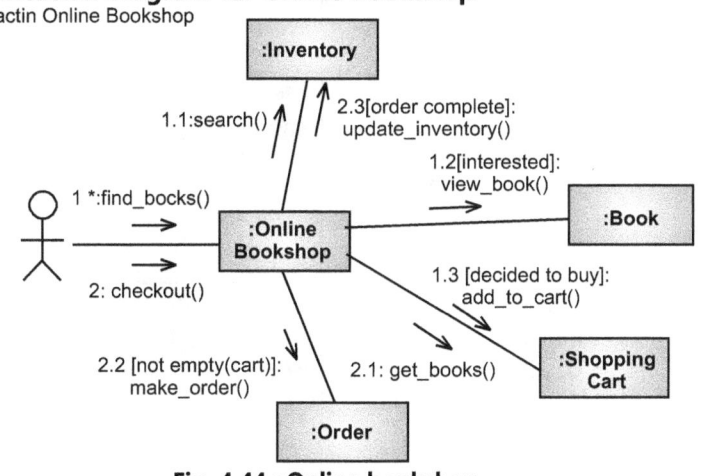

Fig. 4.44 : Online bookshop

4.4.8 Comparing Sequence and Communication Diagrams

Feature	Sequence Diagrams	Communication Diagrams	The Result
Shows participants effectively	Participants are mostly arranged along the top of page, unless the drop-box participant creation notation is used. It is easy to gather the participants involved in a particular interaction.	Participants as well as links are the focus, so they are shown clearly as rectangles.	Communication diagrams barely win. Although both types of diagram can show participants as effectively as each other, it can be argued that communication diagrams have the edge since participants are one of their main focuses.
Showing the links between participants	Links are implied. If a message is passed from one participant to another, then it is implied that a link must exist between those participants.	Explicitly shows the links between participants. In fact, this is the primary purpose of these types of diagram.	Communication diagrams win because they explicitly and clearly show the links between participants.
Showing message signatures	Message signatures can be fully described.	Message signatures can be fully described.	Draw! Both types of diagram can show messages as effectively as each other.
Supports parallel messages	With the introduction of sequence fragments, sequence diagrams are much better.	Shown using the number-letter notation on message sequences.	Draw! Both types of diagram show parallel messages equally well.

Supports asynchronous messages (fire and forget)	Achieved using the asynchronous arrow.	Communication diagrams have no concept of the asynchronous message since its focus is not on message ordering.	Sequence diagrams are a clear winner here because they explicitly support asynchronous messages.
Easy to read message ordering	This is a sequence diagram's forte(forte). Sequence diagrams clearly show message ordering using the vertical placement of messages down the diagram's page.	Shown using the number-point-nested notation.	Sequence diagrams are a clear winner here since they really show-off message ordering clearly and effectively.
Easy to create and maintain the diagram	Creating a sequence diagram is fairly simple. However, maintaining sequence diagrams can be a nightmare unless a helpful UML tool is being used.	Communication diagrams are simple enough to create; however, maintenance, especially if message numbering needs to be changed, still ideally needs the support of a helpful UML tool.	This is a difficult one to judge and is largely based on personal preference. However, communication diagrams do have the edge on the ease-of-maintenance stakes.

Note :
- Use sequence diagrams if you are mainly interested in the flow of messages throughout a particular interaction.
- Use communication diagrams if you are focusing on the links between the different participants involved in the interaction.

4.5 TIMING DIAGRAMS

A timing diagram allows you to show the interaction of objects and changes in state for those objects along a time axis. A timing diagram provides a convenient way to show active objects and their state changes during their interactions with other active objects and system resources. The X-axis of the timing diagram has the time units, while the Y-axis shows the objects and their states.

Sequence diagrams focus on message order and communication diagrams show the links between participants, so far there has been no place on these interaction diagrams to model detailed timing information. You may have an interaction that must take no longer than 10 seconds to complete, or a message that should take no more than half the interaction's total time to return. If this type of information is important to an interaction that you are modeling, then timing diagrams are probably for you.

In a timing diagram, each event has timing information associated with it that accurately describes when the event is invoked, how long it takes for another participant to receive the event and how long the receiving participant is expected to be in a particular state. Interaction timing is most commonly associated with real-time or embedded systems, but it certainly is not limited to these domains. In fact, the need to capture accurate timing information about an interaction can be important regardless of the type of system being modeled.

Timing diagrams provide a helpful tool for sorting out race conditions, priority inversions, deadlocks and other communication issues. When you are trying to sort out such complex executions, use a timing diagram. Timing diagrams will look strangely familiar to anyone with a little experience of the analysis of electronic circuit boards. This is because a timing diagram looks very similar to a plot that you had expect to see on a logic analyzer. Timing diagrams perform a similar job for the participants within your system. On a timing diagram, events are the logic analyzer's signals and the states are the states that a participant is placed in when an event is received.

4.5.1 Building Timing Diagram

Following steps build the complete Timing Diagram :

Step 1 : Add Participants to a Timing Diagram.

Step 2 : Add States to a Timing Diagram.

Step 3 : Add Time Measurement (that's Important!).

Step 4 : Add Participant state-lines.

Step 5 : Add Events and Signals.

By using these steps we can render Timing diagram. Here is requirement set for which will apply above steps and build Timing diagram.

Requirement

The content management system shall allow an administrator to create a new regular blog account within five seconds of the information being entered, provided the personal details of the author are verified using the Author Credentials Database.

Step 1 : Add Participants to a Timing Diagram

First, you need to create a timing diagram that incorporates all of the participants involved in the particular interaction.

Format to write participant

<name>:<type>

Timing Diagram does not support creation and destruction messages of sequence diagram. Details of these participants have been left out because timing diagrams focus on timing in relation to state changes.

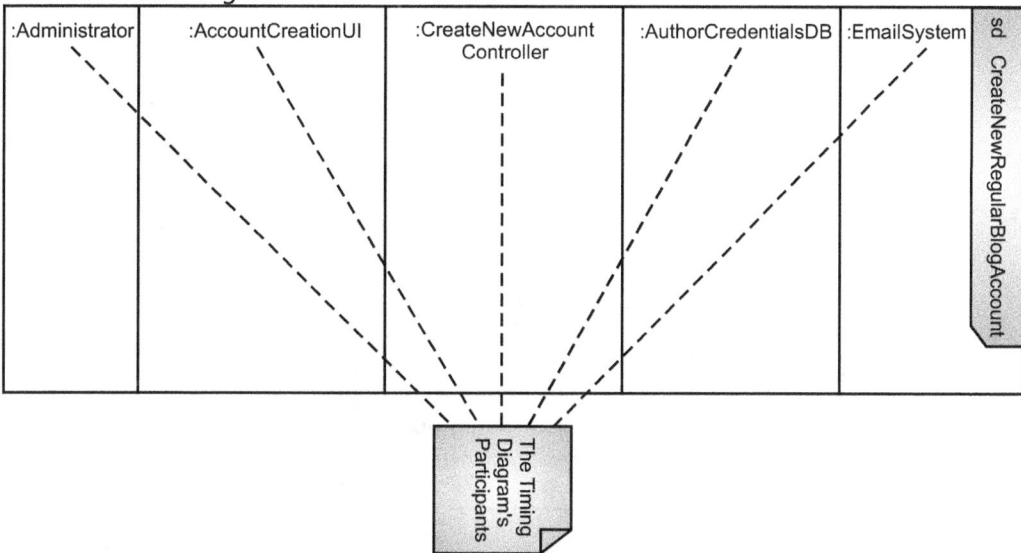

Fig 4.45 : The names of the main participants involved in an interaction are written either vertically (here) or horizontally

Step 2 : Add States to a Timing Diagram

During an interaction, a participant can exist in any number of states. A participant is said to be in a particular state when it receives an event (such as a message). The participant can then be said to be in that state until another event occurs (such as the return of that message). Placed the States on a timing diagram next to their corresponding participant.

Step 3 : Add Time Measurement

So far, we have just been setting the stage, adding participants and the states that they can be put in, but to really model the information that's important to a timing diagram, it's now time to add time. Time on a timing diagram runs from left to right across the page.

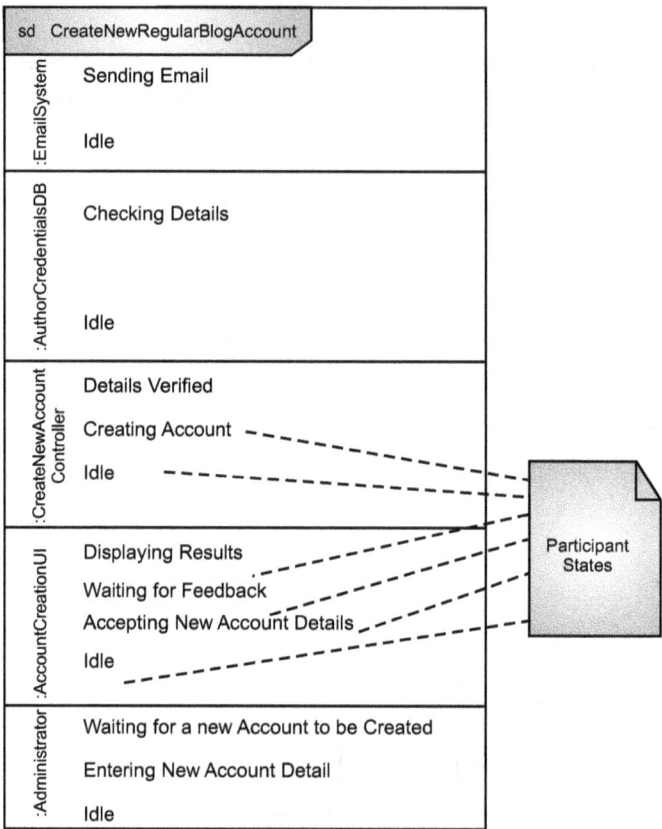

Fig. 4.46 : States are written horizontally on a timing diagram and next to the participant that they are associated with

A. Exact Time Measurements

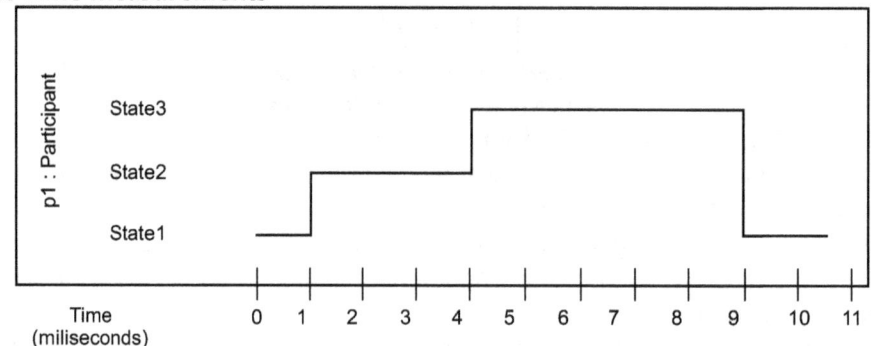

Fig. 4.47 : Time measurements are placed on a timing diagram as a ruler along the bottom of the page

B. Relative Time Indicators

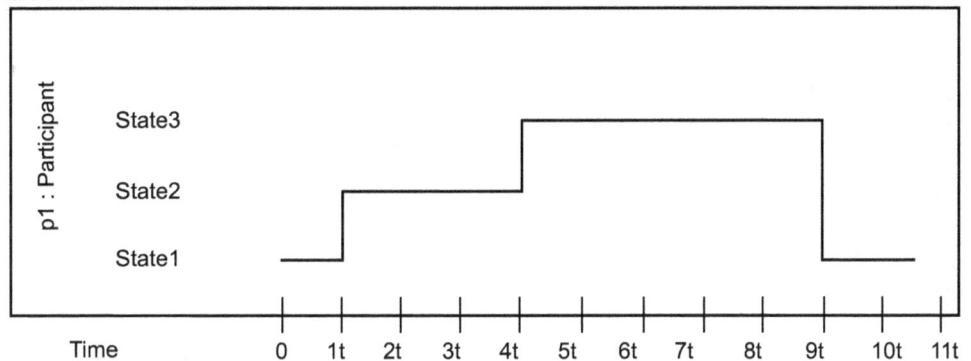

Fig. 4.48 : Relative time indicators are particularly useful when you have timing considerations such as "Participant A will be in State1 for half of the time that Participant B is in State 2".

In a timing diagram, t represents a point in time that is of interest.

Step 4 : Add Participant State-Lines

You can connect state with a horizontal line that is called the *state-line*.

At any given time in the interaction, a participant's state-line is aligned with one of the participant's states.

Step 5 : Add Events and Signals

Participants change state on a timing diagram in response to events. These events might be the invocation of a message or they might be something else such as a message returning after it has been invoked. The important thing to remember is that whatever the event is, it is shown on a timing diagram to trigger a change in the state of a participant. An event on a timing diagram is as shown in Fig. 4.50, an arrow from one participant's state-line the event source to another participant's state-line the event receiver. (can be made understandable).

Timing constraints describe in detail how long a given portion of an interaction should take. They are usually applied to the amount of time that a participant should be in a particular state or how long an event should take to be invoked and received.

An Alternate Notation

The regular timing diagram notation shows states as a list next to the relevant participant. A state-line is then needed to show what state a participant is in at a given time. Unfortunately, if a participant has many different states, then the amount of space needed to model a participant on the timing diagram will grow quickly.

The alternative notation fixes this problem by removing the vertical list of different states. It places a participant's states directly at the point in time when the participant is in that state. Therefore, the state-line is no longer needed, and all of the states for a particular participant can be placed in a single line across the diagram.

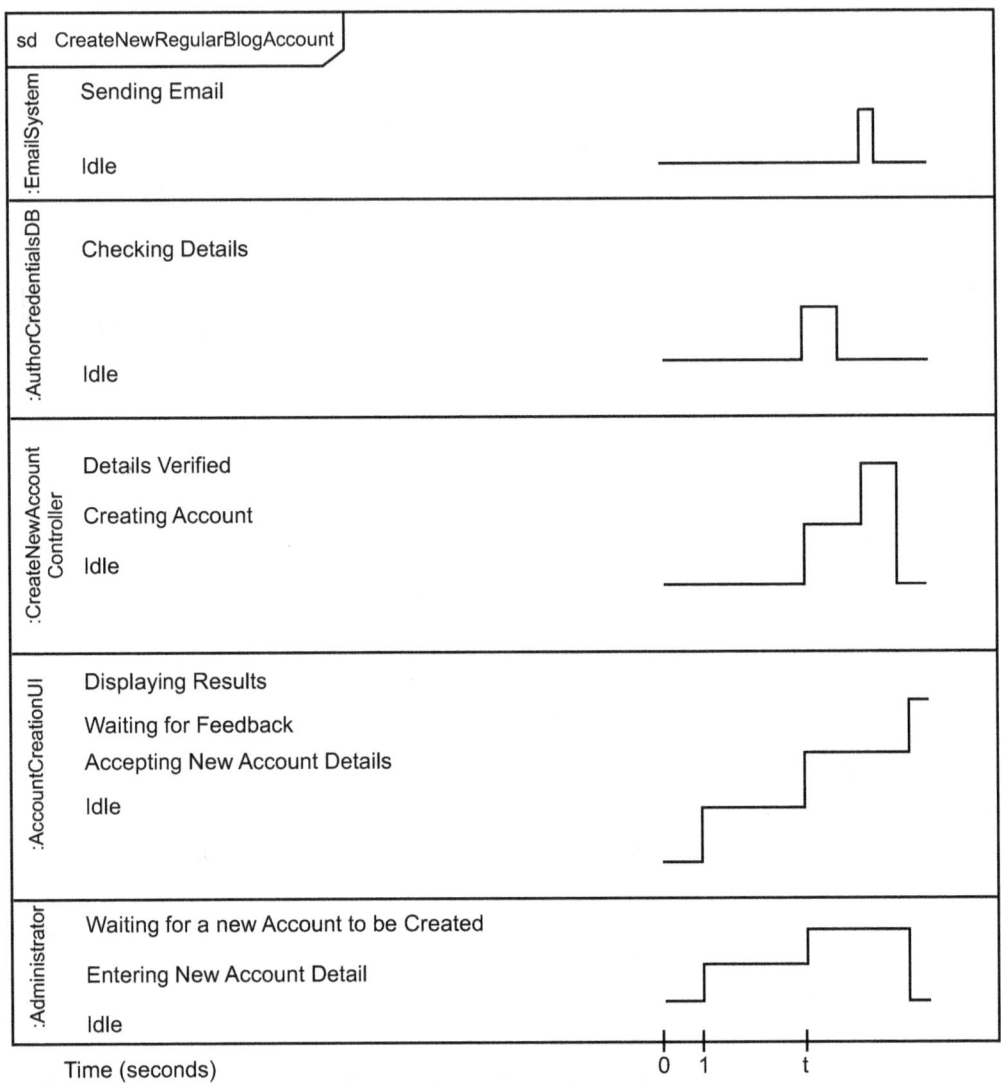

Fig. 4.49 : Each of the participants needs to have a corresponding state-line to indicate their state at any given point in time

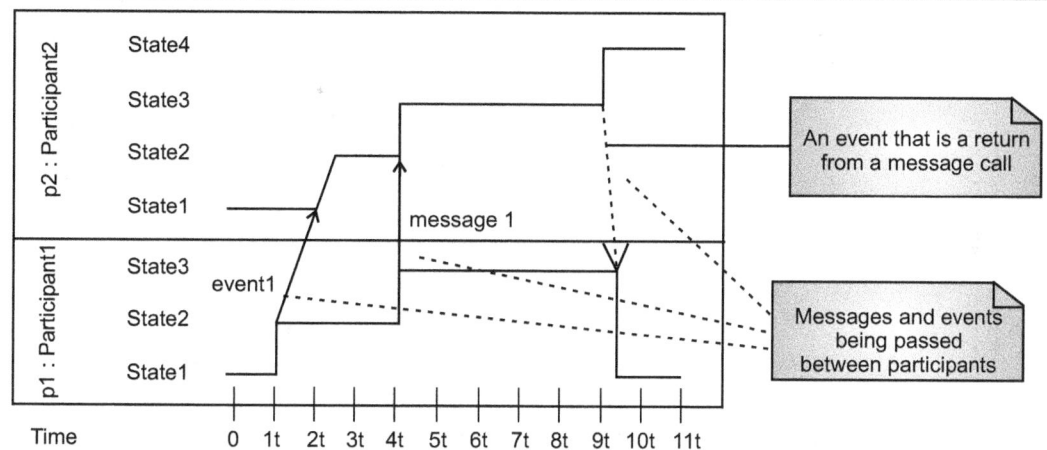

Fig. 4.50 : Events on a timing diagram can even have their own durations, as shown by event1 taking 1 unit of time from invocation by p1:Participant1 and reception by p2:Participant2

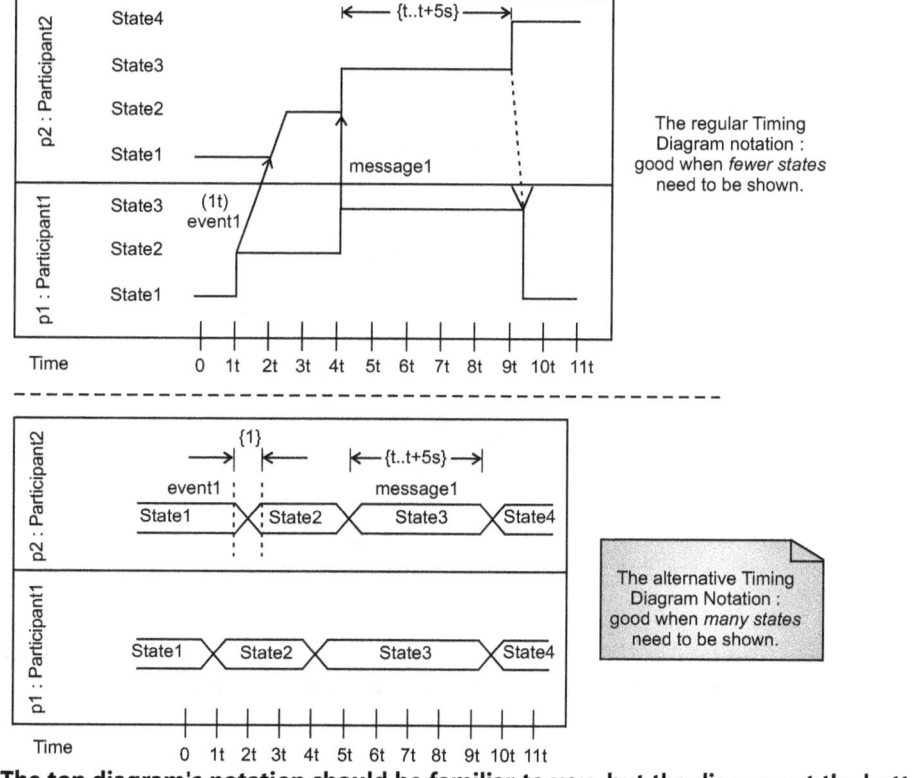

Fig. 4.51 : The top diagram's notation should be familiar to you, but the diagram at the bottom uses the new alternative timing diagram notation

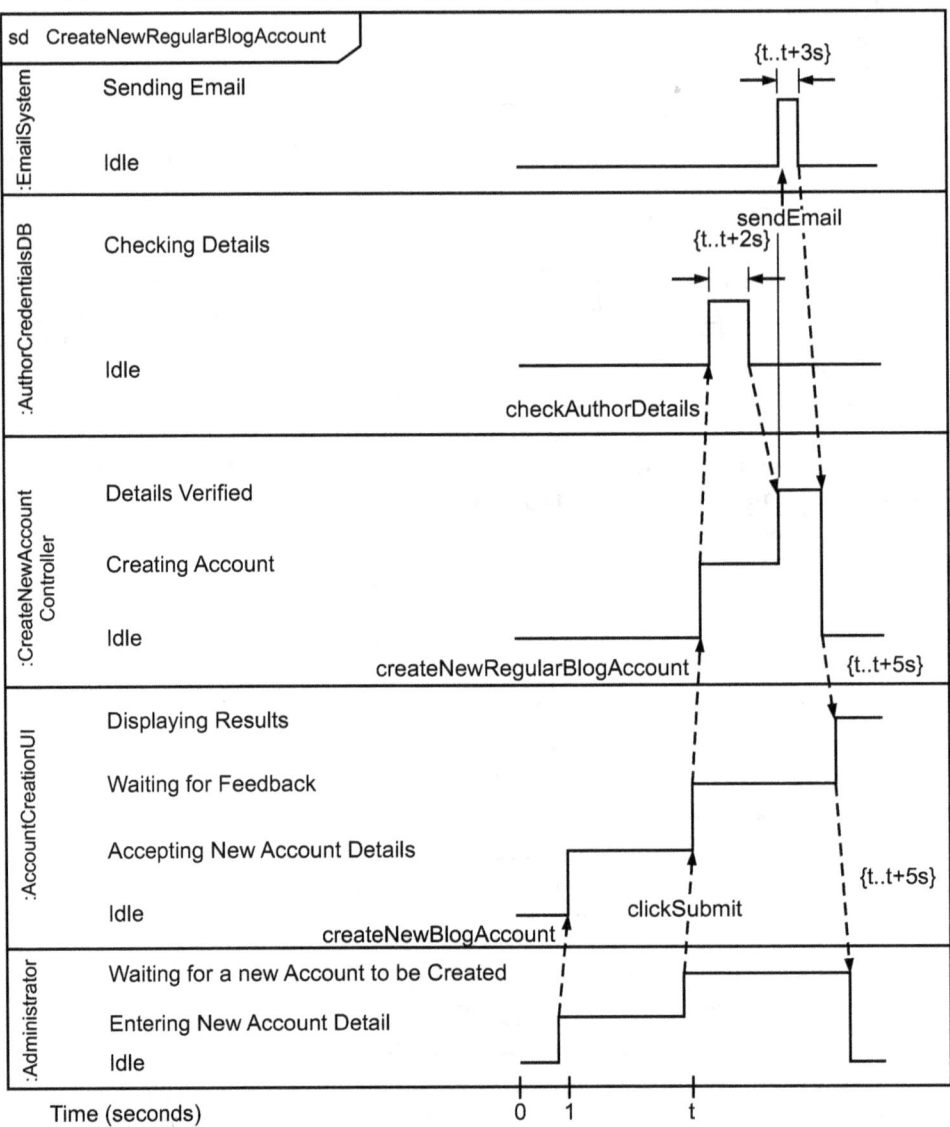

Fig. 4.52 : From when the: Administrator clicks on submit until the point at which the system has created a new account, no more than five seconds have passed

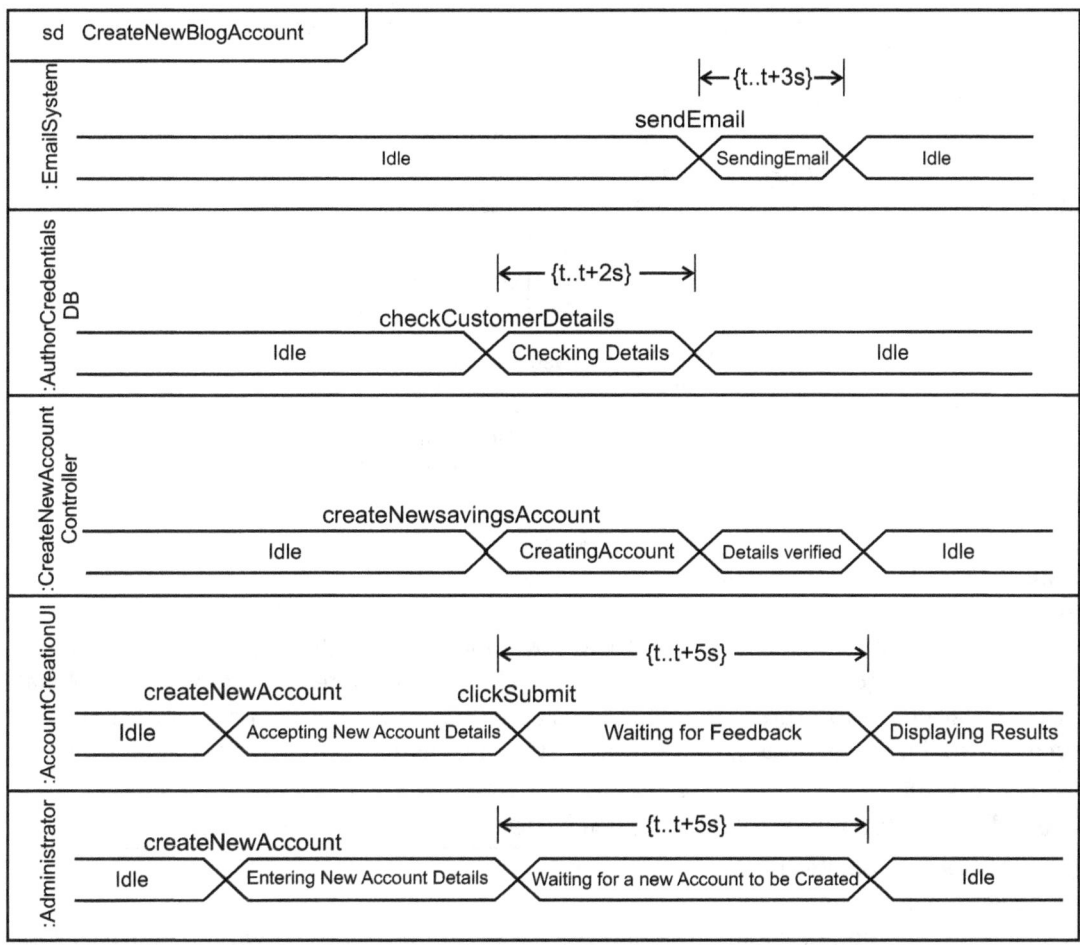

Fig. 4.53 : Create new blog account

4.6 STATE MACHINE DIAGRAM

State machines can be used to model the behavior of a class, subsystem, or entire application. Activity diagrams and interaction diagrams are useful for describing behavior, but there is still a missing piece. Sometimes the state of an object or system is an important factor in its behavior. For example, if the Order Management System required potential customer to submit an application for an order, which could be approved or rejected, then the Order_object may act differently depending on whether it is pending, accepted or rejected. In such situations, it's helpful to model states of an object and the events causing state changes this is what state machine diagrams do best. State machine diagrams capture

the behavior of a software system. State machine diagrams are used in special position of software and hardware systems including the following :
- Real-time/mission-critical systems, such as heart monitoring software.
- Dedicated devices whose behavior is defined in terms of state, such as ATMs.
- First-person shooter games such as Doom or Half-Life.

State machine diagrams are part of the logical model of your system;

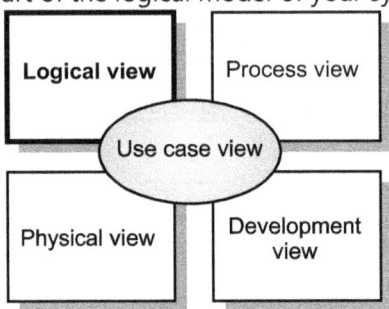

Fig. 4.54 : 4+1 view architecture

UML defines two kinds of state machines—behavioral state machines and protocol state machines. Behavioral state machines capture the life cycles of objects, subsystems and systems. They tell the states an object can have and how events (received messages, time elapsed, errors, and conditions becoming true) affect those states over time. Protocol state machines are used to express the legal transitions that might occur in an abstract classifier such as an interface or a port. Protocol state machines can provide clearer rules for component use.

4.6.1 Basic Elements of State Machine

(1) States and Transitions

All objects have a state.

A state is a condition or situation during the life of an object during which it satisfies some condition, perform some activity or waits for some event. An object remains in a state for a finite amount of time. For example, a Heater in a home might be in any of four states: Idle (waiting for command to start heating the house), Activating (its gas is on, but it's waiting to come-up to temperature), Active (its gas and blower are both on) and Shutting Down (its gas is off but its blower is on, flushing residual heat from the system).

A State is a condition of being at a certain time. The state is a result of previous activities performed by the object and is typically determined by the values of its attributes and links to other objects. A state can be a passive quality, such as on and off for the light object.

A state can also be an active quality, or something that an object is doing. For example, a coffeemaker has the state brewing during which it is brewing coffee. A state is drawn as a rounded rectangle with the name of the state in the center,

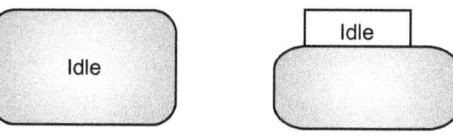

Fig. 4.55 : A rectangle with rounded corners and the name in the center is the most common way to draw a state

(2) Advanced State Behavior

An object transitions (changes) from one state to another state when something happens which is called an event. For example, someone pays an invoice, starts driving the car, or gets married.

A state may contain three kinds of compartments, as shown in Fig. 4.56.

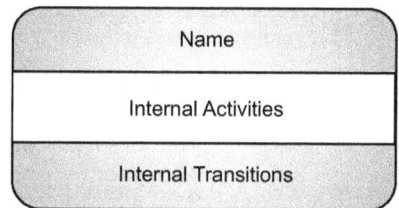

Fig. 4.56 : Name, state variable and activity compartments

Note that the Name compartment cannot be used if the alternate name tab notation is used. The first compartment shows the name of the state, for example, idle, paid and moving.

4.6.1.1 Internal Behavior

- The second compartment is the optional activity compartment, which lists behavior in response to events. You can define your own event such as selecting a Help button, as well as the activity to respond to that event. Three standard events names are reserved in UML: entry, exit, and do.
- The *entry* event can be used to specify actions on the entry of a state; for example, assigning an attribute or sending a message.
- The *exit* event can be used to specify actions on exit from a state.
- The *do* event can be used to specify an action performed while in the state; for example, sending a message, waiting, or calculating.

These standard events cannot be used for other purposes. The formal syntax for the activity compartment is : event-name argument-list '/' action-expression

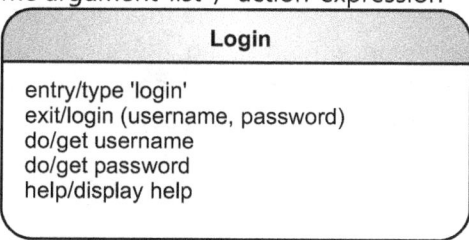

Fig. 4.57 : A state called login, where a number of actions are performed on entry, on exit, and while in the state. The help/display help is a user-defined event and action within the action compartment

4.6.1.2 Internal Transitions

The third compartment is the optional internal transition compartment. This compartment contains a list of internal transitions. A transition can be listed more than once if it has different guard conditions. An internal transition is different from a self transition because self transitions cause entry and exit behavior to occur whereas internal transitions don't.

Internal transitions are written as trigger [guard/behavior, and they are listed inside a state.

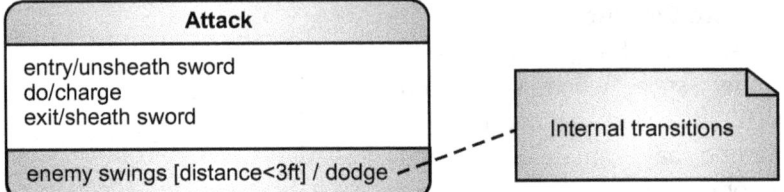

Fig. 4.58 : The Attack has an internal transition: when an opponent swings his weapon and is less than three feet away, the troll dodges

Use internal transitions to model reactions to events that do not cause state changes. For example, you could use internal transitions to show that a pause-and-serve coffee-maker suspends dispensing the coffee when you remove the coffee pot but does not leave the Brewing state, as shown in Fig. 4.59.

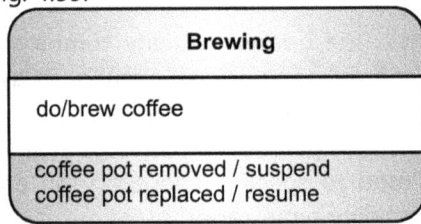

Fig. 4.59 : An internal transition models a reaction while staying in the same state

(3) Transitions

A transition is a relationship between two states indicating that an object in the first state will perform certain actions and enter the second state, when a specified set of events and conditions are satisfied.

Transition is a change of states from a *source state* to a *target state*. A transition, shown with an arrow, a transition description written along the arrow, describes the circumstances causing the state change to occur. The full notation for transition descriptions is Trigger [guard condition]/behavior. Where each element is optional.

(1) Trigger

A *trigger* is an event that may cause a transition. (See Fig. 4.60).

(2) Guard Condition

A guard is a Boolean condition that permits or blocks the transition. When a guard is present, the transition is taken if the guard evaluates to true, but the transition is blocked if the guard is false. If the guard-condition is combined with an event signature, the event must occur, and the guard condition must be true for the transition to fire.

If only a guard condition is attached to a state transition, the transition fires when the condition becomes true. Examples of state transitions with a guard condition are as follows :
[t = 15sec] [Number of invoices > n]
Withdrawal (amount) [balance>=amount]. (See Fig. 4.61).

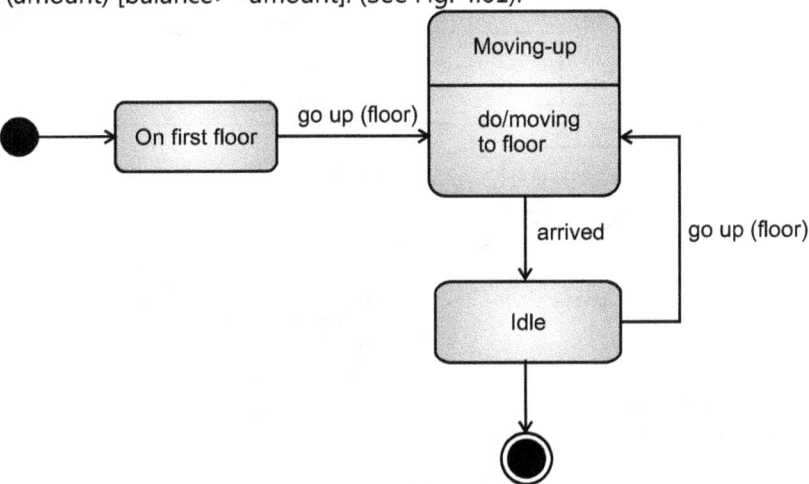

Fig. 4.60 : Shows a trigger go_up with parameter (which is suppressed) which change state from on first floor to Moving-up

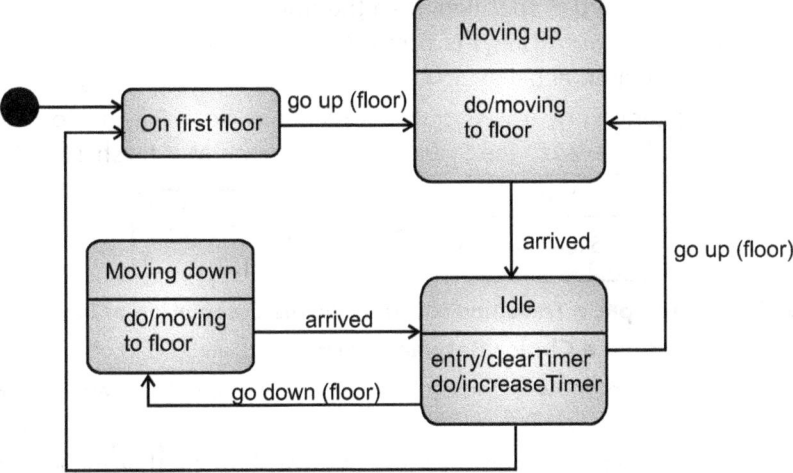

Fig. 4.61 : The state transition between the Idle and on first floor states has a guard condition and an action-expression

From above Fig. 4.61, When the timer attribute is equivalent to the time-out constant, the action *go down* (first floor) is performed; then the state is changed from Idle to on first floor.

4.6.1.3 Transition Variations

Fig. 4.62 shows variety of transition description that shows trigger, guard condition, and combination of both.

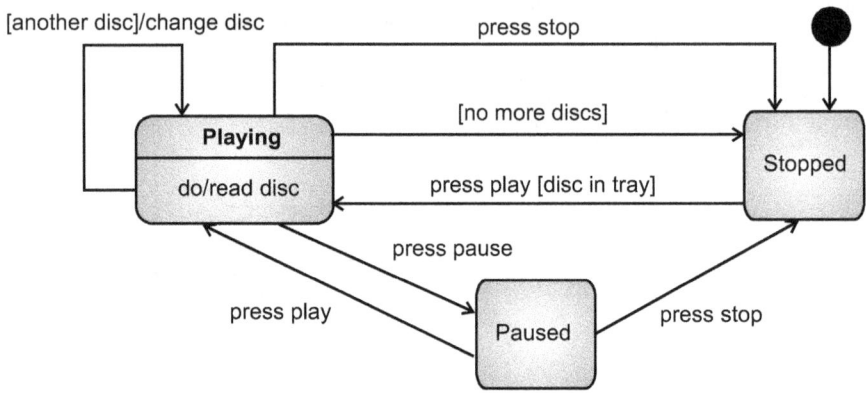

Fig. 4.62 : CD player state diagram, featuring a variety of transition descriptions

1. By the completion of internal behavior.
2. Using guards to model a choice between paths.

(1) By the Completion of Internal Behavior

If neither a trigger nor a guard is specified, then the transition is taken immediately after the source state's internal behavior (if any) is complete. This is useful for modeling a transition caused by completion of internal behavior.

Fig. 4.63 shows a triggerless, guardless transition leading from Playing to Stopped, which means that the CD player moves to the Stopped state as soon as it finishes reading the disc.

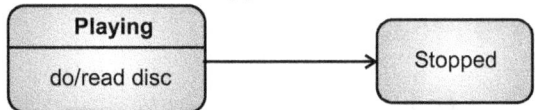

Fig. 4.63 : In this Example, a Transition is Caused by the Completion of Internal Behavior

(2) Using Guards to Model a Choice Between Paths

You can also use guards to show a choice between transitions: the transition whose guard evaluates to true is taken.

In Fig. 4.64, after the CD player is done reading the disc, it will either move to the Stopped state if there are no more discs or transition back to the Playing state if there are more discs. Notice that if there are more discs, the transition includes transition behavior changing the disc.

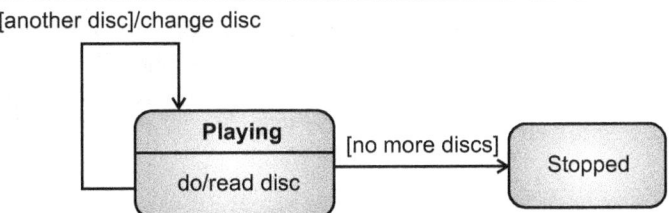

Fig. 4.64 : Using guards to model a choice between paths

4.6.2 Composite States

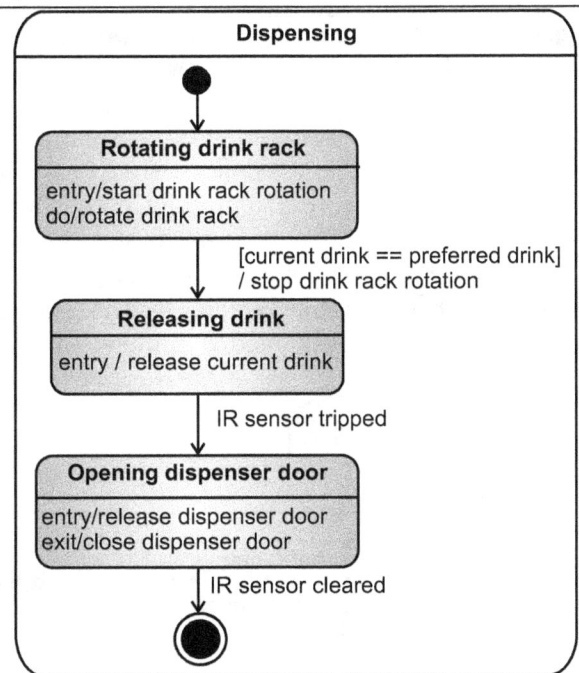

Fig. 4.65 : A composite state with one region

A state may also be decomposition to provide a finer-grained description of the transformation in an object. The decomposition provides opportunities to model not only more detailed states but also concurrent states. A composite state is a state with one or more regions. A *region* is simply a container for substates. A composite state with two or more regions is called orthogonal.

A composite state may have an additional compartment called the decomposition compartment. A *decomposition compartment* is a detailed view of the composite state where you can show a composite state's regions, substates, and transitions. (see Fig. 4.65).

It shows the Composite state for State 'Dispensing' with one region. To increase the clarity of a diagram you may hide the decomposition compartment. If you hide the compartment, you can use the composite icon to indicate that the state's decomposition is not shown on this diagram but further explore. The composite sate notation should situate in the lower right corner of the expanded state. The composite state icon consists of two horizontally aligned rounded rectangles connected by a line. (See Fig. 4.66)

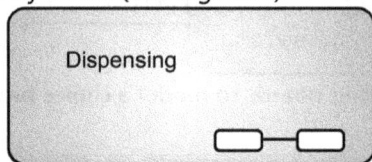

**Fig. 4.66 : Notation for single region composite state
(By hiding decomposition compartment)**

Regions

A region is shown using a dashed line dividing the decomposition compartment. You may name each region by writing its name within the region's area. Each region has its own initial pseudostate and a final state. A transition to a composite state is a transition to the initial pseudostate in each region. Each region within a composite state executes in parallel and it is perfectly acceptable for one region to finish before another. A transition to the final state of a region indicates completing the activity for that region. Once all regions have completed, the composite state triggers a completion event and a completion transition (if one exists) triggers.

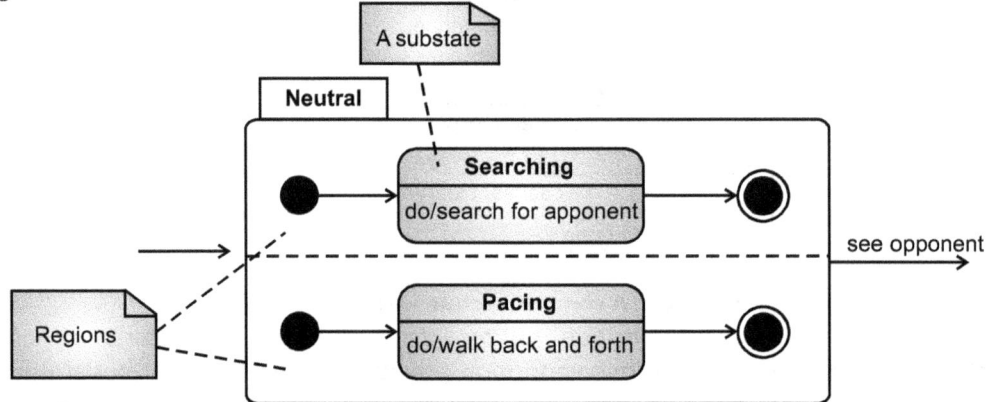

Fig. 4.67 : Composite states contain one or more state diagrams; if they contain more than one state diagram, then the state diagrams execute in parallel

4.6.3 Submachine States

Submachine states are semantically equivalent to composite states in that they are made up of internal substates and transitions. UML defines a submachine state as a way to encapsulate states and transitions so that they can be reused. A submachine state simply means that another state machine, a submachine state machine, is contained by the state.

A submachine state is shown in the same rounded rectangle as any other state, except you show the name of the state, followed by a colon (:) followed by the name of the referenced submachine. Fig. 4.68 shows a submachine state.

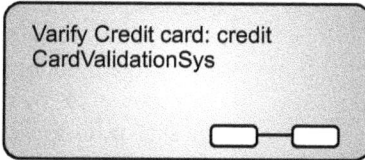

Fig. 4.68 : A submachine state showing the composite icon

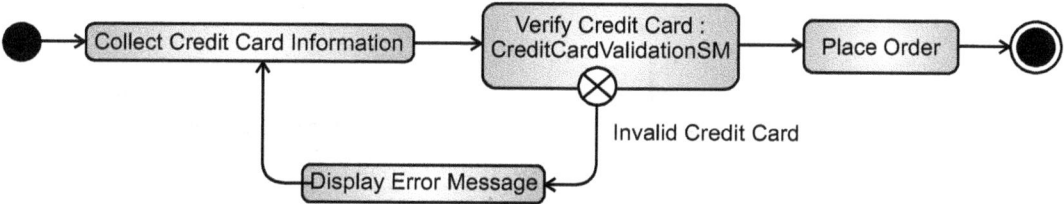

Fig. 4.69 : Details (not required) state machine or sub state machine diagram for above Fig. 4.68

4.6.4 Advanced Pseudostate Notation for State Machine Diagram

Pseudostate Name	Symbol	Description
Initial and Final pseudostate	● (a)	The starting point of a state machine. The transition from the initial pseudostate to the first full state may be labeled with the event that instantiates the object the state machine is modeling.
Final pseudo state	⊙ (b)	This is Final pseudostate of state machine. This is state from which the object may longer change. There may be any number of final states.
Choice	◇ (c)	Allows the execution of a state machine to choose between several different states based on guard conditions on the transitions (see Fig. 4.70).
Deep history	H* (d)	Used inside a state region, a transition to this pseudo state from outside the region indicates the state machine should resume the last sub state it was in within the given region, no matter how "deep" the sub state is within the region.

Shallow history	H (e)	Used inside a state region, a transition to this pseudo state from outside the region indicates the state machine should resume the last substate within the given region. However the sub state must be at the same level as the history pseudostate. You may specify a default "previous state" by showing a single transition from the shallow history pseudo state to an internal sub state. This is used only if the region has never been entered. (see Fig. 4.71)
Fork and join	Fork Join (f)	*Fork* and *join* pseudostates show branching into concurrent states and then rejoining. The fork breaks the incoming transition into two transitions, allowing happening simultaneously. The join then merges its two incoming transitions into one outgoing transition. (see Fig. 4.72).
Signals	Send signal Receive signal (g)	The main purpose of this notation is to visually emphasize sending and receiving signals. The meaning of these symbols are same as Activity Diagram but here the version with the signal icons focuses on the transitions. (see Fig. 4.73)
Entry point	○ (h)	Represents a possible target for a transition into a composite state. An entry point can then transition to an internal substate that may differ from the default transition. You must label entry points by writing their name next to the symbol. (see Fig. 4.74).
Exit point	⊗ (i)	Represents a possible source for a transition from a composite state. Like entry points, exit points are labeled with their names. (see Fig. 4.75)
Junction	● (j)	Brings several possible transitions together into one pseudostate. One or more transitions may then leave the junction to other states. (see Fig. 4.76)
Terminate node	✕ (k)	Causes the state machine to terminate. (see Fig. 4.77)

A Choice Pseudostate

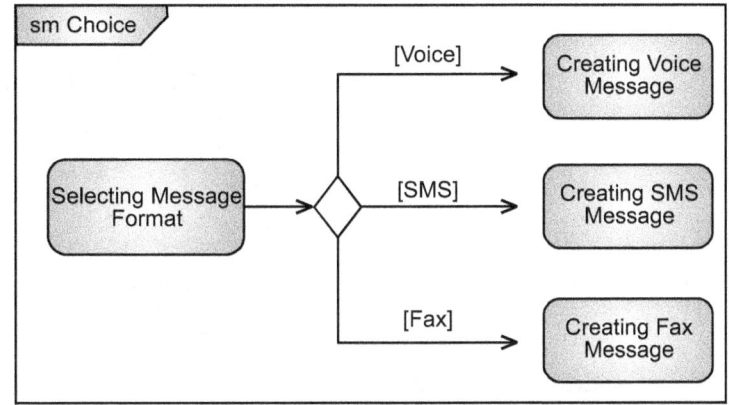

Fig. 4.70 : The path followed after a choice depends on the guard

Shallow History

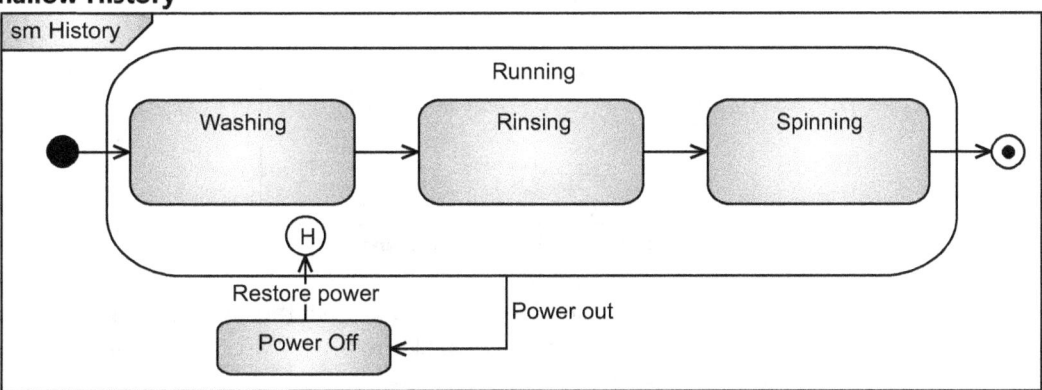

Fig. 4.71 : Shows shallow history

Fork and Join

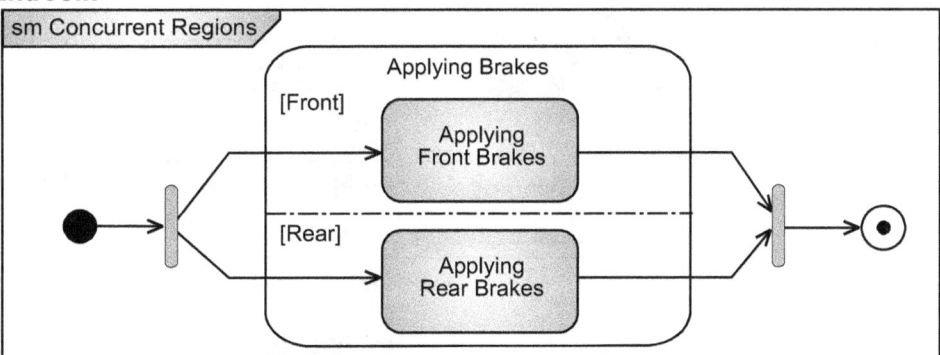

Fig. 4.72 : Shows concurrent event by using fork and join

Signals

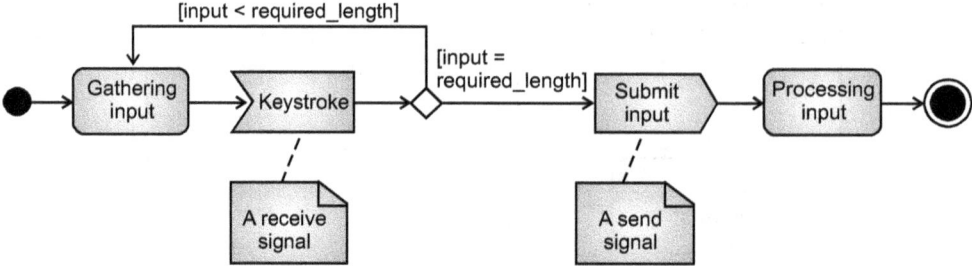

Fig. 4.73 : The bottom diagram draws transitions and transition behavior as receive and send signals

Entry Point

The entry point is used to describe actions that must occur on entry into the state machine. The entry point indicator is shown as a small circle on or optionally within the border of a state machine.

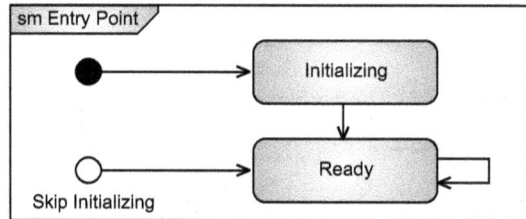

Fig. 4.74 : Shows entry point

Exit Point

The *exit* point is used to describe actions that must occur at the completion of a state machine. The exit point indicator is shown as a small circle with a cross on or optionally within the border of a state machine.

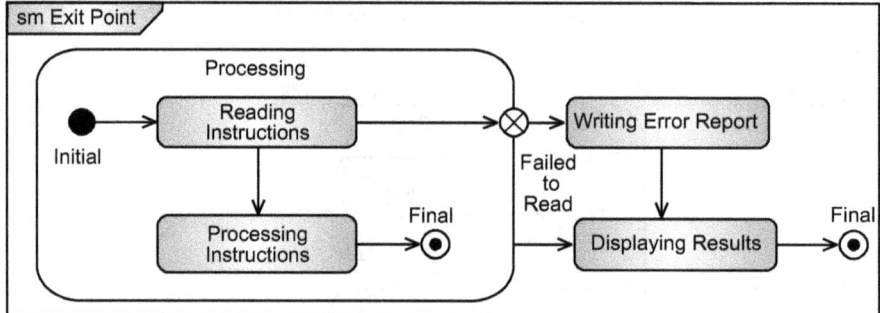

Fig. 4.75 : Shows exit point

Junction Pseudostate

It brings several possible transitions together into one pseudostate. More than one *transitions* may then *leave* the junction to other states.

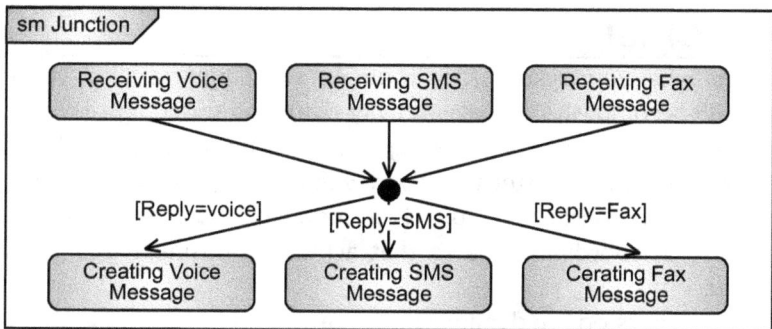

Fig. 4.76 : Shows junction pseudo state

Terminate

Entering in a terminate pseudo-state indicates that the *lifeline of the state machine has ended.*

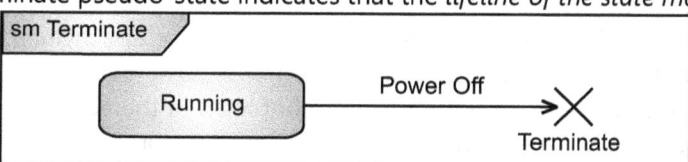

Fig. 4.77 : Shows terminate state

Example of State Machine Diagram

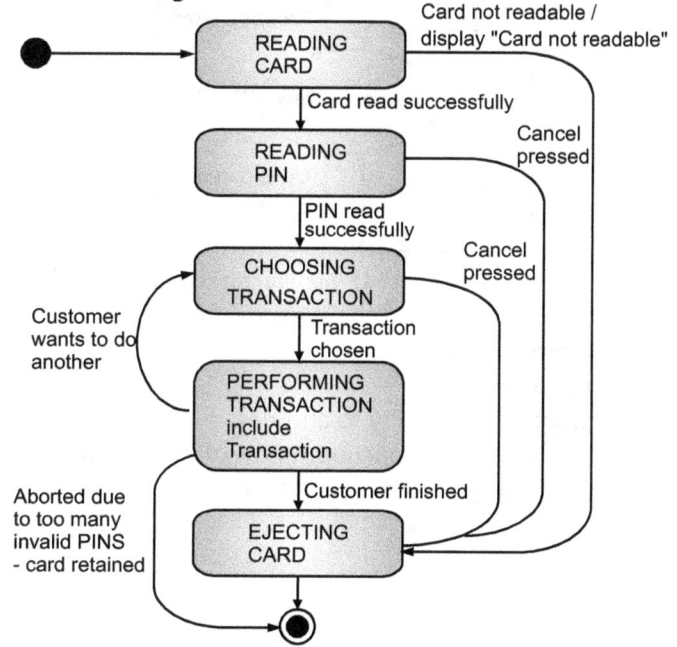

Fig. 4.78 : ATM transaction

4.7 ACTIVITY DIAGRAM

- Use cases show what your system should do. Activity diagrams allow you to specify how your system will accomplish its goals. Activity diagrams show high-level actions chained together to represent a process occurring in your system. For example, you can use an activity diagram to model the steps involved with creating a blog account.
- Activity diagrams are particularly good at modeling business processes. A business process is a set of coordinated tasks that achieve a business goal, such as shipping customers orders.
- Activity diagrams focus on the dynamic flow of a system.
- An activity diagram is essentially a flowchart, showing flow of control from activity to activity. Unlike a traditional flowchart, an activity diagram shows concurrency as well as branches of control.
- In UML, an activity diagram is used to display the sequence of activities. Activity diagrams show the workflow from a start point to the finish point detailing the many decision paths that exist in the progression of events contained in the activity. They may be used to detail situations where parallel processing may occur in the execution of some activities.

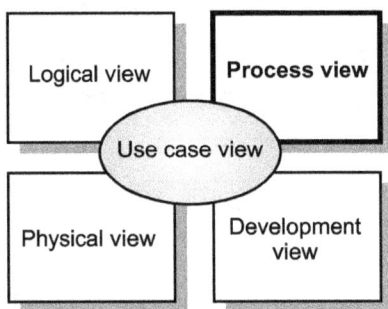

Fig. 4.79 : (4+1) View architecture

Activity diagram shows the process view of the system.

Purpose of Activity Diagram
- Draw the activity flow of a system.
- Describe the sequence from one activity to another.
- Describe the parallel, branched and concurrent flow of the system.

4.7.1 Graphical Notations of Activity Diagram

1. Start Node/Initial Node.
2. Exit Node/Final Node.
3. Action.
4. Activity Frame.
5. Transition/Edge/Path.

6. Decision Node.
7. Merge Node.
8. Fork Node.
9. Join Node.
10. Object Node.
11. Input and output pins.
12. Calling Other Activities.
13. Time Event Node.
14. Interruption Region.
15. Send and Receive Signal.
16. Flow final Node.

1. Start/Initial Node

It shows the starting point of the activity diagram. An initial or start node is depicted by a large black spot, as shown below.

Fig. 4.80 : Start node

2. Final/Exit Node

It shows the exit point of the diagram. An activity diagram can have zero or more activity final nodes. Final node is rendered as two concentric circles with filled inner circle, as shown in Fig. 4.81.

Fig. 4.81 : Exit node

3. Action

- Actions are active steps in the completion of a process. An action can be a calculation, such as Calculate Tax or a task such as Verify Author's Details.
- An action represents a single step within an activity. Actions are denoted by rounded rectangles.
- Action is smallest unit of work which cannot divide into further tasks.

Fig. 4.82 : Action

4. Activity

- An activity is the process being modeled, such as washing a car. An action is a step in the overall activity such as Lather, Rinse and Dry.
- Activity is a set of actions.

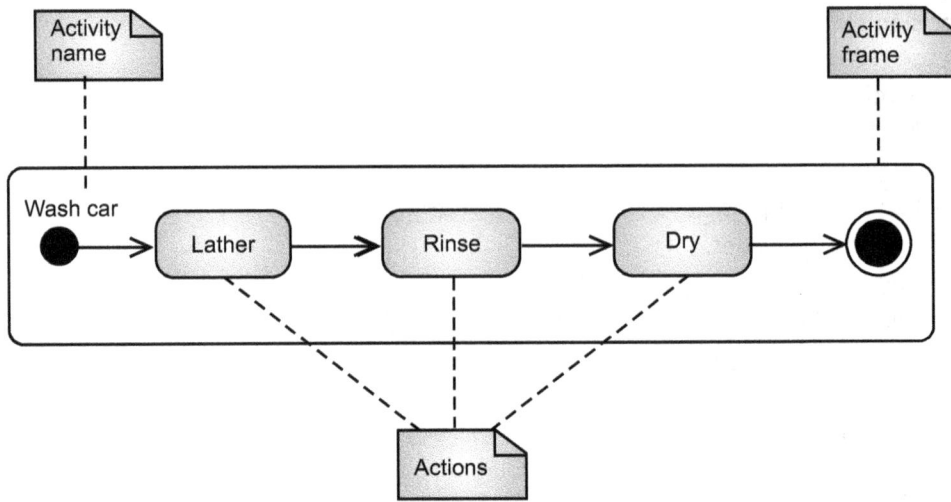

Fig. 4.83 : Activity

5. Transition/Edge/Path

The flow of the activity is shown using arrowed lines called edges or paths. The arrowhead on an activity edge shows the direction of flow from one action to the next. A line going into a node is called an incoming edge, and a line exiting a node is called an outgoing edge.

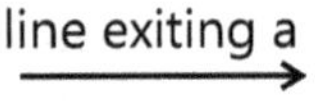

Fig. 4.84 : Transition

6. Decision Node

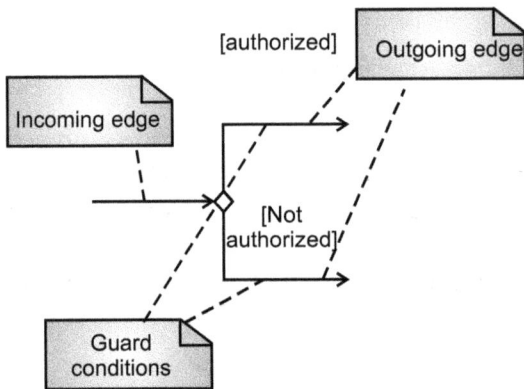

Fig. 4.85 : Decision node

The control flows coming away from a decision node will have guard conditions which will allow control to flow if the guard condition is met. Decisions are used when you want to execute a different sequence of actions depending on a condition. Decisions are drawn as diamond-shaped nodes with one incoming edge and multiple outgoing edges, as shown in

Fig. 4.85. Each branched edge contains a guard condition written in brackets. Guard conditions determine which edge is taken after a decision node.

7. Merge Node

The branched flows join together at a merge node, which marks the end of the conditional behavior started at the decision node. Merges are also shown with diamond-shaped nodes, but they have multiple incoming edges and one outgoing edge, as shown in Fig. 4.86.

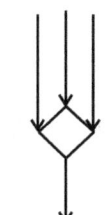

Fig. 4.86 : Merge node

8. Fork Node

Fork Node is used to show the parallel or concurrent actions.

Steps that occur at the same time are said to occur concurrently or in parallel.

Fork has single incoming flow and multiple outing flows.

9. Join Mode

The join means that all incoming actions must finish before the flow can proceed past the join. Forks and joins look identical they are both drawn with thick bars. Join has multiple incoming flows and single outing flow.

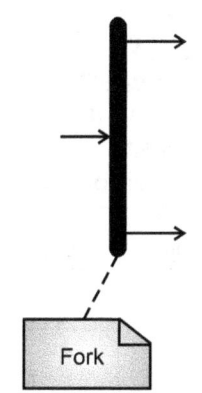

Fig. 4.87 : Fork node

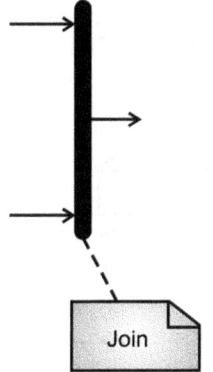

Fig. 4.88 : Join node

10. Object Node

Object nodes to show data flowing through an activity. An object node represents an object that is available at a particular point in the activity and can be used to show that the object is used, created, or modified by any of its surrounding actions. An object node is drawn with a rectangle as shown in the order approval process in Fig. 4.89. The Order object node draws attention to the fact that the Order object flows from the Receive Order Request action to the Approve Payment action.

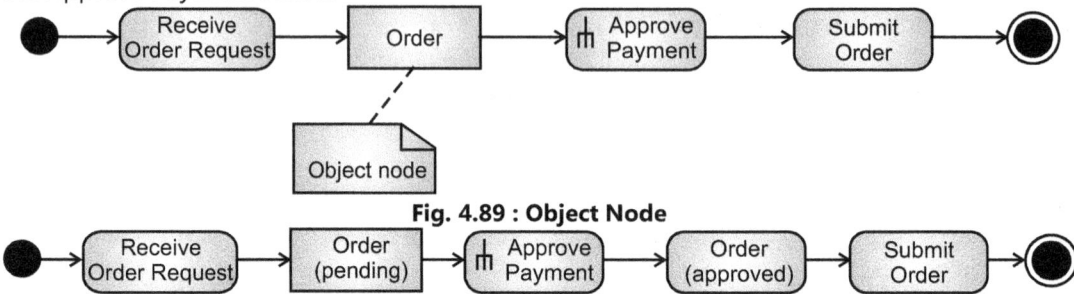

Fig. 4.89 : Object Node

Fig. 4.90 : Shows how objects change state during an activity

11. Input and output pins

An input pin means that the specified object is input to an action. An output pin means that the specified object is output from an action.

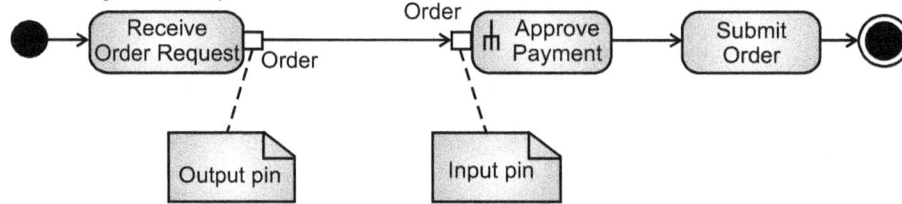

Fig. 4.91 : Input and output pins

12. Transformation

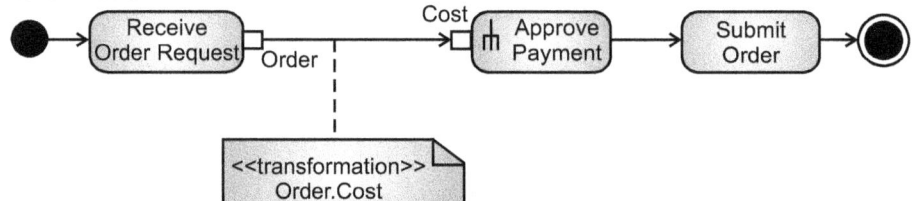

Fig. 4.92 : Transformation

Transformations allow you to show how the output from one action provides the input to another action. If the Approve Payment action needs only parts of the Order object not the whole object you can use a transformation to show which parts are needed.

13. Calling Other Activities

The upside-down pitchfork symbol indicates that it is a call activity node. A call activity node calls the activity corresponding to its node name. This is similar to calling a software procedure.

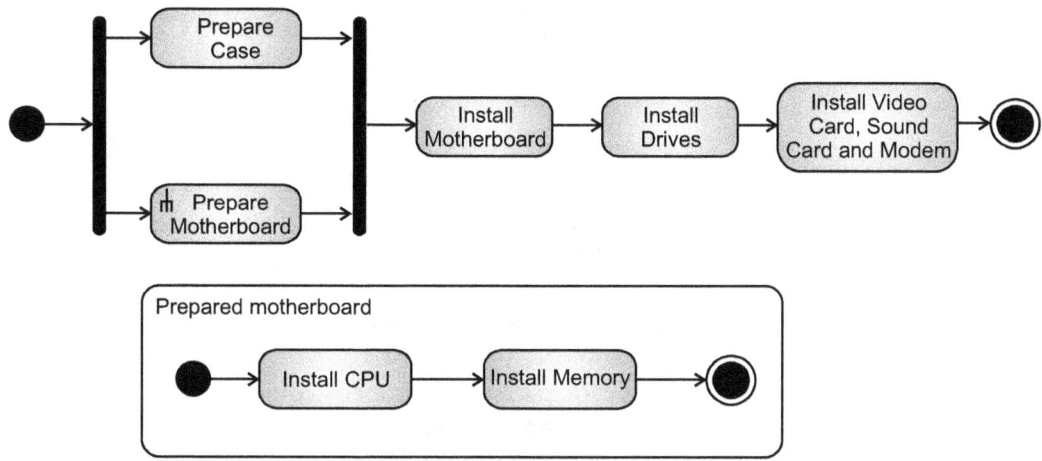

Fig. 4.93 : Calling other activity

14. Time Event Node

You may want to model wait period, such as waiting three days after shipping an order to send a bill. Time events are drawn with an hourglass symbol. Fig. 4.94 shows how to use a time event to model wait period. The text next to the hourglass Wait 3 Days shows the amount of time to wait.

The incoming edge to the time event means that the time event is activated once. In Fig. 4.94 the bill is sent only once not every three days.

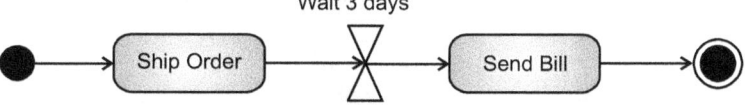

Fig. 4.94 : Time event node

A time event with no incoming flows is a recurring time event, meaning it is activated with the frequency in the text next to the hourglass. In Fig. 4.95, the progress bar is updated every second.

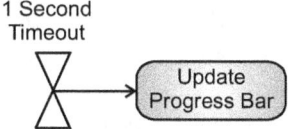

Fig. 4.95 : Recurring time event

15. Interruption Region

The interruption region includes interrupted action and interrupting signal. It is graphically rendered as dash rectangle. The interrupting event is followed by a line that looks like a lightning bolt.

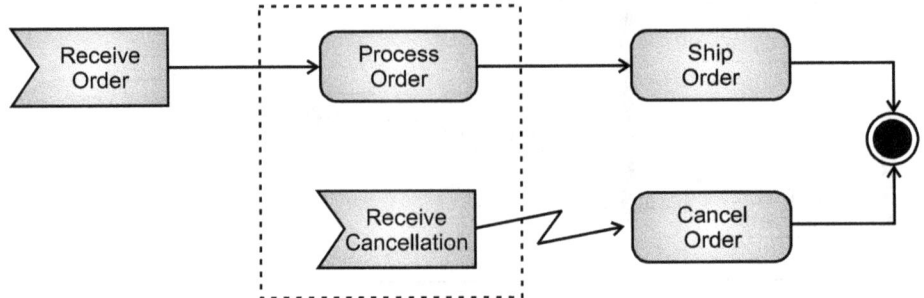

Fig. 4.96 : Interruption region

16. Send and Receive Signal

Send signal is used when your system or part of the system communicates with external participant or vice versa. Receive signal is used when your system receives the response from external participant.

Fig. 4.97 : Send and receive signal

17. Flow Final Node

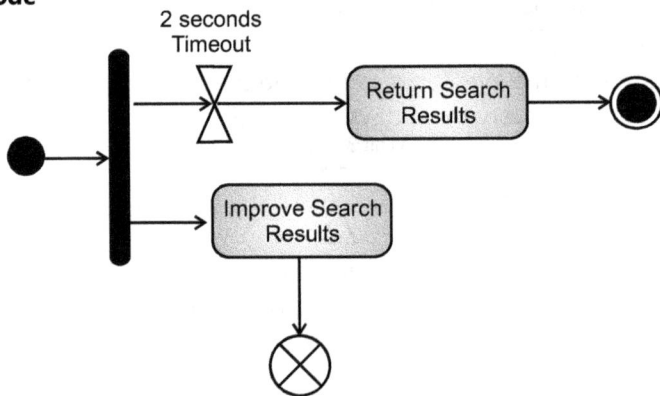

Fig. 4.98 : Flow final node

A flow end node terminates its own path not the whole activity. The flow final node is depicted as a circle with a cross inside. The difference between the two node types is that the flow final node denotes the end of a single control flow; the activity final node denotes the end of all control flows within the activity.

Partitions (or Swimlanes)

Swimlanes are useful, especially when you are modeling workflows of business processes, to partition the activity states on an activity diagram into groups, each group representing the organization responsible for those activities. In UML, each group is called a swimlane because, visually, each group is divided from its neighbour by a vertical solid line. Partition indicates who/what is performing the activities. Activities may involve different participants such as different groups or roles in an organization or system. The following scenarios require multiple participants to complete the activity (participant names are italicized):

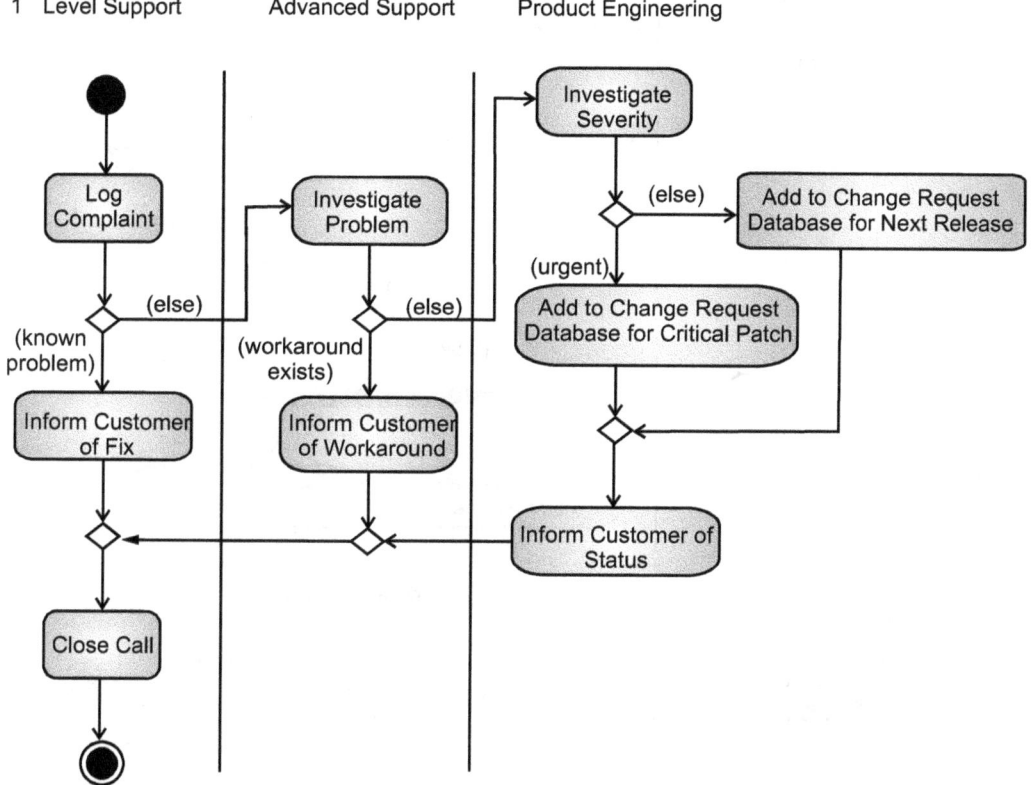

Fig. 4.99 : Complaint system

An order processing activity
Requires the shipping department to ship the products and the accounts department to bill the customer.

A technical support process
Requires different levels of support, including 1st level Support, Advanced Support and Product Engineering. You use partitions to show which participant is responsible for which actions. Partitions divide the diagram into columns or rows (depending on the orientation of your activity diagram) and contain actions that are carried out by a responsible group. The columns or rows are sometimes referred to as swimlanes.

Examples of Activity Diagrams : (1) Passenger Ticket Booking System

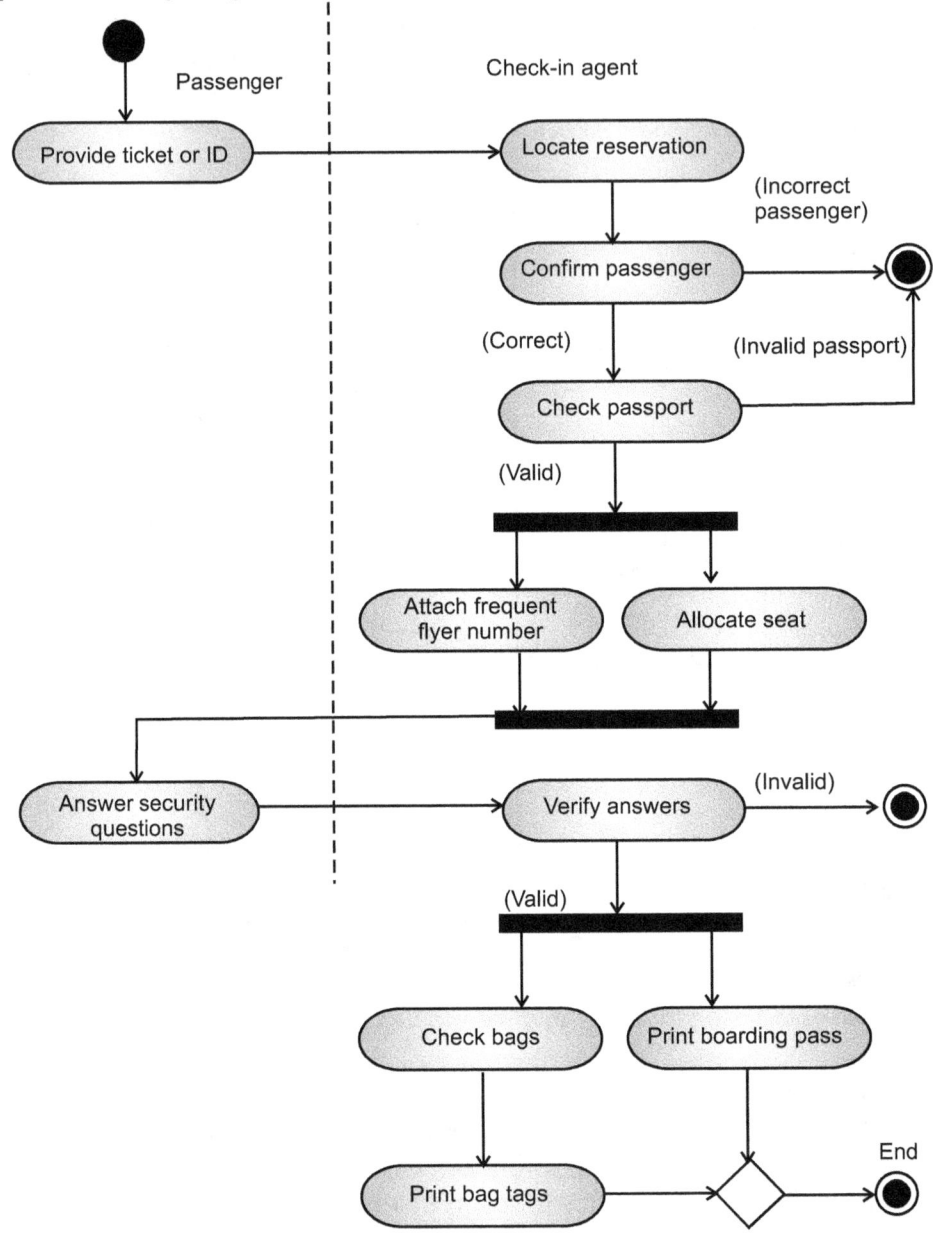

Fig. 4.100 : Ticket booking system

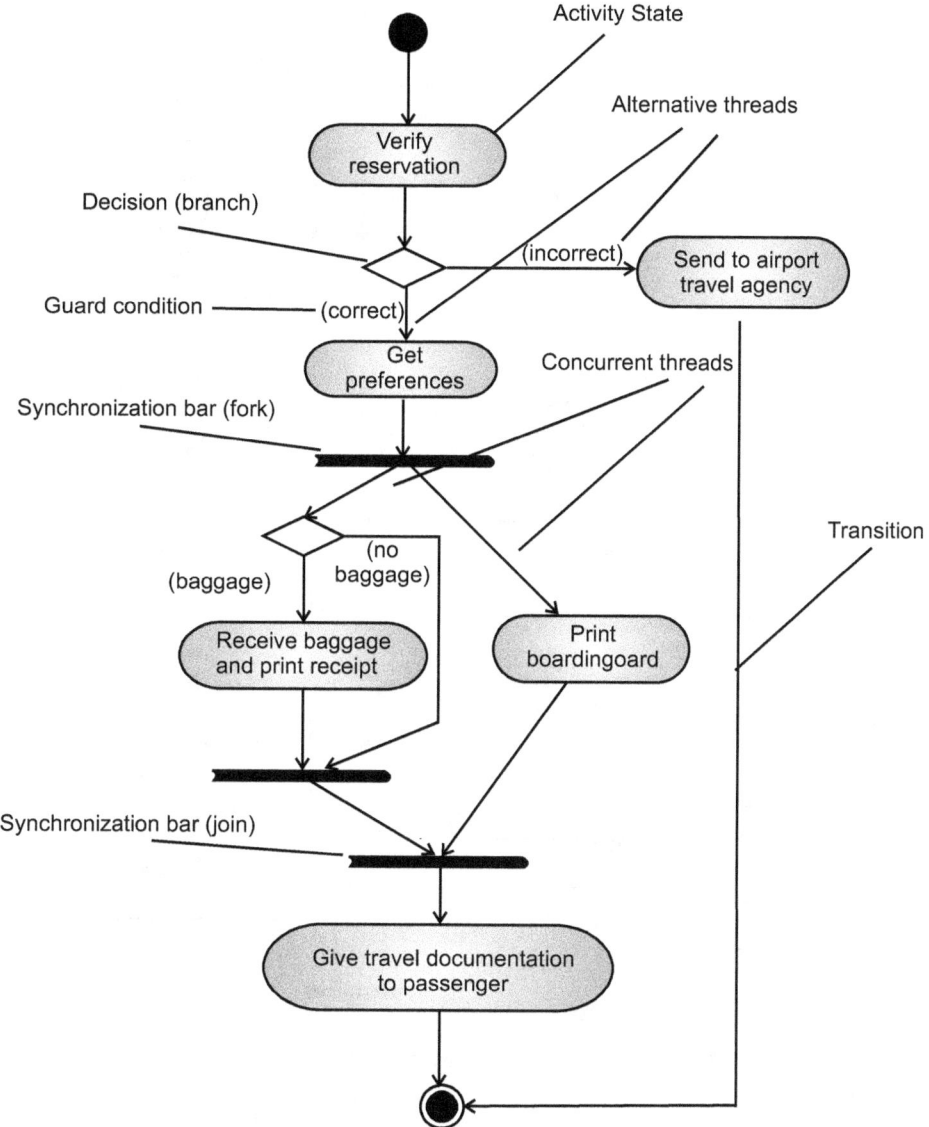

Fig. 4.101 : Reservation system

(2) Order Processing System

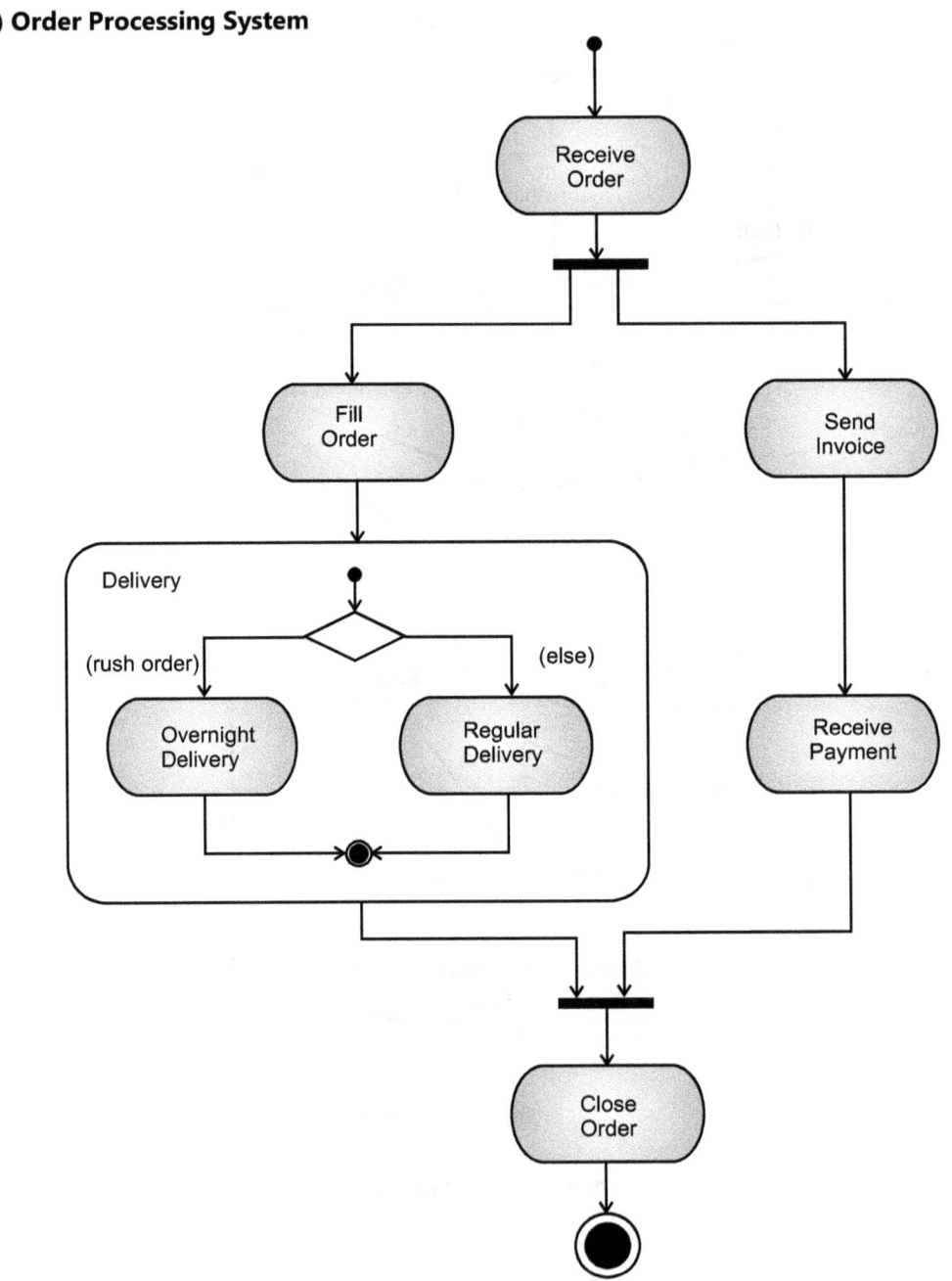

Fig. 4.102 : Order processing system

(3) Complaint System

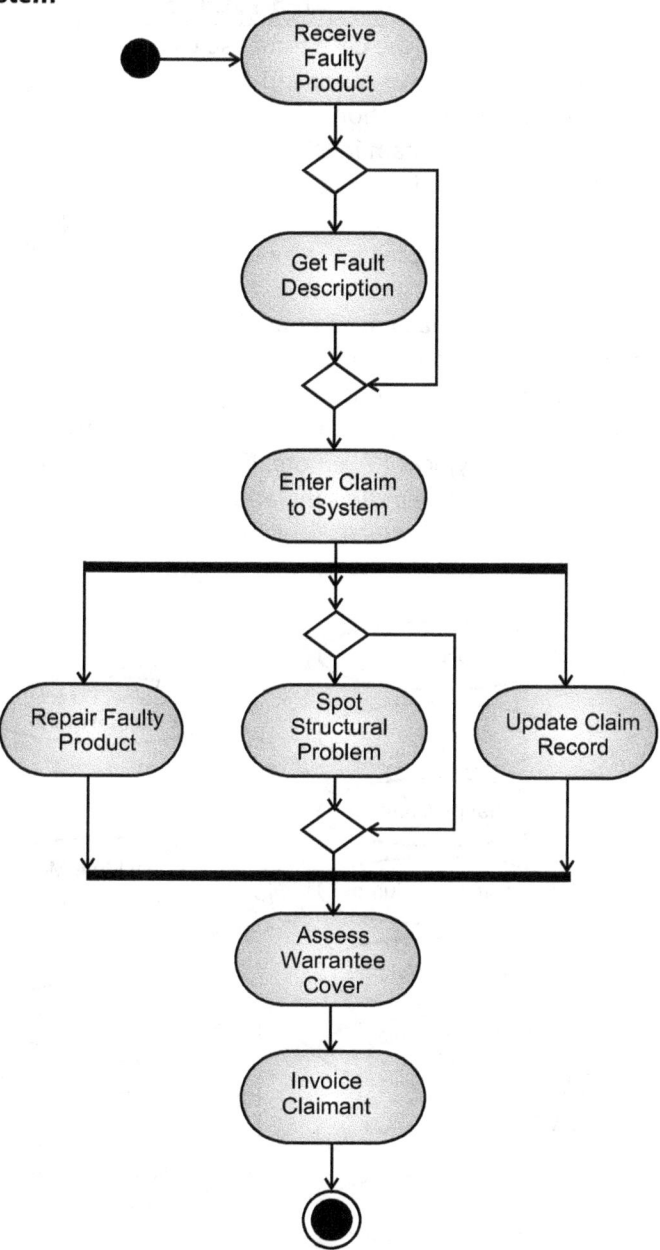

Fig. 4.103 : Complaint system

REVIEW QUESTIONS

1. What is forward engineering of a use case from use case diagram?
2. Explain "Decision and Merge" versus "Fork and Join".
3. What is the purpose of an interaction diagram? Explain with suitable example the different types of interaction diagram in UML 2.0.
4. Compare synchronous and asynchronous messages.
5. How does one model parallel message flows in a sequence diagram?
6. What is recursion? How do we represent recursion in a sequence diagram?
7. Describe Timing diagram.
8. What is importance of a state machine diagram in an embedded application?
9. How does one model parallel message flows in an activity diagram?
10. Explain the difference between sequence diagram and communication diagram.
11. Consider a typical normal television and assume that a software remote simulator is built that behaves like your typical TV remote. If use cases were applied to describe the functionality of the software TV remote simulator, what would be some of the use cases of the software remote control (simulator) of the TV? Draw a use case diagram for this description using full UML notation for use case diagrams.

Ans. :

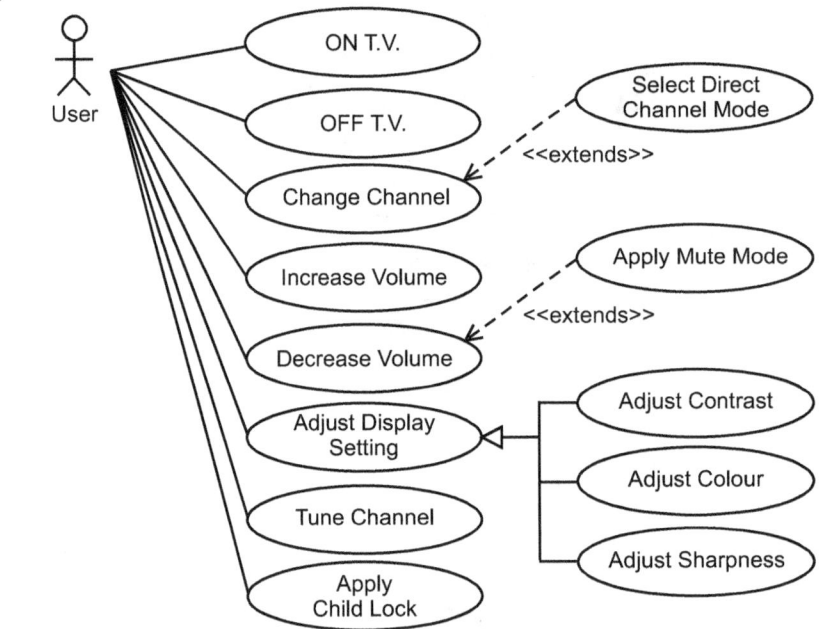

Fig. 4.104

12. Can an activity diagram be drawn to represent a business process? Justify your answer. Draw an ACTIVITY diagram for describing how selling a two wheeler to a customer takes place at a dealers place. Customers can enquire about the two wheeler models available, a salesperson is assigned to show the customer the vehicles, the salesperson shows the available two wheelers, customer chooses a model for purchase, he can optionally take accessories like rearguard etc., ask for a quotation and choose to purchase a vehicle if interested. Explain notation used in a sentence each.

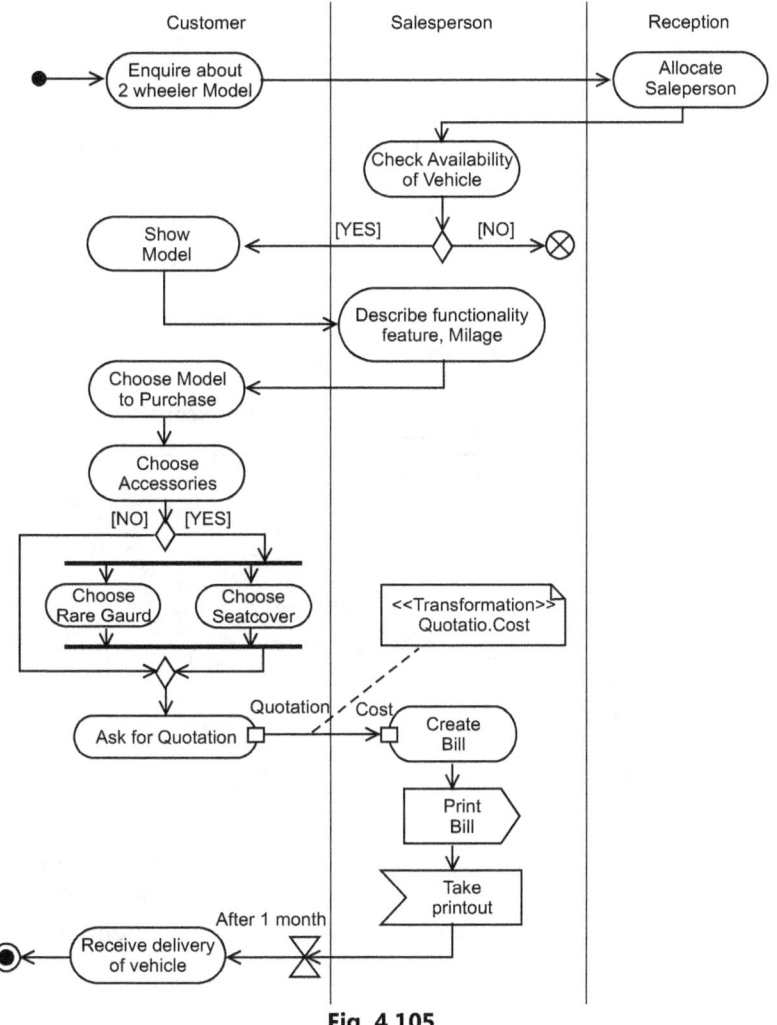

Fig. 4.105

Symbols used in above activity diagram [Refer Section 5.1.1 (Page 128)]

(a) Decision and Merge Node
(b) Fork, Join
(c) Send, Receive Signal Node
(d) Input transformation / Output object pin
(e) Time Node

13. Draw neat fragments on one of the (state/activity/timing) diagrams to represent the following. Explain the concept too
    (a) Deep history.
    (b) Sending signal in activity diagram.
    (c) Event occurrence in timing diagram.
    (d) Data store.

14. In the context of communication diagrams show how to model the following statements (assume a typical bank loan system).
    (a) a student requests for a bank loan.
    (b) a note to explain that loan cannot be given to minors, the note is attached to the request message.
    (c) a request object is temporarily created to hold request details.
    (d) the college (a third party system) system can be requested details about the student's year of passing.

Ans.:

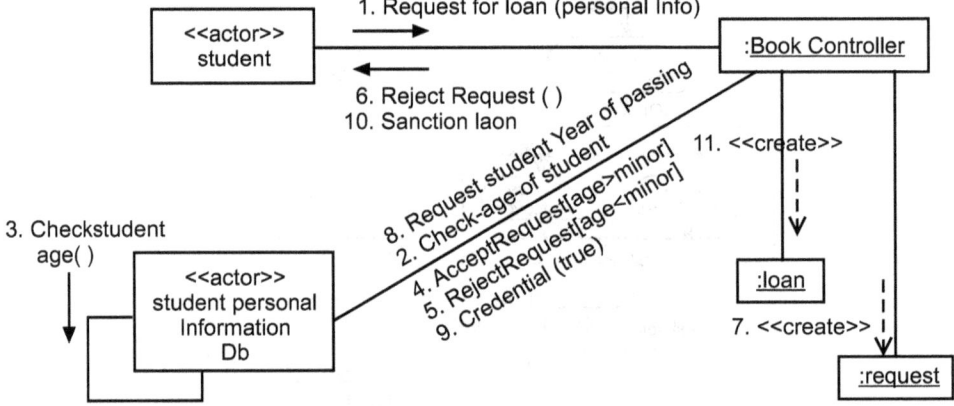

Fig. 4.106

15. Consider a use case "Check My Marks". The possible actor in the system is student. The possible classes in the system are MARKSHEET, LOGIN, DISPLAY and ENQUIRY. The student if authenticated can enquire personal makes of any semester and results are shown on display. Please make additional assumptions if relevant and appropriate. Identify classes, actors and Model a SEQUENCE diagram for above system with best use of UML notation.

Ans.

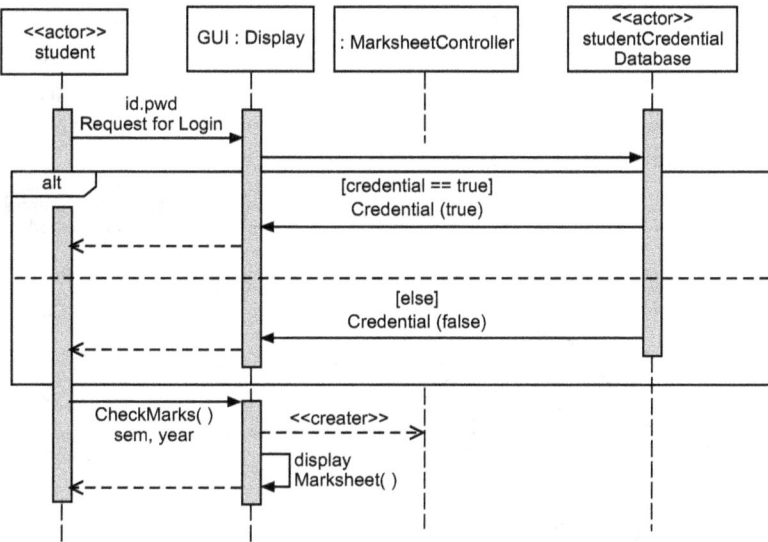

Fig. 4.107

16. Draw a simple COMMUNICATION diagram fragment to show that a customer can interact with the system to check availability of reservation for a particular flight on a day. Please make additional assumptions if relevant and appropriate.

Ans.:

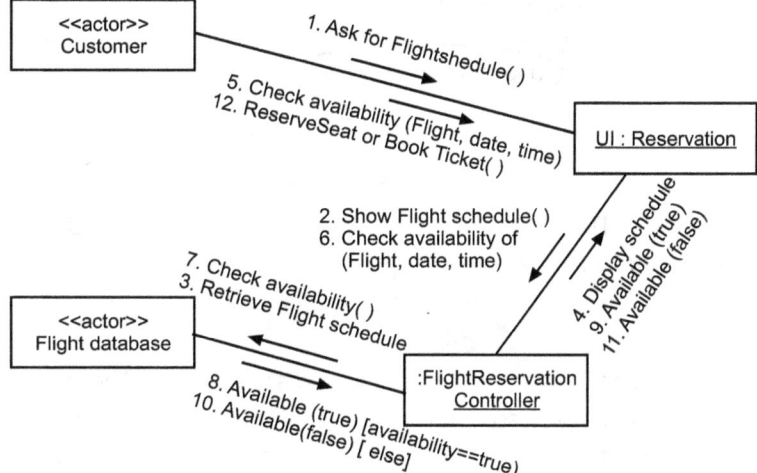

Fig. 4.108

17. In the context of sequence diagrams with examples: explain the concept of
    (a) Lifeline, (b) Entity object.
    (a) Entity object.

(b) Consider software Personal Diary application described below. We can use the diary to manage our daily. To-Do tasks, our personal appointments, personal contacts. The application will run on our mobile phone. Add further appropriate assumptions about the scope of the application. Draw a use case diagram for this description using full UML notation or use case diagrams.

Ans.:

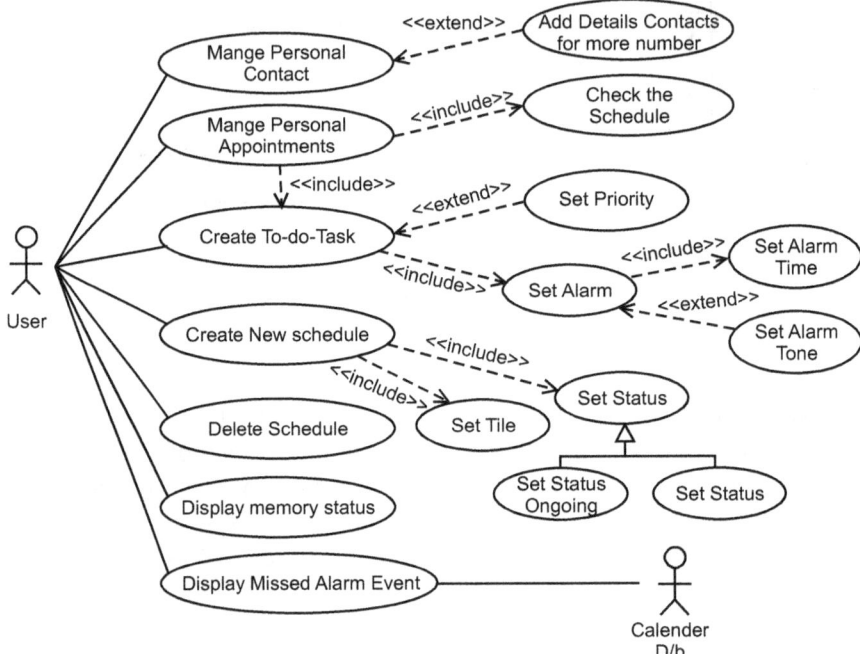

Fig. 4.109

18. Draw and ACTIVITY diagram for a system process described below. A college has different student associations like sports, literary, science club etc. A student can login to college website, look at the various available associations and choose one of them to join.

    All the associations expect you to be a valid student first. The joining process could be different for different associations for example sports association expects you to undergo a fitness test too. The associations organize various events. A member can register for the event online for free.

    Non-members need to pay nominal fees by credit card to register and in either case one gets a confirmation of registration of event. The registrations information needs to be passed onto the activity that sends the email confirmations.

Ans.:

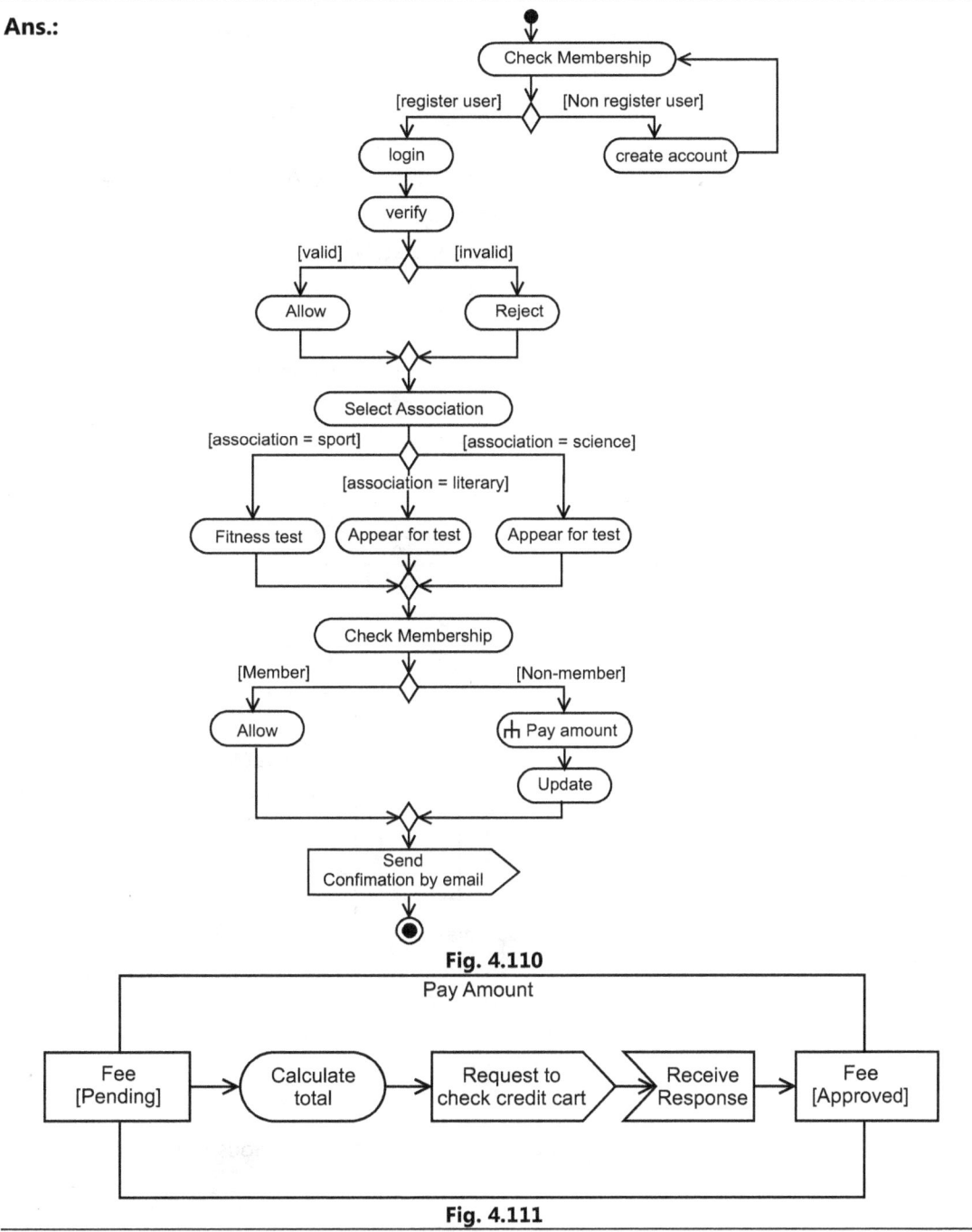

Fig. 4.110

Fig. 4.111

19. Consider a use case "take back-up of machine data". The possible actor in the system is machine owner. The owner interacts with the application to choose the directories to be backed up. The application then proceeds to take a backup of directories one-by-one.

The files in the chosen directories are also backed-up one by one. For each file a decision is taken to back-up only if file has changed from last back-up. Time status of the file change is maintained for each file separately.

Once the backup is completed a report is shown to he user about the number of files backed up, total time taken etc.

A log of all the backup activities is maintained for reference in future. Please make additional assumptions if relevant and appropriate. Identify classes, actors and model a SEQUENCE diagram for above system with best use of UML notation.

Ans. :

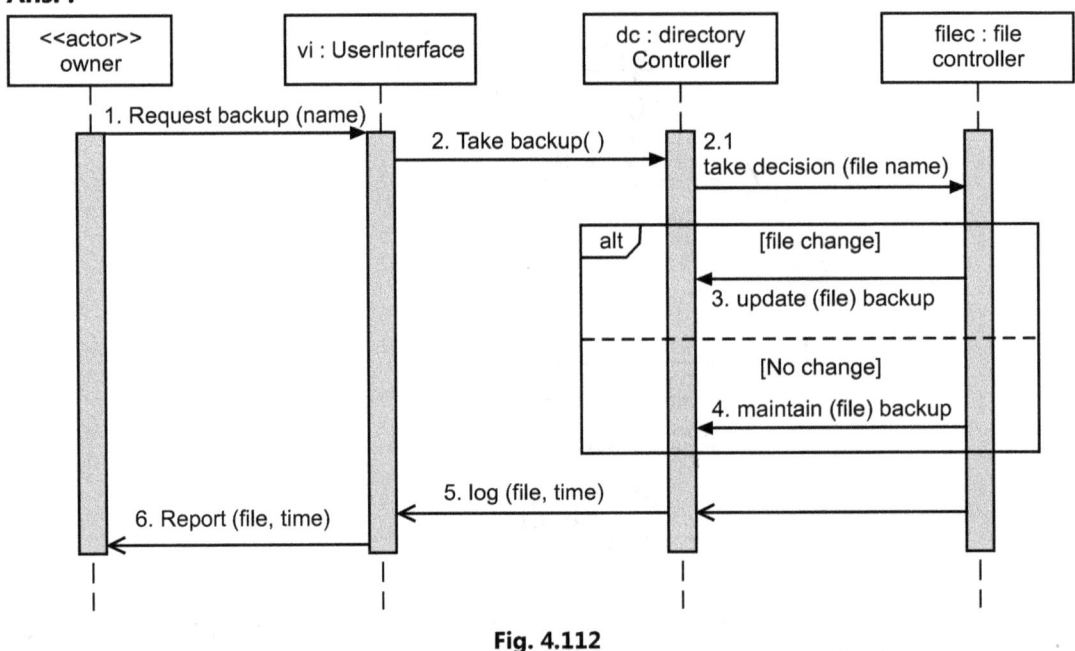

Fig. 4.112

20. For an "Online Railway Reservation System". Identify the various use cases and draw the use case diagram.

Ans. :

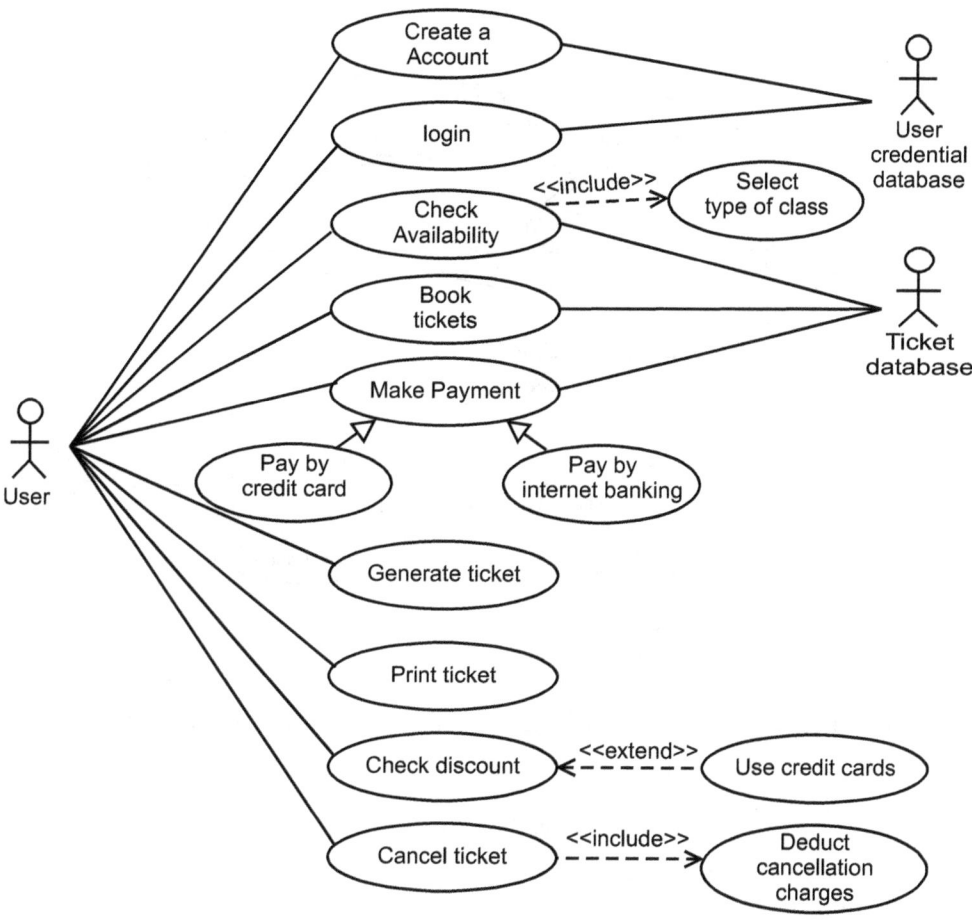

Fig. 4.1113

21. What is the importance of a state diagram in an embedded application?

    Consider a "Student Attendance System" having use cases like "View Attendance", "View Practical Attendance", Input Student-Id", "Attendance Report" etc.

    Make use of use case relationship to model above use cases and their relationships in context of use case diagram.

Ans. :

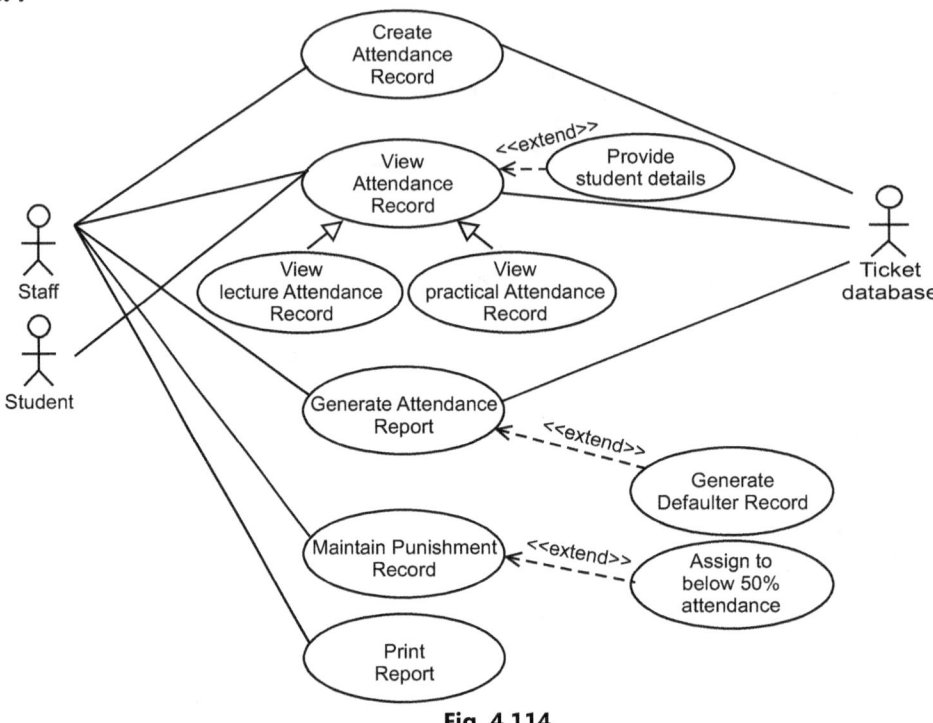

Fig. 4.114

21. Explain the concepts and notations through simple examples for following terms in UML:

    (i) Concurrent states.

    (ii) Substate.

    (iii) History state.

    (iv) Exceptions in activity diagram.

22. Model a software system for controlling a water purifier which can be either ON or OFF. In the ON state it can be ARO or UV mode. There are buttons to change from one mode to other or this mode can change automatically based on the hardness of the water cut-offs. (ARO when pH value < 1.5 and UV when pH value > 1.5). User can manually override any modes through by pressing appropriate buttons. All the buttons function only if power is on. For the above described system draw state machine diagram.

Ans. :

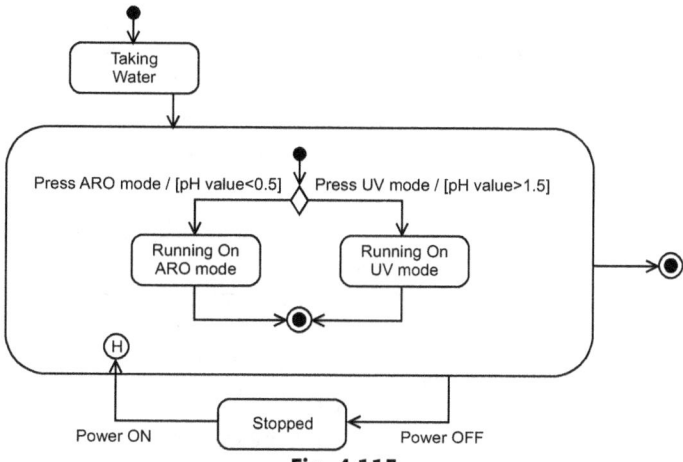

Fig. 4.115

23. Draw an activity diagram to explain the way one would create a presentation for a seminar using power point. Show the activities that are optional.

Ans. :

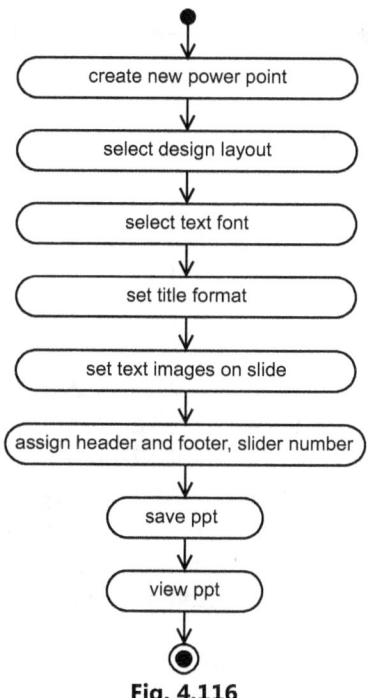

Fig. 4.116

24. (a) Draw a communication diagram for a "schedule of one day workshop" in the information technology department of a engineering institute organized for the students of final year. Make assumptions of possible classes.

Ans. :

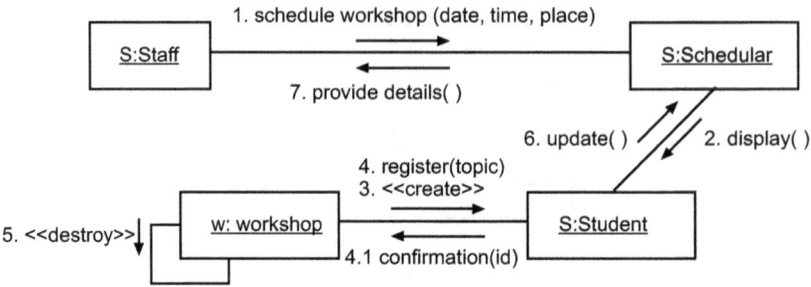

Fig. 4.117

(b) Compare synchronous and asynchronous messages.

(c) How does one model parallel message flows in a sequence diagram?

25. What is recursion? How do we represent recursion in a sequence diagram? Consider a suitable example and draw a complete sequence diagram.

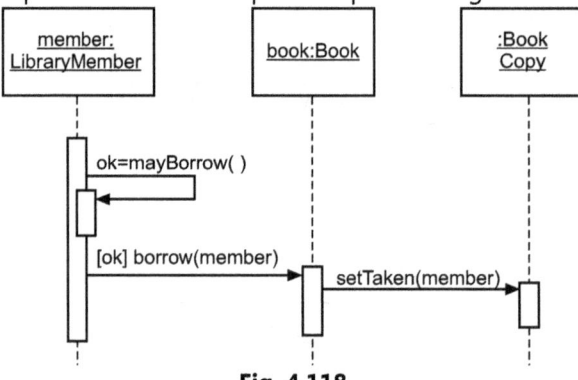

Fig. 4.118

Ans. : Recursive programming is a powerful technique that can greatly simplify some programming tasks. In summary, recursive programming is the situation in which a procedure calls itself, passing in a modified value of the parameter(s) that was passed in to the current iteration of the procedure. Typically, a recursive programming environment contains (at least) two procedures: first, a procedure to set-up the initial environment and make the initial call to the recursive procedure, and second, the recursive procedure itself that calls itself one or more times.

Nesting of Control - Recursion

Sometimes an object can tell itself to do something. This is considered recursion, caused by the object calling a self-operation, or receiving a callback from another object. To model recursion, you nest, or stack, the focus of control -- draw a smaller Focus of Control rectangle on top of, and slightly to the right of, the original one that sits on the object lifeline.

26. Consider an online web based "Computer Rental System". Draw a sequence diagram for "Rent a computer" use case with the following assumptions. The customer need to first select the type of computer he wants to rent. The computer system database is maintained in the system organized in to types like: Desktop, Laptop, Notepad, Pocket PC etc. Based on the availability of the computer system, the rates of rent are displayed, the booking is done, confirmed, the booking details are stored and the customer is issued an electronic configuration of the book.

Ans. :

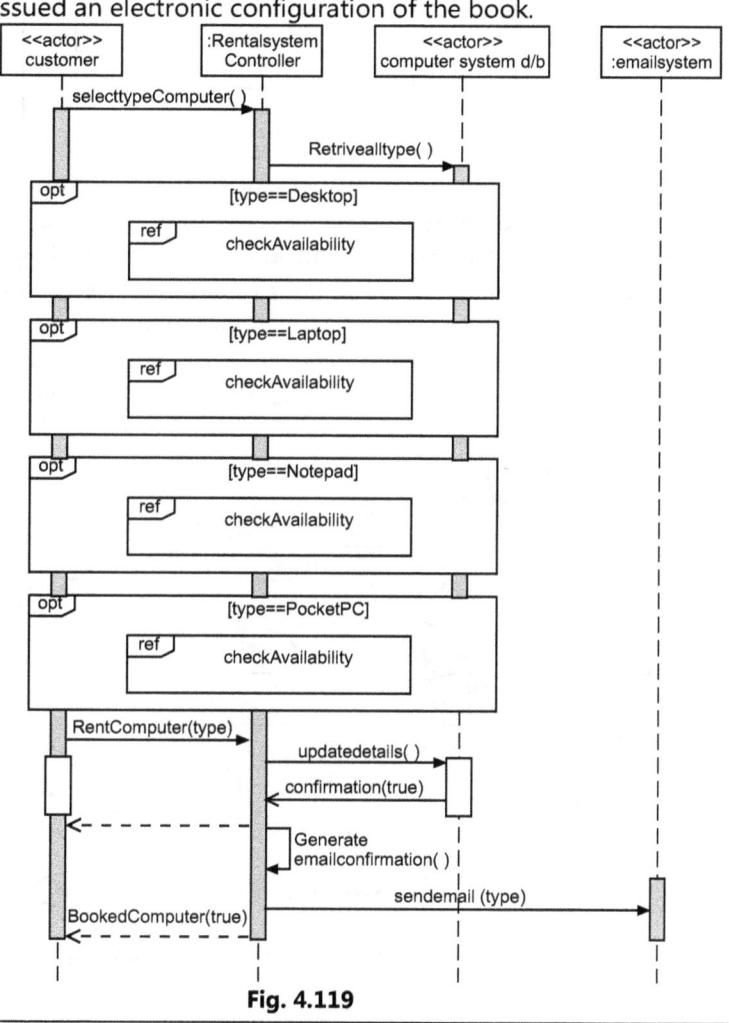

Fig. 4.119

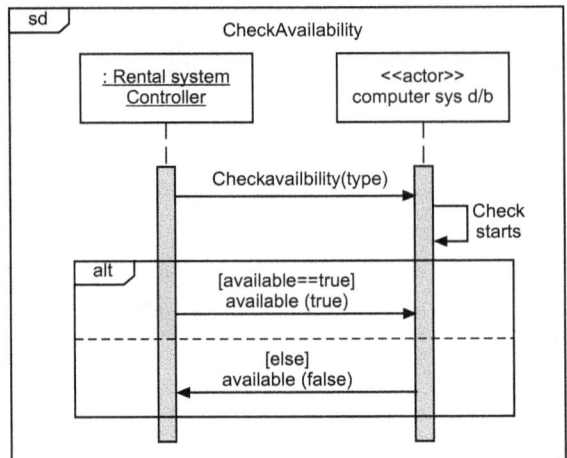

Fig. 4.120

27. Consider a railway reservation and enquiry system. Passengers can book tickets of different categories, book at personal ticket history, check status of reservation, check schedules, check availability, compute fares for plans, Railway authorities can add trains, decide quotes and change stations for a route, even change train timings. Add further assumptions about the scope of application if necessary. Draw a USE CASE diagram for this description using full UML notation for use case diagrams.

Ans. :

Fig. 4.121

28. What are protocol state machines in UML?

Ans.: UML Protocol state machine diagrams are a subset of state machine diagrams that display a sequence of events an object responds to, without having to show the specific behavior. Protocol state machines are most often used to describe complex protocols, such as database access through a specific interface, or communication protocols such as TCP/IP.

For example Database Access, the open, close, query, fetch, cancel, create, and kill operations just be implemented in the order specified by the DBaccess interface's protocol (shown in Figure).

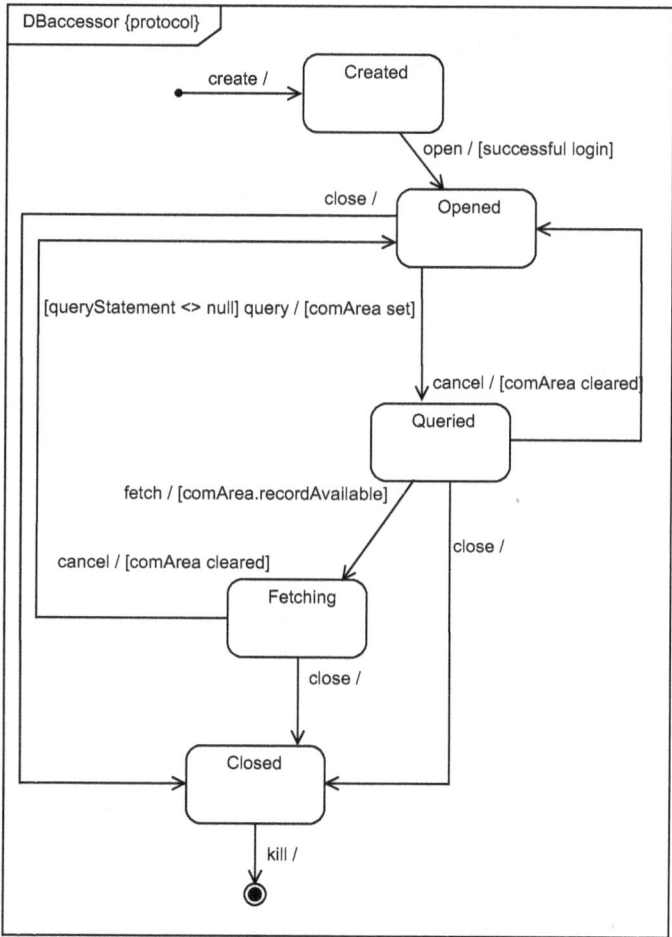

Fig. 4.122

29. Draw an INTERACTION OVERVIEW Diagram for a typical college Library system. (Hint: Typical library has membership, issuing of books, returning of books, fine calculations as some example use cases with their own sequence diagrams.) Make suitable assumptions about scope.

Ans. : Note : Explore the set of interaction for following interaction diagram.

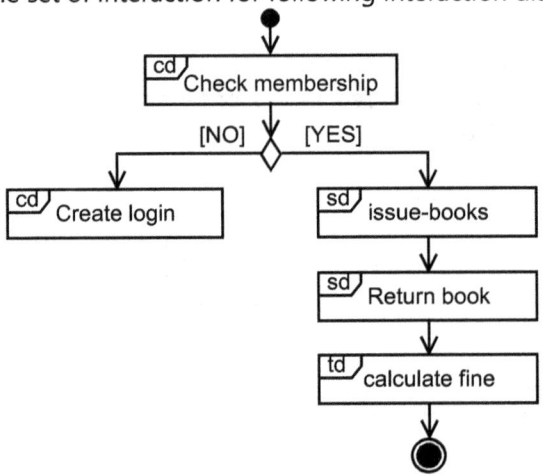

Fig. 4.123

30. How does one model 'data/objects' in an Activity diagram? Illustrate with meaningful examples. [4]

Ans.:

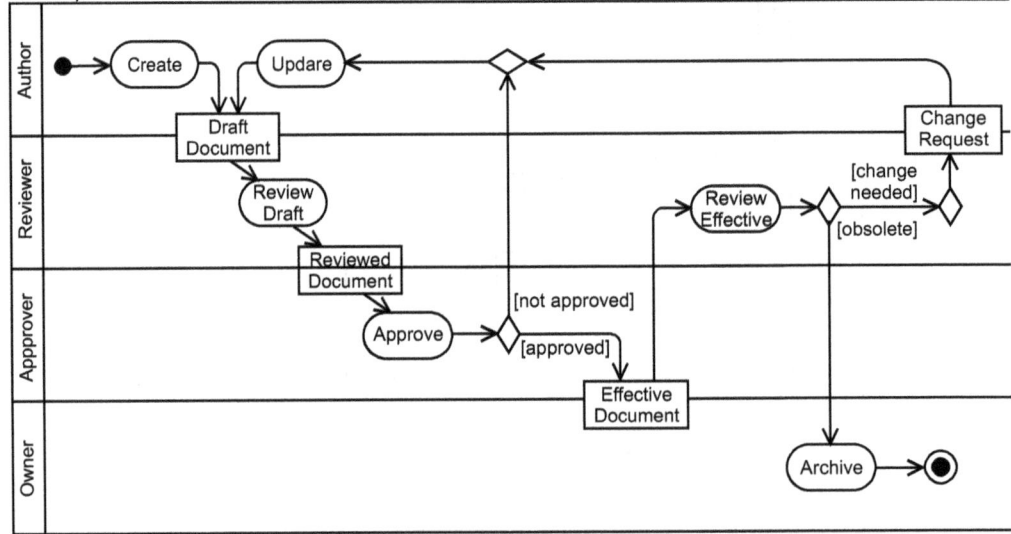

Fig. 4.124

31. Consider a use of a "Rent a Car". A partial description of usecase follows. Customers rent online from choice of cars. A transaction of renting car further involves aspects like sources, destination, number of days car is hired, rate of hiring etc. Payments can be done in various ways. Loyal customers with repeat business may be given discounts. Some of the likely classes are Cars, Types of cars, Rates card, Customers, Transaction for renting the car, RentingCar a controller object, Payment, Rental GUI object to interact etc. Make additional suitable assumptions about the scope and DRAW the SEQUENCE DIAGRAMS showing actors, lifelines, objects, messages/parameters, return values, iterations.

Ans.:

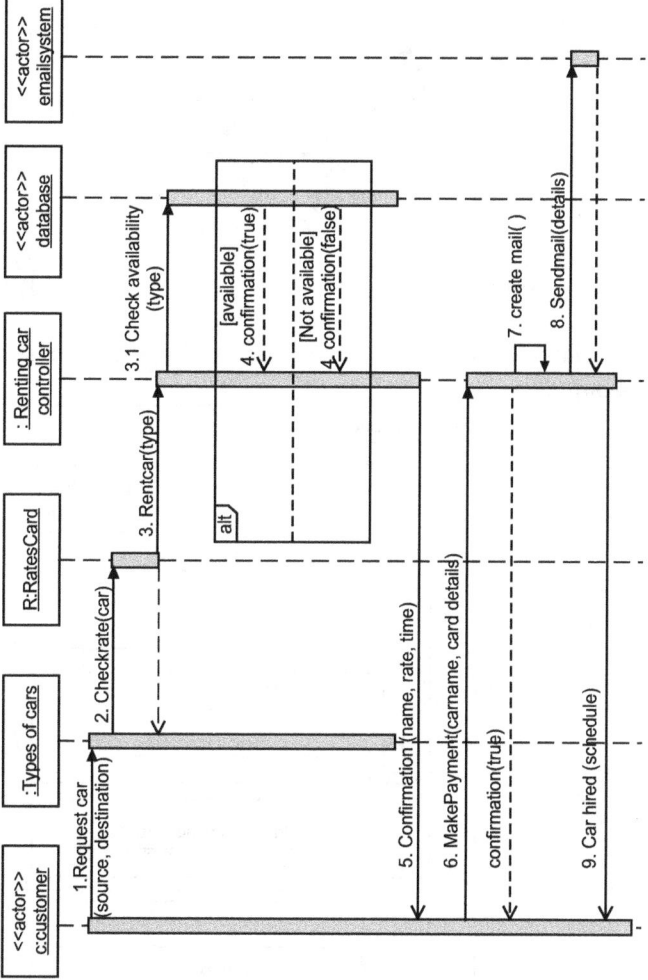

Fig. 4.125

32. For use case "Rent A Car" described in (question number 11 a) draw a COMMUNICATION diagram. Please make additioanl assumptions if relevant and appropriate. First Identify classes, actors for above system and THEN DRAW a COMMUNICATION diagram for above usecase with best use of UML2 Notation.

Ans. :

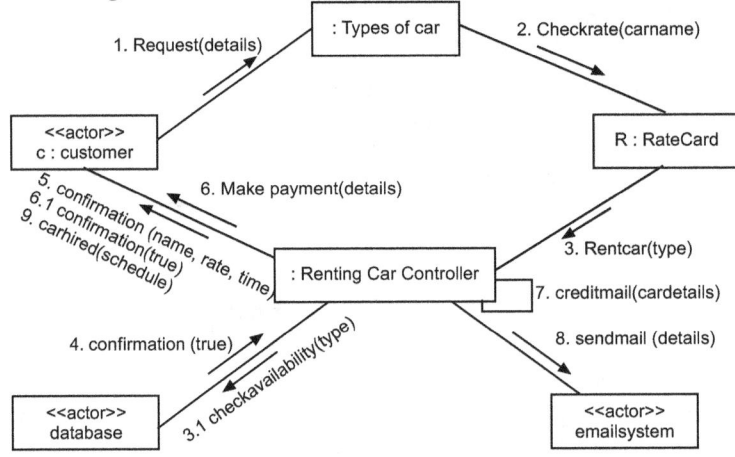

Fig. 4.126

33. Show two different ways to model/depict 'Iteration' in sequence diagrams, with suitable examples.

Ans. :

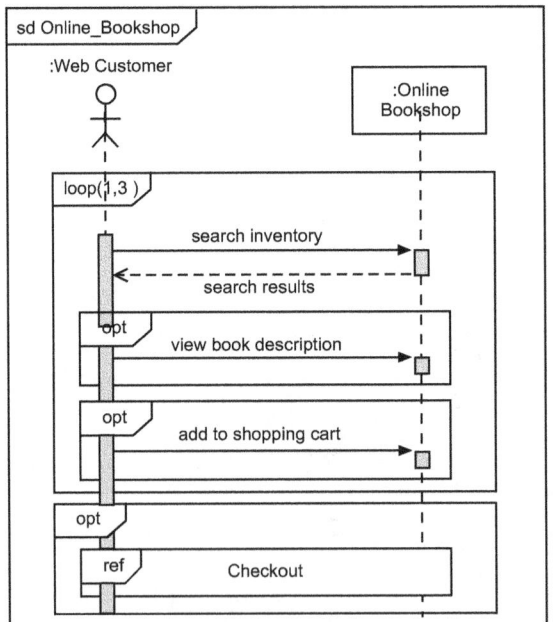

Fig. 4.127

34. The project leader schedules a meeting of members of project group by using a meeting scheduler. These are some of the assumptions :

The project leader interacts though a GUI form to schedule the meeting. A scheduler dose the automated scheduling of meeting based on the free slots in the timetable. All the members involved in the meeting will get an invitation though SMS on their mobiles The system depends on an external mobile gateway to forward SMS. Draw a sequence diagram that describes the above system.

Ans.:

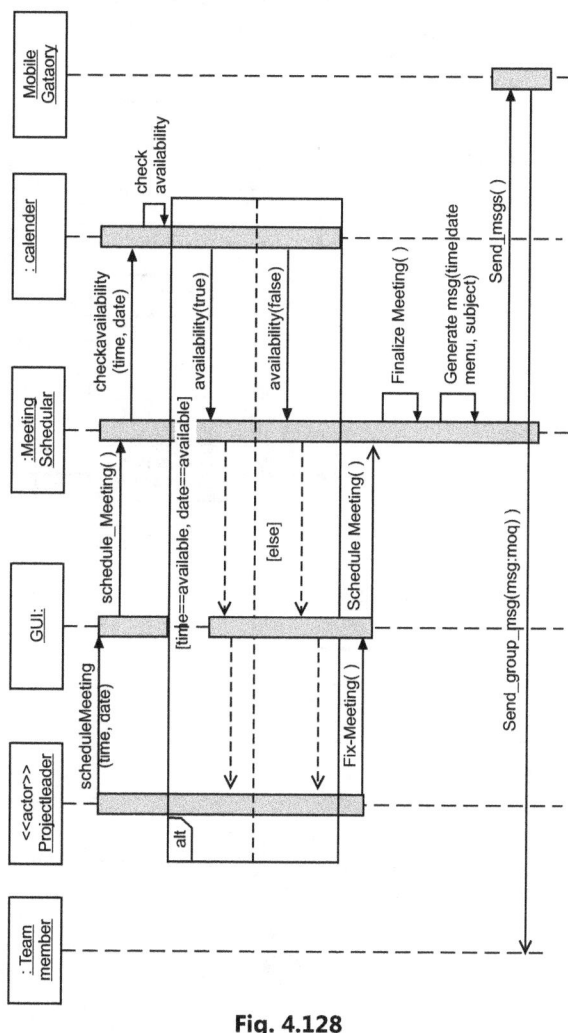

Fig. 4.128

35. A candidate applies in a placement call for placement in a company. He can be placed in one of the companies registered with the placement call. The candidates applications are sorted on aggregate percentage basis. Top students are selected for placements in the registered companies on merit basis. The joining process involves candidate being shown available companies. Candidate selects membership of health club, food club and entertainment club. On successful placement he is given a selection letter and a copy of company schedule. A candidate not placed can select to register himself for waitlist. Draw an activity diagram for the above described system making suitable assumptions about scope.

Ans. :

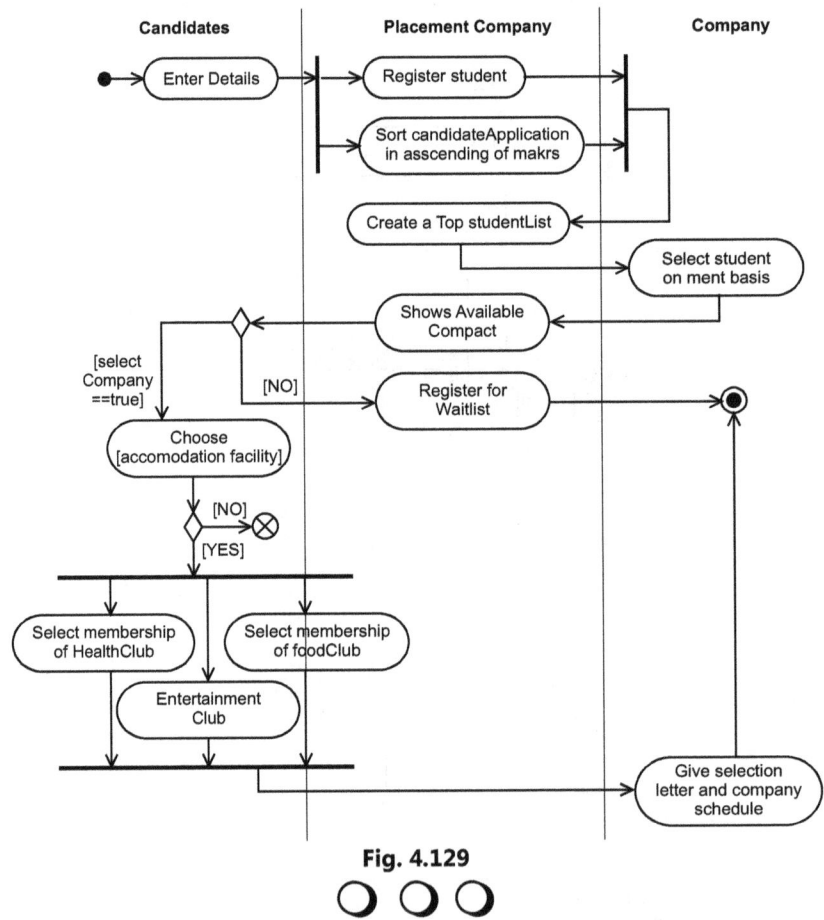

Fig. 4.129

UNIT - V
PACAKAGE DIAGRAM, COMPONENT DIAGRAM, DEPLOYMENT DIAGRAM

5.1 PACKAGE DIAGRAM

5.1.1 Introduction to Packages

A package name must be unique within its enclosing package. In UML, groups of classes are modeled with packages.

Most object-oriented languages have an analog of UML packages to organize and avoid name collision among classes. For example, Java has packages, C# has namespaces (although Java packages and C# namespaces differ significantly in other details). You can use UML packages to model these structures.

Package diagrams are often used to view dependencies among packages. Since a package can break if another package on which it depends changes, understanding dependencies between packages is vital to the stability of your software.

Packages can organize almost any UML element not just classes. For example, packages are also commonly used to group use cases. Package diagrams form part of the development view, which is concerned with how your system's parts are organized into modules and packages, as shown in Fig. 5.1.

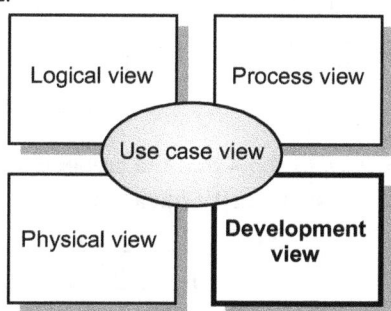

Fig. 5.1 : (4+1) Architecture view

The Development View describes how your system's parts are organized into modules, which are represented as packages in UML. Suppose that during the design of a CMS, you decide to keep classes related to security (for example, performing user authentication) grouped together.

Fig. 5.2 shows the security package and a few other packages from the CMS in UML. The symbol for a package is a folder with a tab. The name of the package is written inside the folder.

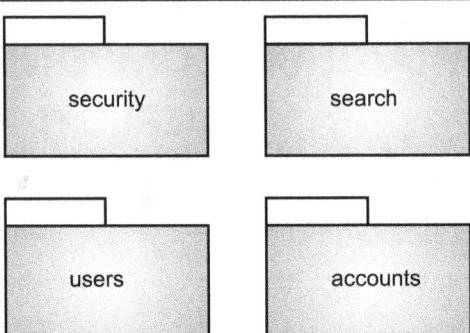

Fig. 5.2 : Packages in a CMS; each package corresponds to a specific system concern

5.1.1.1 Contents of a Package

Packages organize UML elements, such as classes, and the contents of a package can be drawn inside the package or outside the package attached by a line, as shown in Fig. 5.5. If you draw the elements inside the package, write the name of the package in the folder tab.

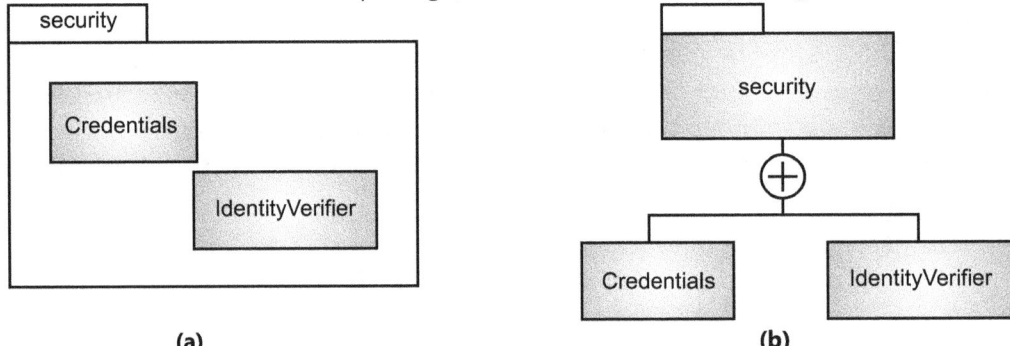

(a)   (b)

Fig. 5.3 : Two ways to show that the credentials and identity Verifier classes are contained in the security package

Packages can also contain other packages, as shown in Fig. 5.4 (a).

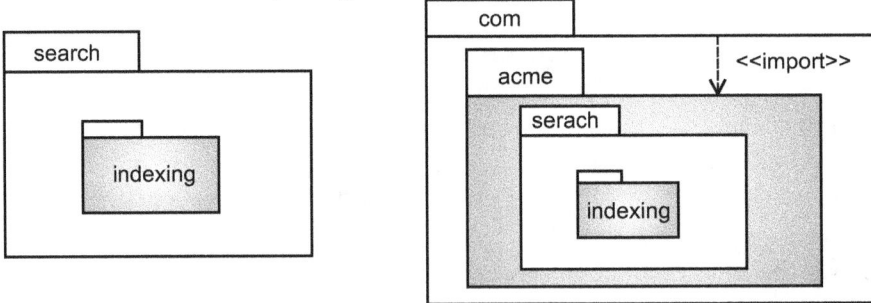

Fig. 5.4 (a) : A package that contains another package

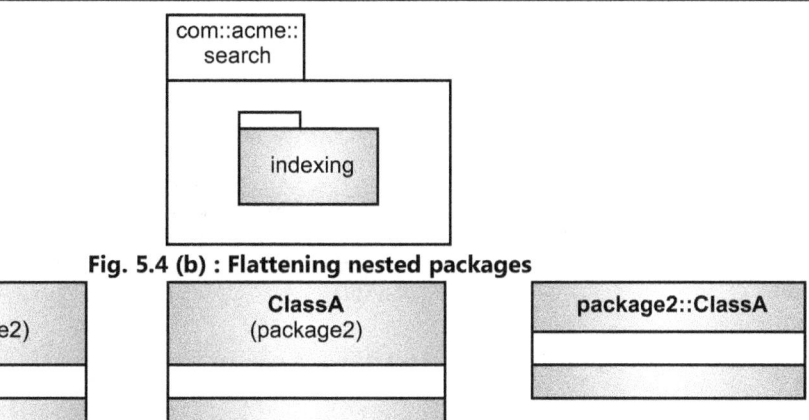

Fig. 5.4 (b) : Flattening nested packages

Fig. 5.5 : Common ways UML tools show that a class belongs to a package

5.1.1.2 Element Visibility

Elements in a package may have public or private visibility. Elements with *public visibility* are accessible outside the package. Elements with *private visibility* are available only to other elements inside the package. You can model public or private visibility in UML by writing a plus or minus symbol in front of the element's name, as shown in Fig. 5.6.

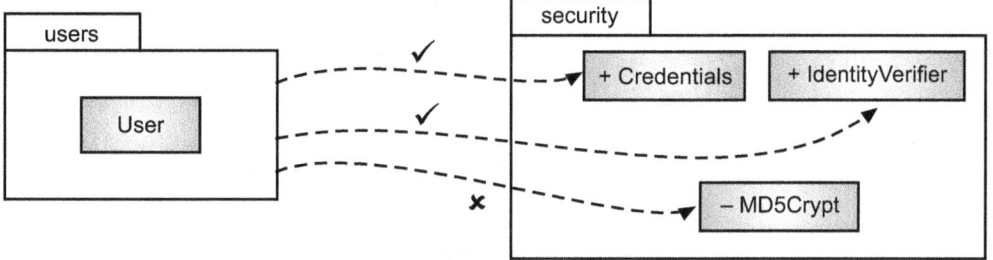

Fig. 5.6 : Since MD5 crypt has private visibility, it is not accessible outside the security package

5.1.2 Relationships in Packages

5.1.2.1 Package Dependency

The previous sections showed that, a class in one package needs to use a class in another package. This causes a dependency between packages :

If an element in package A uses an element in package B, then package A depends on package B, as shown in Fig. 5.7.

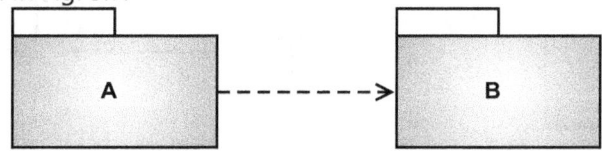

Fig. 5.7 : Package A depends on package B

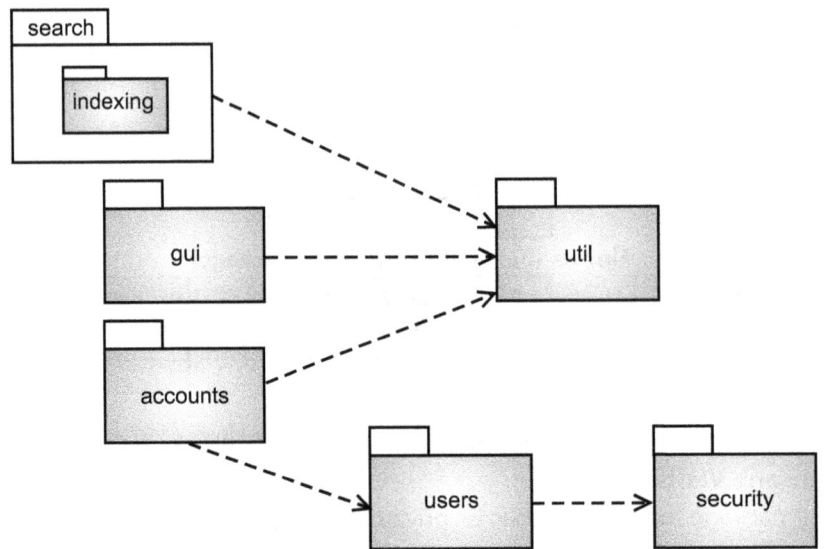

Fig. 5.8 : A typical package diagram featuring core packages and dependencies

5.1.2.2 Importing and Accessing Packages

When a package *imports* another package, elements in the importing package can use elements in the imported package without having to use their fully scoped names. This feature is similar to a Java import, in which a class can import a package and use its contents without having to provide their package names. In an import relationship, the imported package is referred to as the *target package*. To show the import relation, draw a dependency arrow from the importing package to the target package with the stereotype import (see Fig. 5.9).

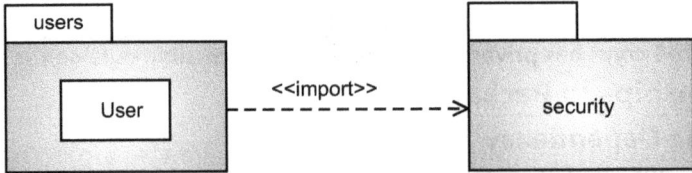

Fig. 5.9 : The package users imports security, so classes in users may use public classes in security without having to specify the package name

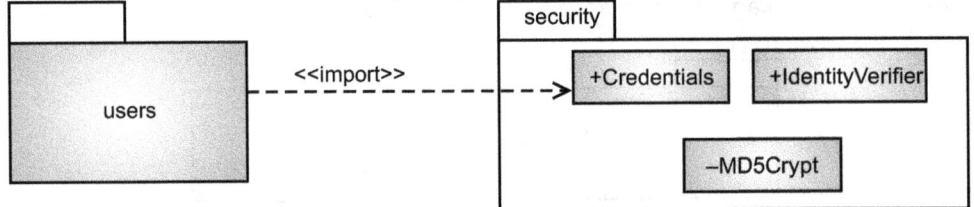

Fig. 5.10 : The users package imports only the credentials element from the security package

A package can also import a specific element in another package instead of the whole package, as shown in Fig. 5.10. When importing a package, only public elements of the target package are available in the importing namespace. For example, in Fig. 5.11 elements in users can see Credentials and Identity Verifier but not MD5Crypt.

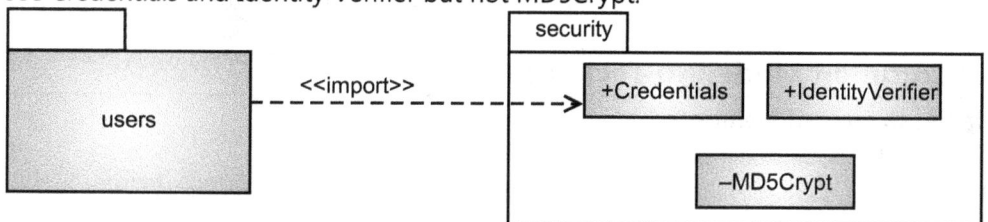

Fig. 5.11 : Private visibility causes a class not to be seen even though its package is imported

In Fig. 5.12 package B imports C and accesses D, so B can see public elements in C and D. Package A imports B, so A can see public elements in B. A can also see public elements in C because C is publicly imported into B, but A cannot see anything in D because D is privately imported into B.

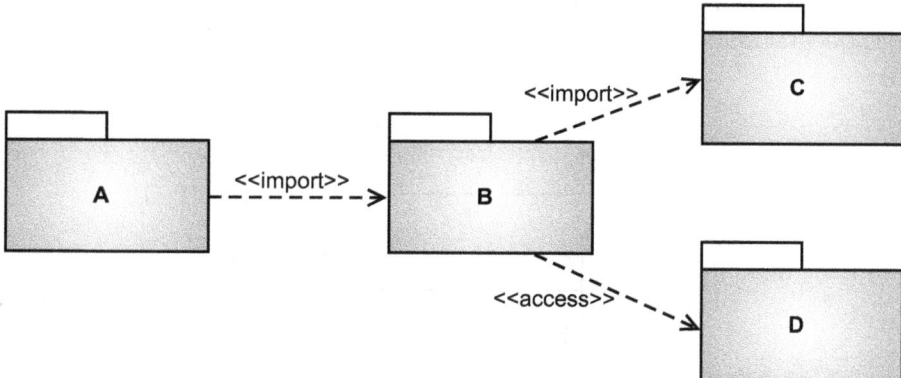

Fig. 5.12 : Package A can see public elements in C but not D

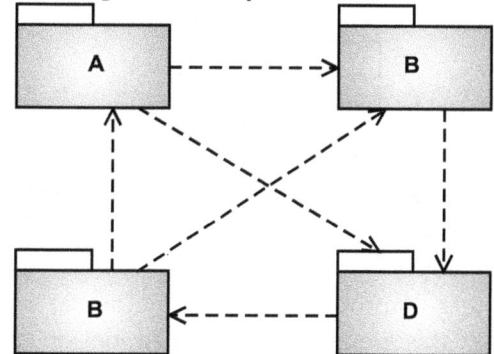

Fig. 5.13 : Directly or indirectly, a change in any one package could affect every other package

5.1.2.3 Managing Package Dependencies

Having complicated dependencies among packages can lead to brittle software since changes in one package can cause its dependent packages to break. Fig. 5.13 shows a dependency disaster: a change in any one package could ultimately affect every other package.

5.1.3 Common Modeling Techniques

Modeling Groups of Elements

- To model groups of elements,
- Examine the elements in a particular architectural view and form the clusters defined by elements that are conceptually or semantically close to one another.
- Surround each of these clusters in a package.
- For each package, distinguish which elements should be accessible outside the package.
- Mark them public, and all others protected or private. When in doubt, hide the element.
- Explicitly connect packages that build on others via import dependencies.
- In the case of families of packages, connect specialized packages to their more general part via generalizations.

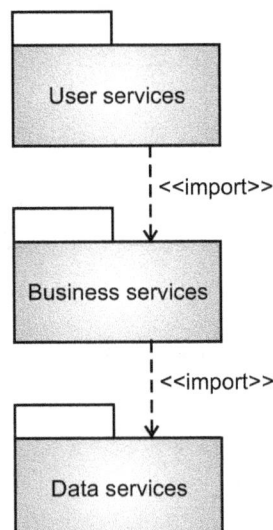

Fig. 5.14 : Modeling groups of elements

Modeling Architectural Views

- To model architectural views,
- Considering your context of problem, identify the set of architectural views that are significant. In practice, this generally includes a design view, a process view, an implementation view, a deployment view, and a use case view.

- Put the necessary and sufficient elements to visualize, specify, construct, and document the semantics of each view into the appropriate package.
- Furthermore, as per requirements group these elements into their own packages.
- There will typically be dependencies across the elements in different views. So, in general, let each view at the top of a system be open to all others at that level.

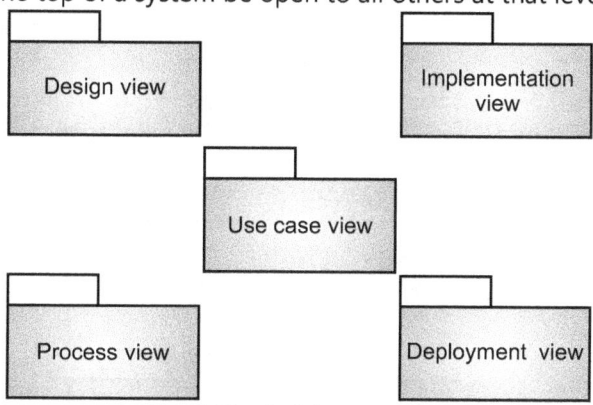

Fig. 5.15 : Architecture view

When you draw a package in the UML

- Use the simple form of a package icon unless it's necessary for you to explicitly reveal the contents of that package.
- When you do reveal a package's contents, show only elements that are necessary to understand the meaning of that package in context.
- Especially if you are using packages to model things under configuration management, reveal the values of tags associated with versioning.

5.2 COMPONENT DIAGRAM

- A component is an encapsulated, reusable, and replaceable part of your software. When modeling large software systems it is common to break the software into manageable subsystems. UML provides the component classifier for exactly this purpose. The functionality provided by a component is specified by a set of provided interfaces that the component realizes In addition to providing interfaces, a component may require interfaces in order to function. These are called required interfaces.
- The functionality of a component's provided interfaces is implemented with one or more internal classifiers. These are typically classes but can be other components. Components should be designed to be reused, with dependencies on external interfaces, strong encapsulation, and high cohesion.
- The main difference between a class and a component is that a component generally has bigger responsibilities than a class. For example, you might create a user information

class that contains a user's contact information (her name and email address) and a user management component that allows user accounts to be created and checked for authenticity. Furthermore, it is common for a component to contain and use other classes or components to do its job.
- Since components are major players in your software design, it's important that they are loosely coupled so that changes to a component do not affect the rest of your system.
- A component is an autonomous unit within a system.
- The components can be used to define software systems of arbitrary size and complexity.
- UML component diagrams enable to model the high-level software components, and the interfaces to those components.
- It shows the development view of the system.

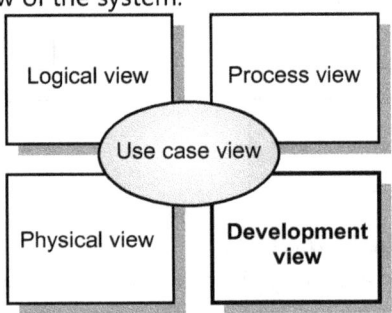

Fig. 5.16 : (4+1) view architecture

Drawing component diagrams has several benefits:
- Thinking of your design with regard to the major blocks helps the development team to understand an existing design and create a new one.
- By thinking of your system as a collection of components with well-defined provided and required interfaces, you improve the separation between the components. This in turn makes the design easier to understand and easier to change when requirements change.

Purpose

The component diagram's main purpose is to show the structural relationships between the components of a system. In UML 1.1, a component represented implementation items, such as files and executables. Unfortunately, this conflicted with the more common use of the term component," which refers to things such as COM components. Over time and across successive releases of UML, the original UML meaning of components was mostly lost. UML 2 officially changes the essential meaning of the component concept; in UML 2, components are considered autonomous, encapsulated units within a system or subsystem that provide one or more interfaces. Although the UML 2 specification does not strictly state it, components are larger design units that represent things that will typically be implemented using replaceable" modules. But, unlike UML 1.x, components are now strictly logical, design-time constructs. The idea is that you can easily reuse and/or substitute a different component implementation in your designs because a component encapsulates behavior and implements specified interfaces. [Note: The physical items that UML 1.x called components are now called "artifacts" in UML 2. An artifact is a physical unit, such as a file, executable, script, database, etc. Only artifacts live on physical nodes; classes and components do not have "location." However, an artifact may manifest components and other classifiers (i.e., classes). A single component could be manifested by multiple artifacts, which could be on the same or different nodes, so a single component could indirectly be implemented on multiple nodes.

5.2.1 A Basic Component in UML

A component is drawn as a rectangle with the <<component>> stereotype and an optional tabbed rectangle icon in the upper right hand corner.

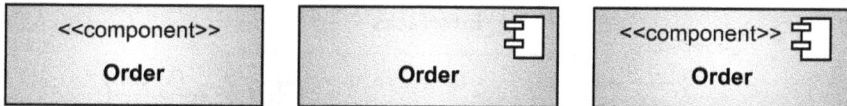

Fig. 5.17 : The different ways to draw a component's name compartment

You can show that a component is actually a subsystem of a very large system by replacing <<component>> with <<subsystem>>. A *subsystem* is a secondary or subordinate system that's part of a larger system. UML considers a subsystem as a special kind of component and is flexible about how you use this stereotype.

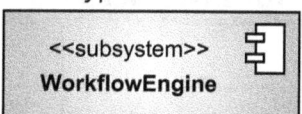

Fig. 5.18 : You can substitute the <<subsystem>> stereotype to show the largest pieces of your system

5.2.2 Provided and Required Interfaces of a Component

- Components need to be loosely coupled, so that they can be changed without forcing changes on other parts of the system. This is where interfaces are introduced. Components interact with each other through provided and required interfaces to control dependencies between components and to make components swappable.
- A provided interface of a component is an interface that the component realizes. Other components and classes interact with a component through its provided interfaces. A component's provided interface describes the services provided by the component.
- A required interface of a component is an interface that the component needs to function. More precisely, the component needs another class or component that realizes that interface to function. But to stick with the goal of loose coupling, it accesses the

class or component through the required interface. A required interface declares the services a component will need.

There are three standard ways to show provided and required interfaces in UML : ball and socket symbols, stereotype notation, and text listings.

Fig. 5.19 : The ball and socket notation for showing a component's provided and required interfaces

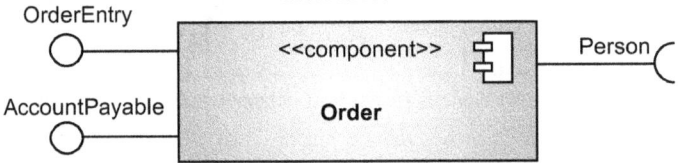

Fig. 5.20 : An alternative approach (compare with Fig. 5.21) to showing a component's provided/required interfaces using interface symbols

5.2.3 Stereotype Notation for Interfaces

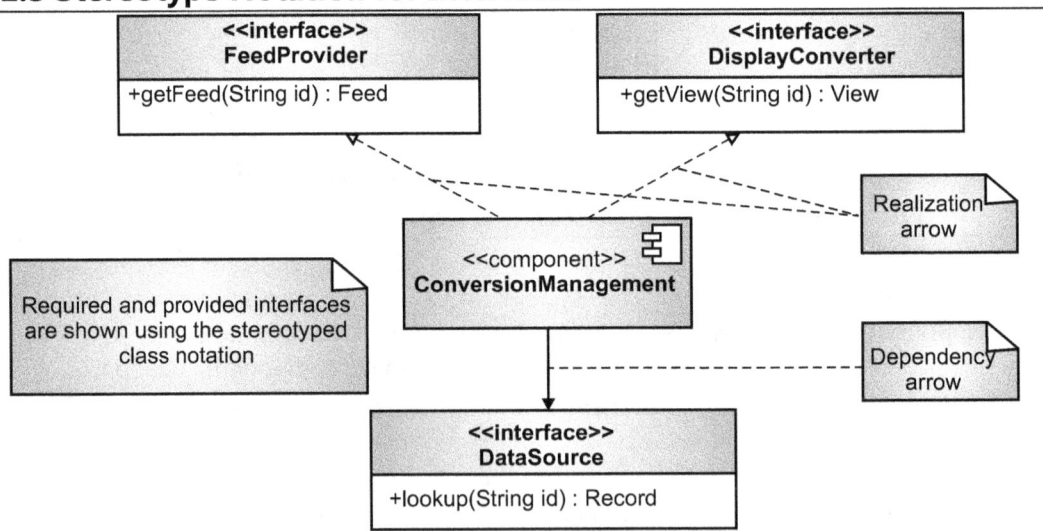

Fig. 5.21 : The stereotyped class notation, showing operations of the required and provided interfaces

5.2.4 Component Dependencies

Components may need other components to implement their functionality. You can show component dependencies using the dependency relation (a dashed line with an open arrow) between the two components.

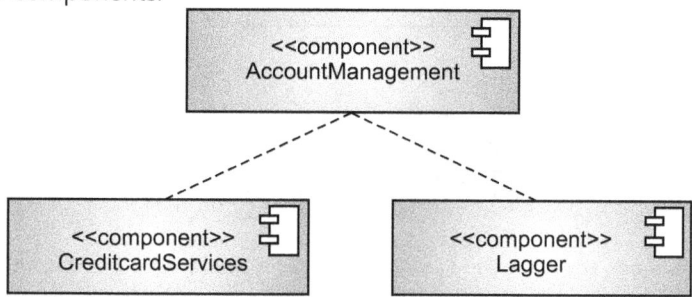

Fig. 5.22 : Component dependency

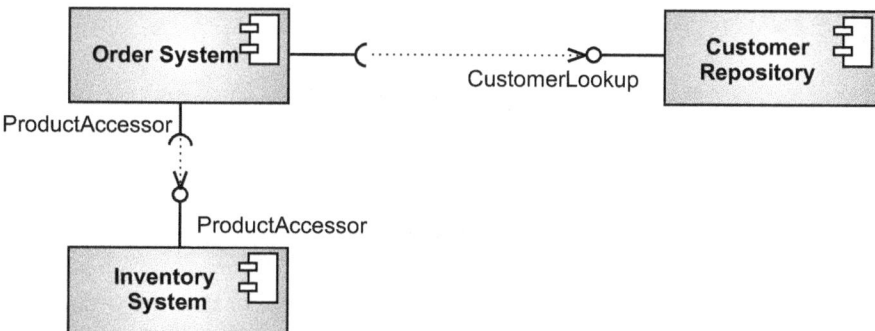

Fig. 5.23 : A component diagram that shows how the Order System component depends on other components

5.2.5 Classes That Realize a Component

A component often contains and uses other classes to implement its functionality. Such classes are said to *realize* a component. They help the component do its job. You can show realizing classes by drawing them (and their relationships) inside the component.

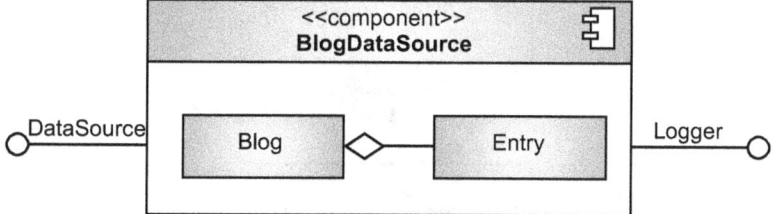

Fig. 5.24 : The blog and entry classes realize the blog data source component

You can also show a component's realizing classes by drawing them outside the component with a dependency arrow from the realizing class to the component, as shown in Fig. 5.25.

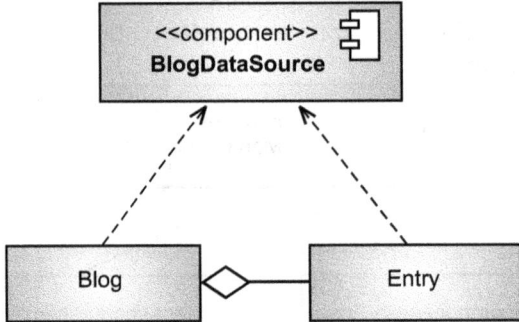

Fig. 5.25 : Alternate view, showing the realizing classes outside with the dependency relationship

The final way to show realizing classes is to list them in a <<realizations>> compartment inside the component, as shown in Fig. 5.26.

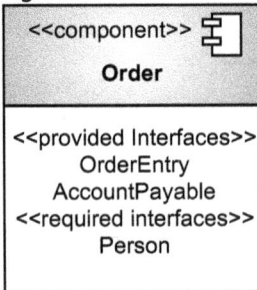

Fig. 5.26 : The additional compartment here shows the interfaces that the Order component provides and requires

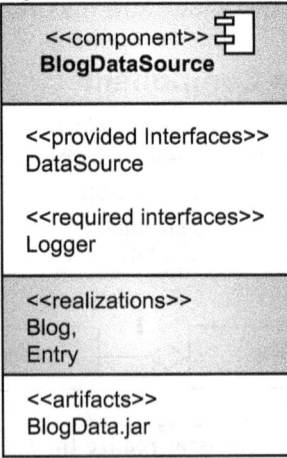

Fig. 5.27 : You can also list the realizing classes inside the component

5.2.6 Ports and Internal Structure

Components can also have ports and internal structure. You can use ports to model distinct ways that a component can be used with related interfaces attached to the port.

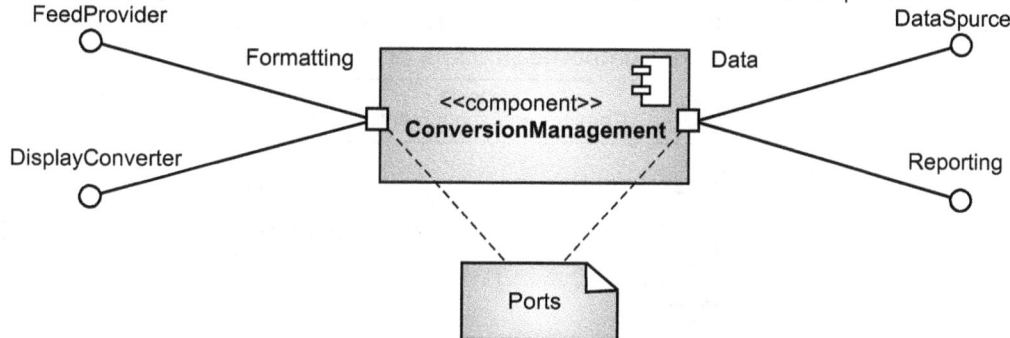

Fig. 5.28 : Ports show unique uses of a component and group "like" interfaces

5.2.7 Delegation Connectors

A component's provided interface can be realized by one of its internal parts. Similarly, a component's required interface can be required by one of its parts. In these cases, you can use *delegation connectors* to show that internal parts realize or use the component's interfaces. Delegation connectors are drawn with arrows pointing in the "direction of traffic," connecting the port attached to the interface with the internal part. If the part realizes a provided interface, then the arrow points from the port to the internal part.

If the part uses a required interface, then the arrow points from the internal part to the port.

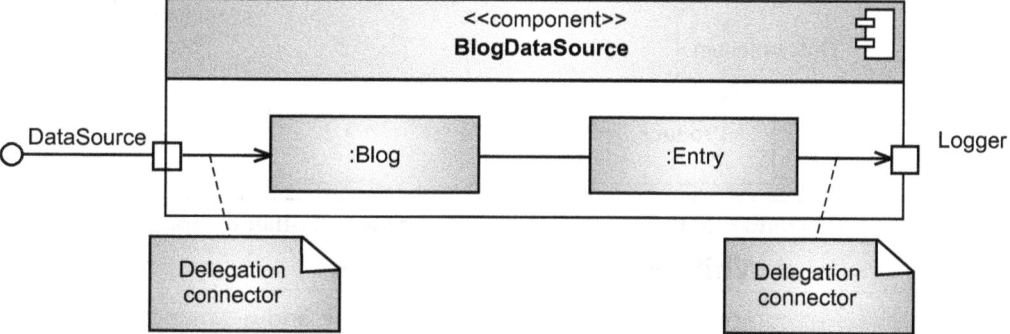

Fig. 5.29 : Delegation connectors show how interfaces correspond to internal parts

You can think of the delegation connectors as follows : The port represents an opening into a component through which communications pass, and delegation connectors point in the direction of communication. So, a delegation connector pointing from a port to an internal part represents messages being passed to the part that will handle it.

5.2.8 Assembly Connectors

Assembly connectors show that a component requires an interface that another component provides. Assembly connectors snap together the ball and socket symbols that represent required and provided interfaces. Assembly connectors are special kinds of connectors that are defined for use when showing composite structure of components.

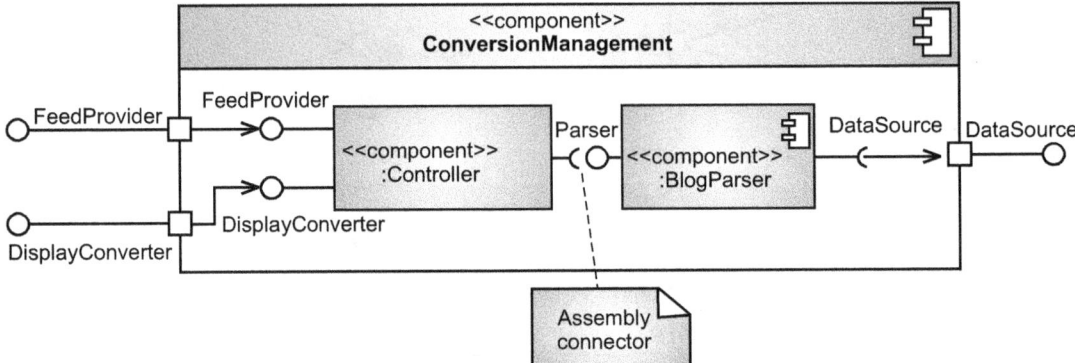

Fig. 5.30 : Assembly connectors show components working together through interfaces

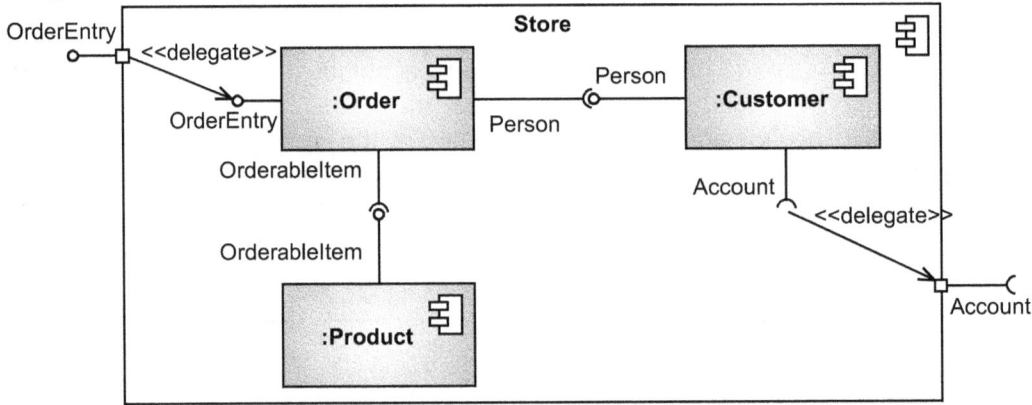

Fig. 5.31 : This component's inner structure is composed of other components

5.2.9 Black-Box and White-Box Component Views

There are two views of components in UML : a black-box view and a white-box view. The black-box view shows how a component looks from the outside, including its required interfaces, it's provided interfaces, and how it relates to other components.

A black-box view specifies nothing about the internal implementation of a component. The white-box view, on the other hand, shows which classes, interfaces, and other components help a component achieve its functionality.

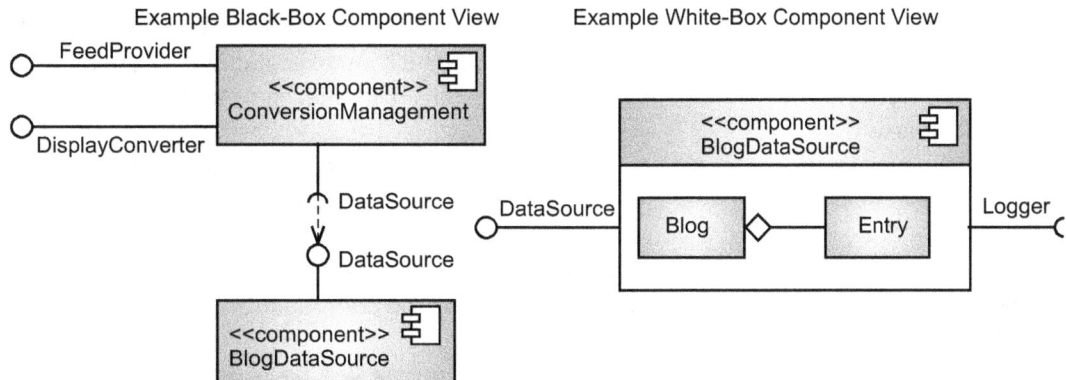

Fig. 5.32 : Black-box component views are useful for showing the big picture of the components in your system, whereas white-box views focus on the inner workings of a component

Note : The component diagram is a very important diagram that architects will often create early in a project. However, the component diagram's usefulness spans the life of the system. Component diagrams are invaluable because they model and document a system's architecture. Because component diagrams document a system's architecture, the developers and the eventual system administrators of the system find this work product-critical in helping them understand the system.

5.2.10 Common Uses

- To model source code.
- To model executable releases.
- To model physical databases.
- To model adaptable systems.

Common Modeling Techniques:

- Modeling Source Code. To model a system's source code,
- Either by forward or reverse engineering, identify the set of source code files of interest and model them as components stereotyped as files.
- For larger systems, use packages to show groups of source code files.
- Consider exposing a tagged value indicating such information as the version number of the source code file, its author, and the date it was last changed. Use tools to manage the value of this tag.
- Model the compilation dependencies among these files using dependencies. Again, use tools to help generate and manage these dependencies.

Modeling an Executable Release

- Identify the set of components you'd like to model. Typically, this will involve some or all the components that live on one node, or the distribution of these sets of components across all the nodes in the system.

- Consider the stereotype of each component in this set. For most systems, you'll find a small number of different kinds of components (such as executables, libraries, tables, files, and documents). You can use the UML's extensibility mechanisms to provide visual cues for these stereotypes.
- For each component in this set, consider its relationship to its neighbors. Most often, this will involve interfaces that are exported (realized) by certain components and then imported (used) by others. If you want to expose the seams in your system, model these interfaces explicitly. If you want your model at a higher level of abstraction, elide these relationships by showing only dependencies among the components.

Modeling a Physical Database
- Define a separate table for each class. This is a simple but naive approach because it introduces maintenance headaches when you add new child classes or modify your parent classes. Collapse your inheritance lattices so that all instances of any class in a hierarchy has the same state. The downside with this approach is that you end up storing superfluous information for many instances.
- Separate parent and child states into different tables. This approach best mirrors your inheritance lattice, but the downside is that traversing your data will require many crosstable joins.

Given these general guidelines, to model a physical database,
- Identify the classes in your model that represent your logical database schema.
- Select a strategy for mapping these classes to tables. You will also want to consider the physical distribution of your databases. Your mapping strategy will be affected by the location in which you want your data to live on your deployed system.
- To visualize, specify, construct, and document your mapping, create a component diagram that contains components stereotyped as tables. Where possible, use tools to help you transform your logical design into a physical design.

Modeling Adaptable Systems

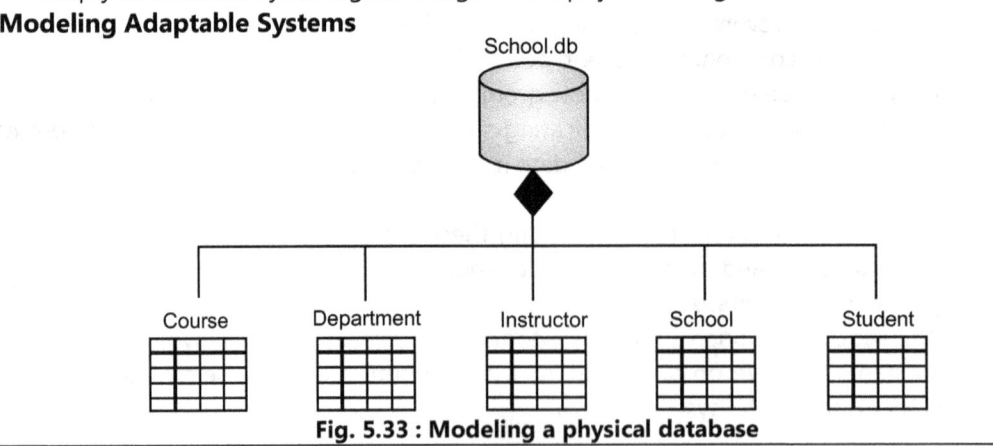

Fig. 5.33 : Modeling a physical database

Consider the physical distribution of the components that may migrate from node to node. You can specify the location of a component instance by marking it with a location tagged value, which you can then render in a component diagram (although, technically speaking, a diagram that contains only instances is an object diagram).

If you want to model the actions that cause a component to migrate, create a corresponding interaction diagram that contains component instances. You can illustrate a change of location by drawing the same instance more than once, but with different values for its location tagged value.

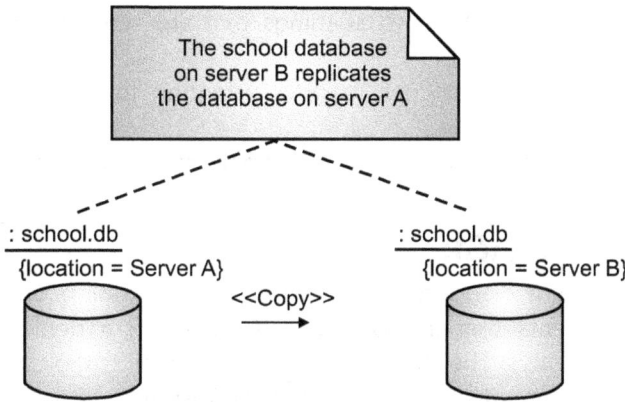

Fig. 5.34 : Modelling adaptables

Forward and Reverse Engineering : To forward engineer a component diagram,
- For each component, identify the classes or collaborations that the component implements.
- Choose the target for each component. Your choice is basically between source code (a form that can be manipulated by development tools) or a binary library or executable (a form that can be dropped into a running system).

Use Tools to Forward Engineer Your Models

To reverse engineer a component diagram,
- Choose the target you want to reverse engineer. Source code can be reverse engineered to components and then classes. Binary libraries can be reverse engineered to uncover their interfaces. Executables can be reverse engineered the least.
- Using a tool, point to the code you'd like to reverse engineer. Use your tool to generate a new model or to modify an existing one that was previously forward engineered.
- Using your tool, create a component diagram by querying the model. For example, you might start with one or more components, then expand the diagram by following relationships or neighboring components. Expose or hide the details of the contents of this component diagram as necessary to communicate your intent.

A Well-Structured Component Diagram
- Is focused on communicating one aspect of a system's static implementation view.
- Contains only those elements that are essential to understanding that aspect.
- Provides detail consistent with its level of abstraction, with only those adornments that are essential to understanding exposed.
- Is not so minimalist that it misinforms the reader about important semantics.

When you draw a component diagram,
- Give it a name that communicates its purpose.
- Lay out its elements to minimize lines that cross.
- Organize its elements spatially so that things that are semantically close are laid out physically close.
- Use notes and color as visual cues to draw attention to important features of your diagram.
- Use stereotyped elements carefully. Choose a small set of common icons for your project or organization and use them consistently.

5.3 DEPLOYMENT DIAGRAM

A deployment diagram is a diagram that shows the configuration of run time processing nodes and the components that live on them. Graphically, a deployment diagram is a collection of vertices and arcs. The deployment diagram depicts the runtime architecture of devices, execution environments, and artifacts that reside in this architecture. It is the ultimate physical description of the system topology, describing the structure of the hardware units and the software that executes on each unit.

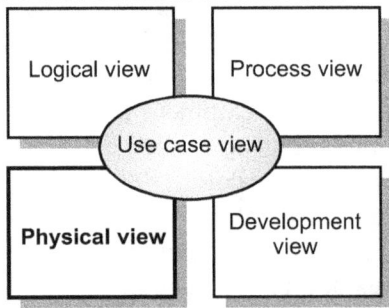

Fig. 5.35 : Deployment diagrams focus on the Physical View of your system

In such an architecture, it should be possible to look at a specific node in the topology, see which components are executing in that node and which logical elements (classes, objects, collaborations, and so on) are implemented in the component, and finally trace those elements to the initial requirement analysis of the system (which could have been done through use-case analysis). The deployment diagram shows how a system will be physically deployed in the hardware environment. Its purpose is to show where the different components of the system will physically run and how they will communicate with each other. Since the diagram models the physical runtime, a system's production staff will make considerable use of this diagram.

5.3.1 Nodes

A node is a hardware or software resource that can host software or related files. You can think of a software node as an application context; generally not part of the software you developed, but a third-party environment that provides services to your software.

The following items are reasonably common examples of hardware nodes :
- Server
- Desktop PC
- Disk drives

The following items are examples of execution environment nodes :
- Operating system
- J2EE container
- Web server
- Application server

Nodes are computational resources upon which artifacts may be deployed for execution. These resources include devices such as computers with processors, as well as card readers, mobile devices, communication devices, and so on. A node can be shown both as a type and an instance (a node is a classifier), where a type describes the characteristics of a processor or device type and an instance represents actual occurrences (machines) of that. The detailed definition of the capability of the system can be defined either as attributes or as properties defined for nodes. A node is drawn as a three dimensional cube with the name inside it, and just as for the notation of classes and objects, if the symbol represents an instance, the name is underlined.

When nodes are used to represent physical computational resources, they are shown with the <<device>> stereotype. Distinct execution environments within these nodes are shown with the <<execution environment>> stereotype (see Fig. 5.37). An execution environment is a specialized node that represents a software configuration hosting specific types of artifacts. An execution environment is expected to provide specific services to hosted artifacts by means of mutually agreed upon interfaces.

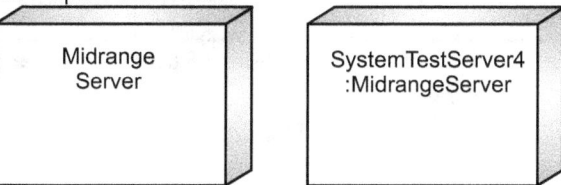

Fig. 5.36 : The MidrangeServer is a node type, and SystemTestServer4 is an instance of that type

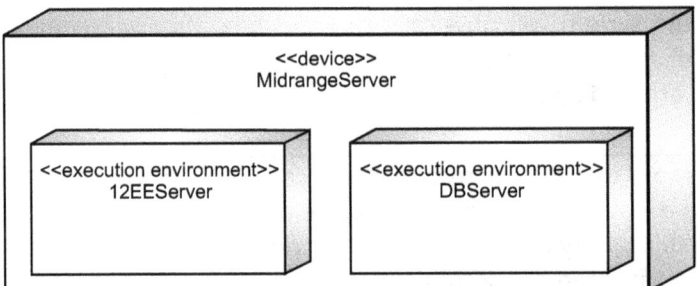

Fig. 5.37 : Device nodes with embedded execution environments

5.3.2 Communication Paths

Nodes are connected to each other by communication paths, as shown in Fig. 5.38. They are drawn as normal associations with a straight line, indicating that there is some sort of communication between them and that the nodes exchange objects or send messages through that path. The communication type can be represented by a stereotype that identifies the communication protocol or the network used.

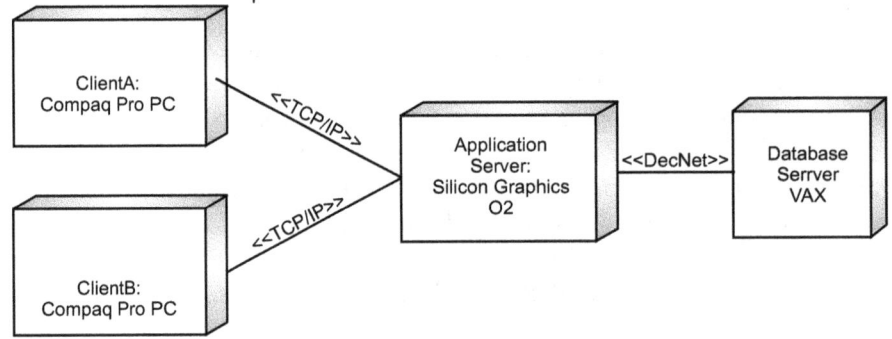

Fig. 5.38 : Communication associations between nodes

5.3.3 Artifacts

Artifacts are physical files that execute or are used by your software. Common artifacts you will encounter include :

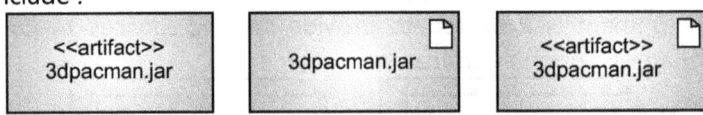

Fig. 5.39 : Equivalent representations of a 3dpacman.jar artifact

- Executable files, such as .exe or .jar files
- Library files, such as .dlls (or support .jar files)
- Source files, such as .java or .cpp files
- Configuration files that are used by your software at runtime, commonly in formats such as .xml, .properties, or .txt

An artifact is shown as a rectangle with the stereotype <<artifact>>, or the document icon in the upper right hand corner, or both, as shown in Fig. 5.39. For the rest of the book, an artifact will be shown with both the stereotype <<artifact>> and the document icon.

5.3.4 Deploying an Artifact to a Node

An artifact is deployed to a node, which means that the artifact resides on (or is installed on) the node. Using the classifier/instance idiom, these artifacts are shown with their name underlined. An artifact deployed onto a node might be presented with a set of properties describing execution parameters for that artifact on that particular node. Fig. 5.40 shows the 3dpacman.jar artifact from the previous example deployed to a Desktop PC hardware node by drawing the artifact symbol inside the node.

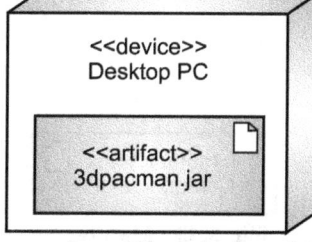

Fig. 5.40 : The 3dpacman.jar artifact deployed to a Desktop PC node

You can model that an artifact is deployed to a node in two other ways. You can also draw a dependency arrow from the artifact to the target node with the stereotype <<deploy>>, as shown in Fig. 5.41.

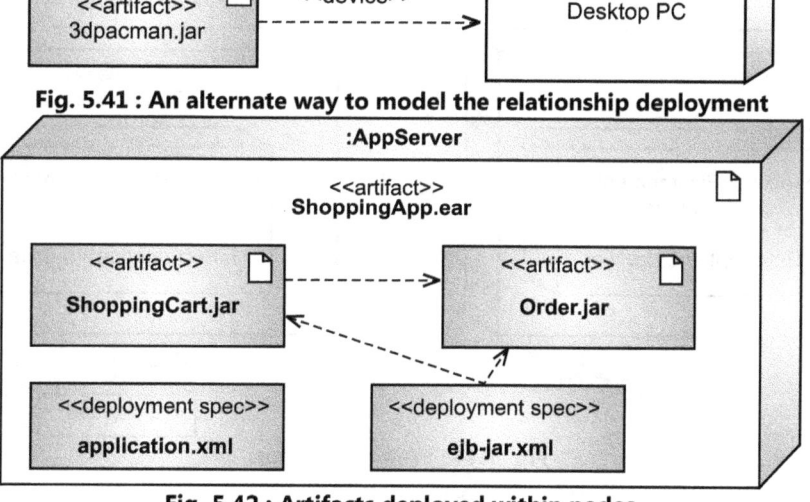

Fig. 5.41 : An alternate way to model the relationship deployment

Fig. 5.42 : Artifacts deployed within nodes

- An artifact manifest one or more model elements.
- A <<manifestation>> is the concrete physical of one or more model elements by an artifact.
- This model element often is a component.
- A manifestation is notated as a dashed line with an open arrow-head labeled with the keyword <<manifest>>.

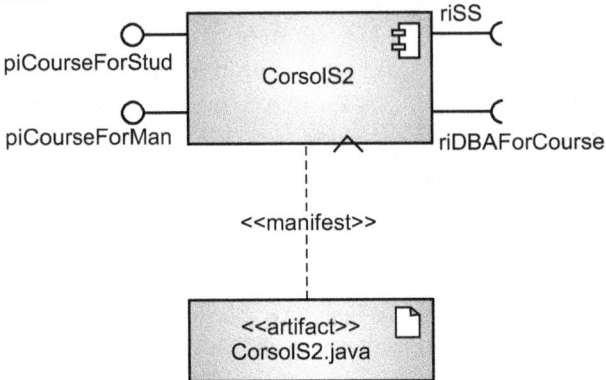

Fig. 5.43 : Manifest

Examples of Deployment Diagram :
(1) Web Application

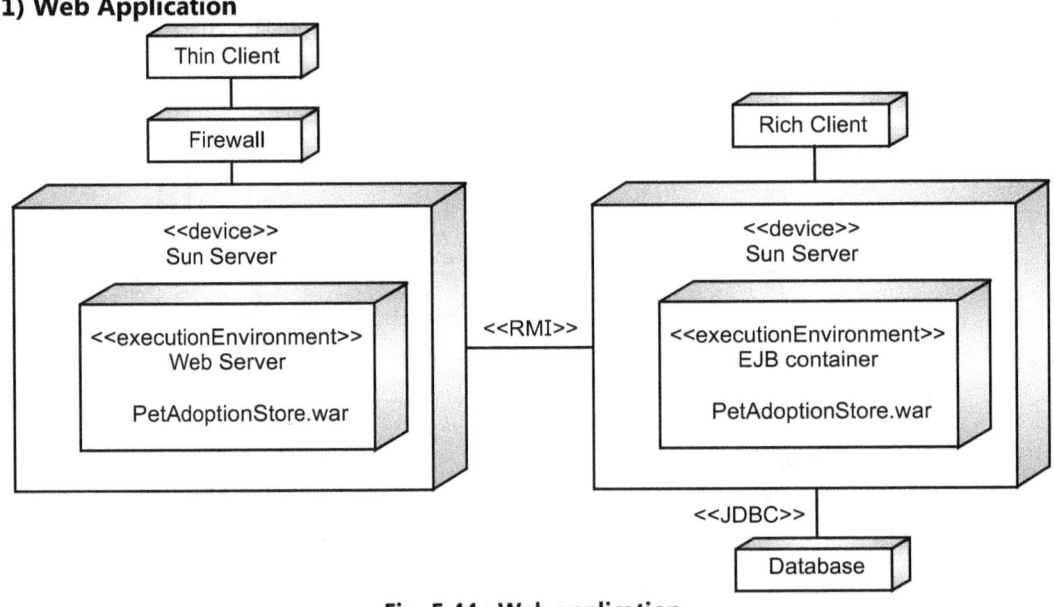

Fig. 5.44 : Web application

(2) Client–Server System

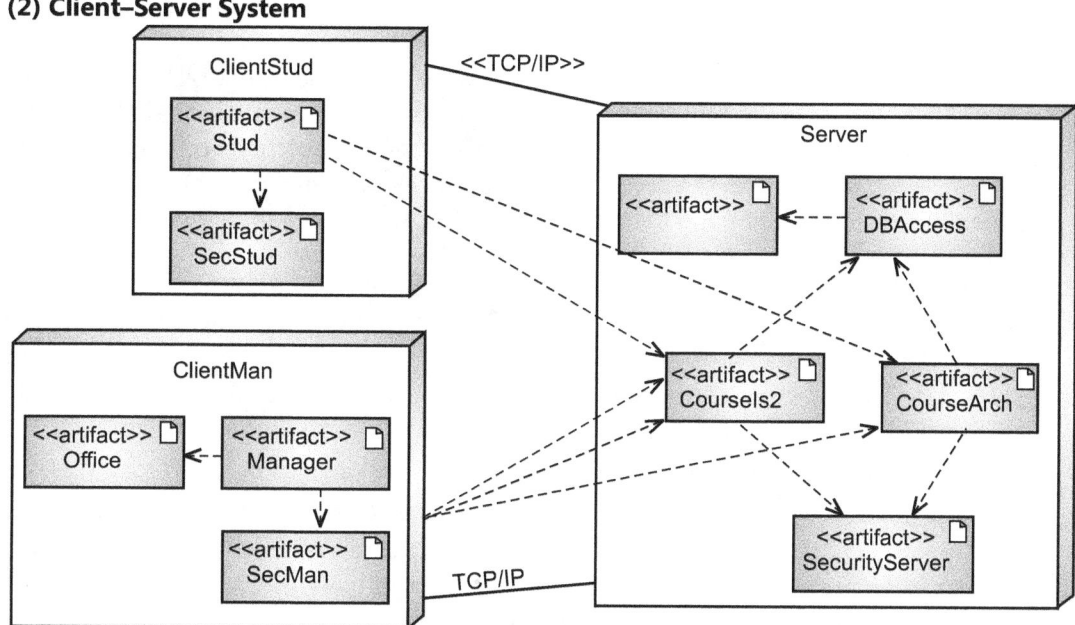

Fig. 5.45 : Client server system

5.3.5 Common Modeling Techniques

5.3.5.1 Modeling an Embedded System

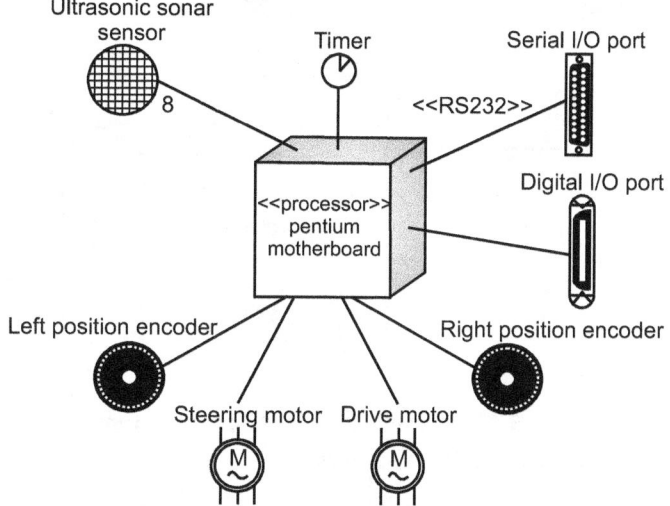

Fig. 5.46 : Modeling an embedded system

To model an embedded system,
- Identify the devices and nodes that are unique to your system.
- Provide visual cues, especially for unusual devices, by using the UML's extensibility mechanisms to define system-specific stereotypes with appropriate icons. At the very least, you'll want to distinguish processors (which contain software components) and devices (which, at that level of abstraction, don't directly contain software).
- Model the relationships among these processors and devices in a deployment diagram.
- Similarly, specify the relationship between the components in your system's implementation view and the nodes in your system's deployment view.
- As necessary, expand on any intelligent devices by modeling their structure with a more detailed deployment diagram.

5.3.5.2 Modeling a Client/Server System

To model a client/server system,
- Identify the nodes that represent your system's client and server processors.
- Highlight those devices that are germane to the behavior of your system. For example, you'll want to model special devices, such as credit card readers, badge readers, and display devices other than monitors, because their placement in the system's hardware topology are likely to be architecturally significant.
- Provide visual cues for these processors and devices via stereotyping.
- Model the topology of these nodes in a deployment diagram. Similarly, specify the relationship between the components in your system's implementation view and the nodes in your system's deployment view.

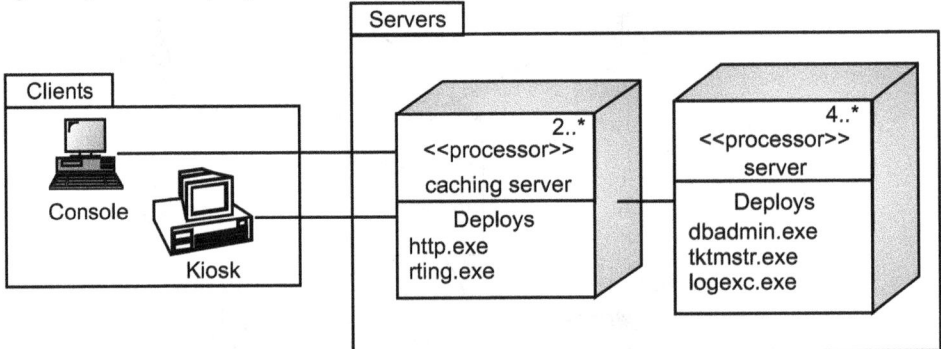

Fig. 5.47 : Modeling a client/server system

5.3.5.3 Modeling a Fully Distributed System

To model a fully distributed system,
- Identify the system's devices and processors as for simpler client/server systems.

- If you need to reason about the performance of the system's network or the impact of changes to the network, be sure to model these communication devices to the level of detail sufficient to make these assessments.
- Pay close attention to logical groupings of nodes, which you can specify by using packages.
- Model these devices and processors using deployment diagrams. Where possible, use tools that discover the topology of your system by walking your system's network.
- If you need to focus on the dynamics of your system, introduce use case diagrams to specify the kinds of behavior you are interested in, and expand on these use cases with interaction diagrams.

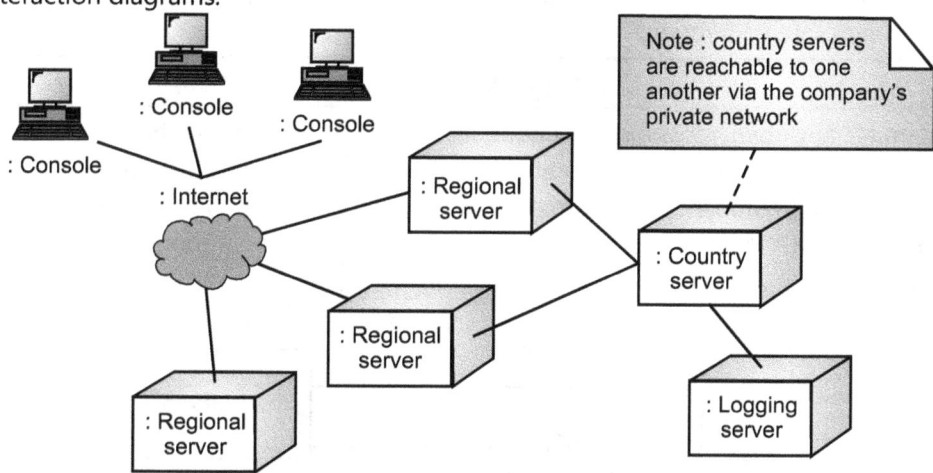

Fig. 5.48 : Modeling a fully distributed system

5.4 FORWARD AND REVERSE ENGINEERING

Forward engineering of deployment diagram is to creation of code from model.

Reverse engineering (the creation of models from code) from the real world back to deployment. diagrams is of tremendous value, especially for fully distributed systems that are under constant change. You will want to supply a set of stereotyped nodes that speak the language of your system's network administrators, in order to tailor the UML to their domain. The advantage of using the UML is that it offers a standard language that addresses not only their needs, but the needs of your project's software developers, as well.

To reverse engineer a deployment diagram,

- Decide the target that you want to reverse engineer.
- Decide also the fidelity of your reverse engineering. In some cases, it's sufficient to reverse engineer just to the level of all the system's processors; in others, you'll want to reverse engineer the system's networking peripherals, as well.

- Use a tool that walks across your system, discovering its hardware topology. Record that topology in a deployment model.
- Along the way, you can use similar tools to discover the components that live on each node, which you can also record in a deployment model. You'll want to use an intelligent search, for even a basic personal computer can contain gigabytes of components, many of which may not be relevant to your system.
- Using your modeling tools, create a deployment diagram by querying the model. For example, you might start with visualizing the basic client/server topology, then expand on the diagram by populating certain nodes with components of interest that live on them. Expose or hide the details of the contents of this deployment diagram as necessary to communicate your intent.

REVIEW QUESTIONS

1. Identify any two possible components and the interfaces they support for a hypothetical typical college library system that issues (returns) books to student members. The students can search for the books details as well as check availability. Draw a COMPONENT diagram to show the two identified components with interfaces they support.

Ans. :

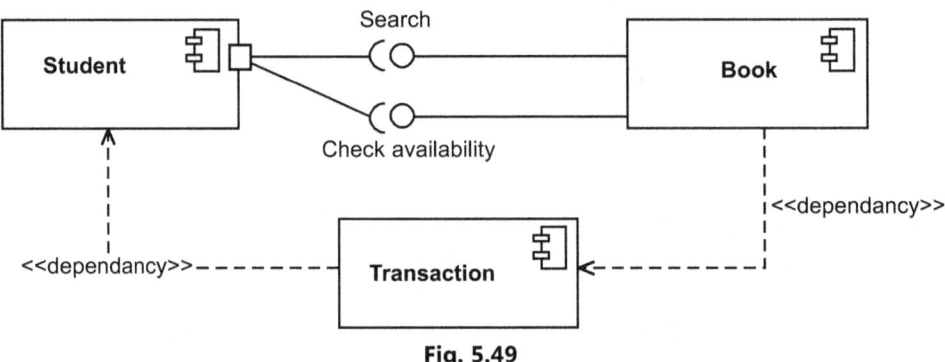

Fig. 5.49

2. An applications has two components. We have defined one interface called ICompare Strings. There is only one service defined which compares with given strings.

   The MYSTRINGS component implements the interface. We have a SEARCHBOOKS components that needs to search based on title, author names.

   The SEARCHBOOKS component can actually reuse the capabilities of comparing strings. Show a fragment of a component diagram showing components and interfaces and various dependencies.

Ans. :

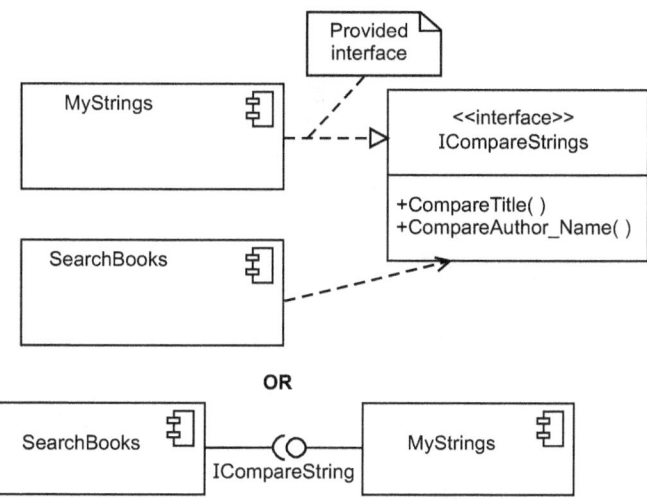

Fig. 5.50

3. Why do we break large systems into subsystems? Taking an example of any large system show how packages can be used to either MODEL grouping of use cases into PACKAGES or grouping of classes components into packages.

Ans. :

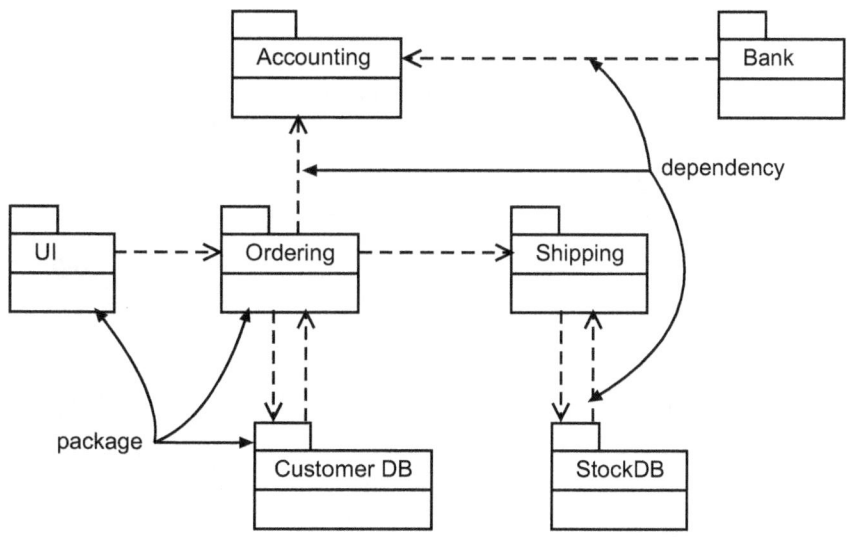

Fig. 5.51

4. Consider a system of your choice to represent a relationship between a component and its interface.

Ans. :

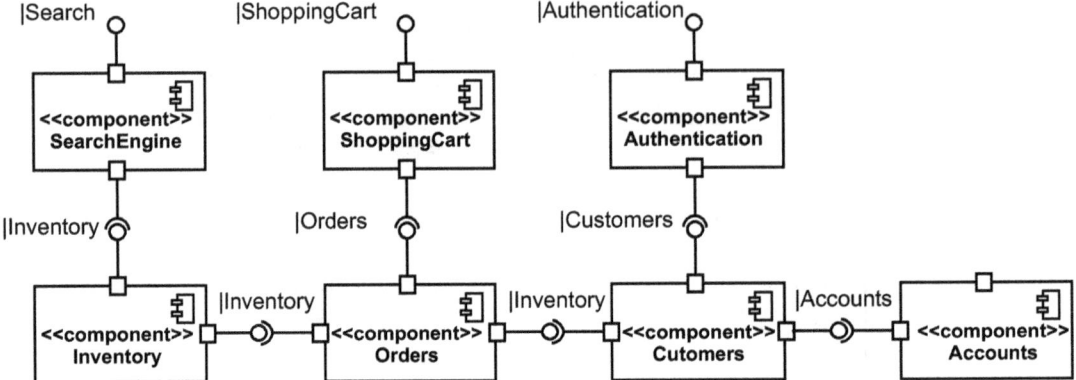

Fig. 5.52

CASE STUDIES

PART - I

1. Use case diagram for Airport Check-In and Security Screening.

This is an example of Business Use Case Diagram which is created during Business Modelling and is rendered here in notation used by Rational Unified Process (RUP).

Business actors are Passenger, Tour Guide, Minor (Child), Passenger with Special Needs (For example, with disabilities), all playing external roles in relation to airport business.

Business use cases are Individual Check-In, Group Check-In (for groups of tourists), Security Screening etc. - representing business functions or processes taking place in airport and serving the needs of passengers.

Business use cases Baggage Check-in and Baggage Handling extend Check-In use cases, because passenger might have no luggage, so baggage check-in and handling are optional.

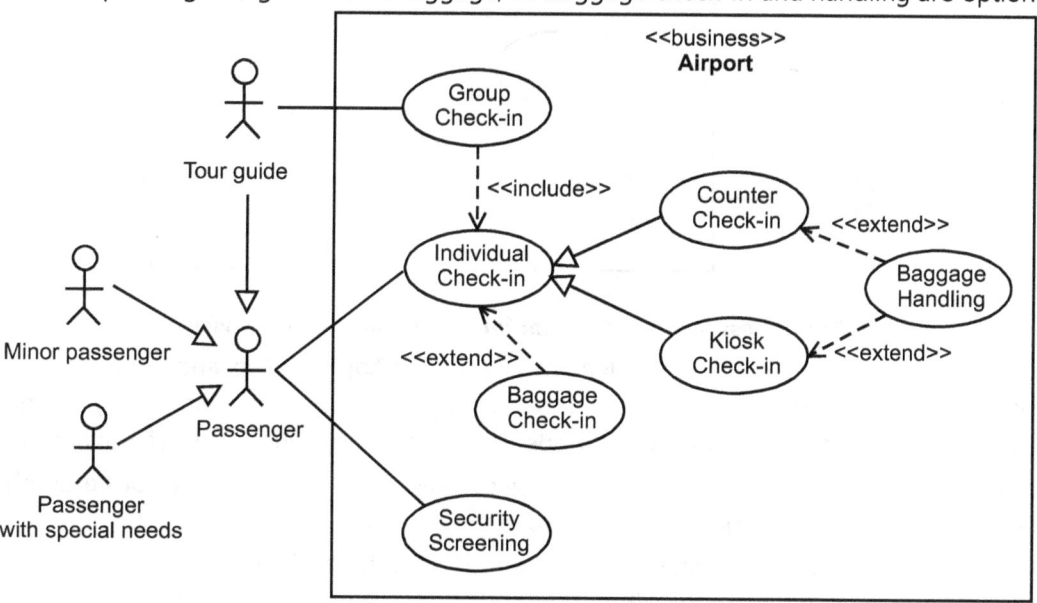

Fig. 1 : An example of use case diagram for airport check-in and security screening

2. Use case diagram for Restaurant

Here we provide two alternative examples of Business Use Case Diagram for a Restaurant rendered in notation used by Rational Unified Process (RUP).

2.1 First example shows external business view of a restaurant.

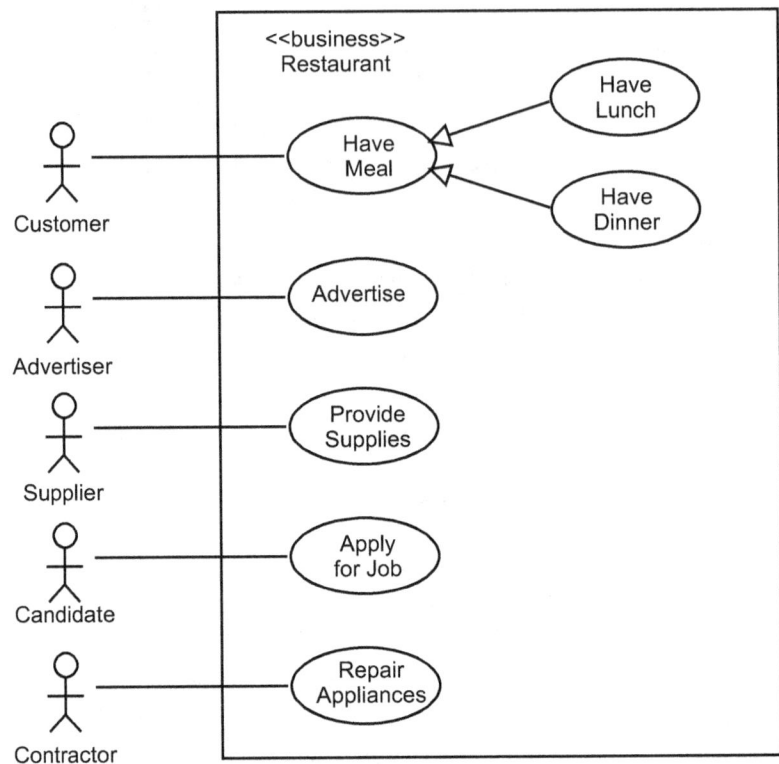

Fig. 2 : Business use case diagram for Restaurant - External view

For example, Customer wants to Have Meal, Candidate - to Apply for Job, and Contractor - to fix some appliances. Note, that we don't have such actors as Chef or Waiter. They are not external roles but part of the business we model - the Restaurant, thus - they are not actors.

2.2 Second example shows internal business view of a restaurant. As in the previous example, actors have some needs and goals as related to the restaurant.

This approach could be more useful to model services that the business provides to different types of customers, but reading this kind of business use case diagrams could be confusing.

For example, Customer is now connected to Serve Meal use case, Supplier - to Purchase Supplies.

We have now new actor Potential Customer participating in Advertise use case by reading ads and getting some information about restaurant. At the same time, Contractor actor is gone because Repair Appliances is not a service usually provided by restaurants.

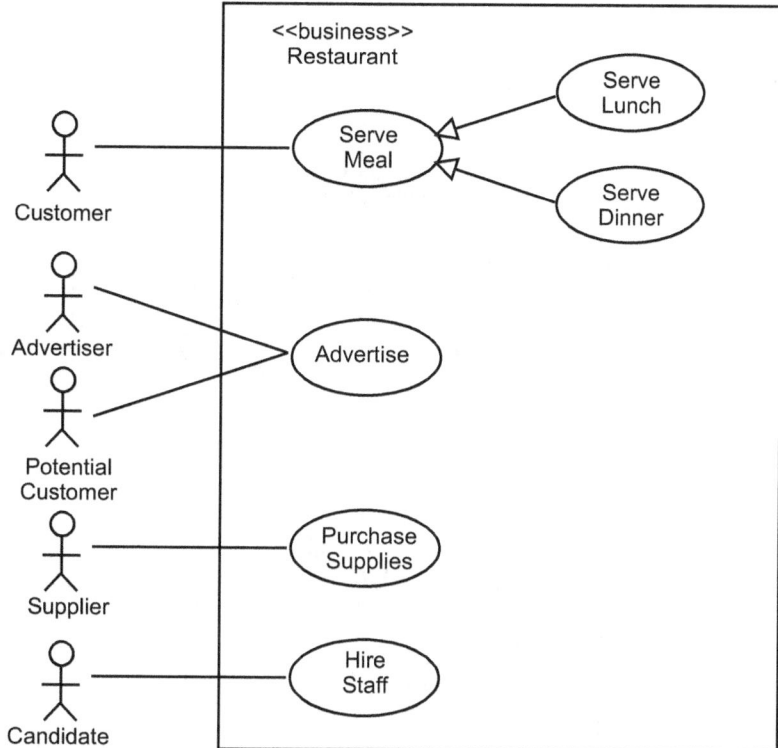

Fig. 3 : Business use case diagram for Restaurant - Internal view

Still, in this example we don't have actors as Chef or Waiter for the same reasons as before - they both are not external roles but part of the business we model.

3. Use case diagram for Online Shopping

Web Customer actor uses some web site to make purchases online. Top level use cases are View Items, Make Purchase and Client Register.

View Items use case could be used by customer as top level use case if customer only wants to find and see some products. This use case could also be used as a part of Make Purchase use case.

Client Register use case allows customer to register on the web site, for example, to get some coupons or be invited to private sales.

Note, that Checkout use case is included use case not available by itself - checkout is part of making purchase.

Except for the Web Customer actor there are several other actors which will be described below with detailed use cases.

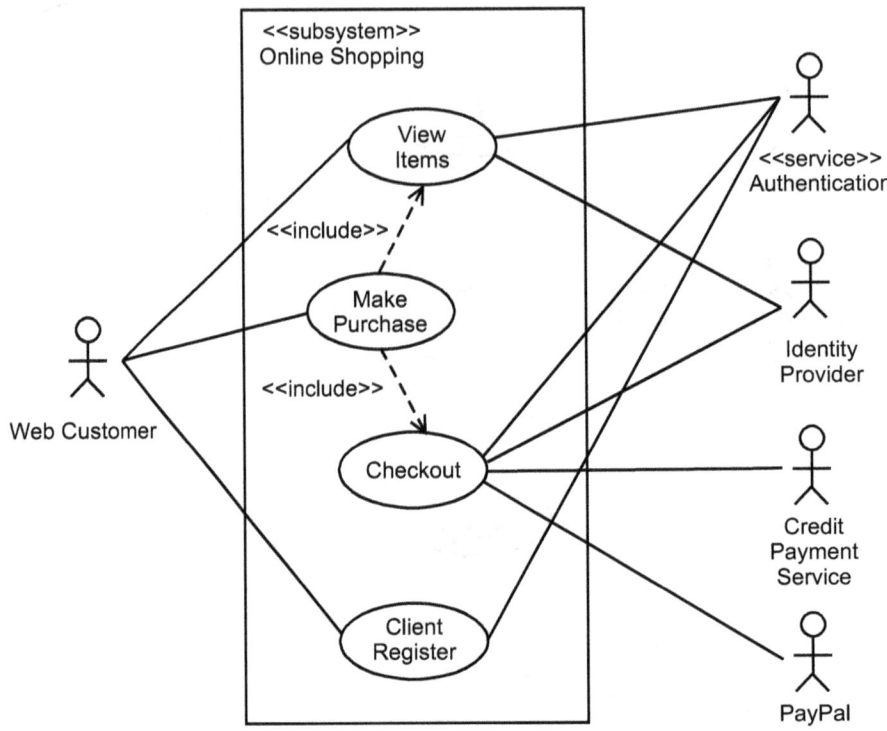

Fig. 4 : Online shopping - top level use cases

View Items use case is extended by several optional use cases - customer may search for items, browse catalog, view items recommended for him/her, add items to shopping cart or wish list.

Customer Authentication use case is included in View Recommended Items and Add to Wish List because both require customer to be authenticated. At the same time, item could be added to the shopping cart without user authentication.

Checkout use case includes several required uses cases. Web customer should be authenticated.

It could be done through user login page, user authentication cookie ("Remember me") or Single Sign-On (SSO). Web site authentication service is used in all these use cases, while SSO also requires participation of external identity provider.

Checkout use case also includes Payment use case which could be done either by using credit card and external credit payment service or with PayPal.

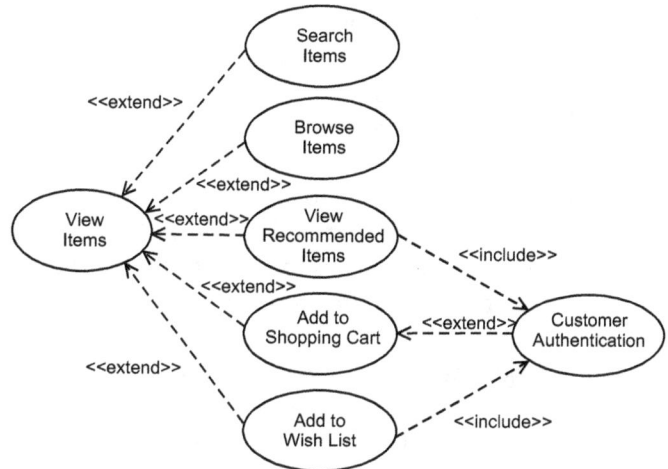

Fig. 5 : Online shopping - view items use case

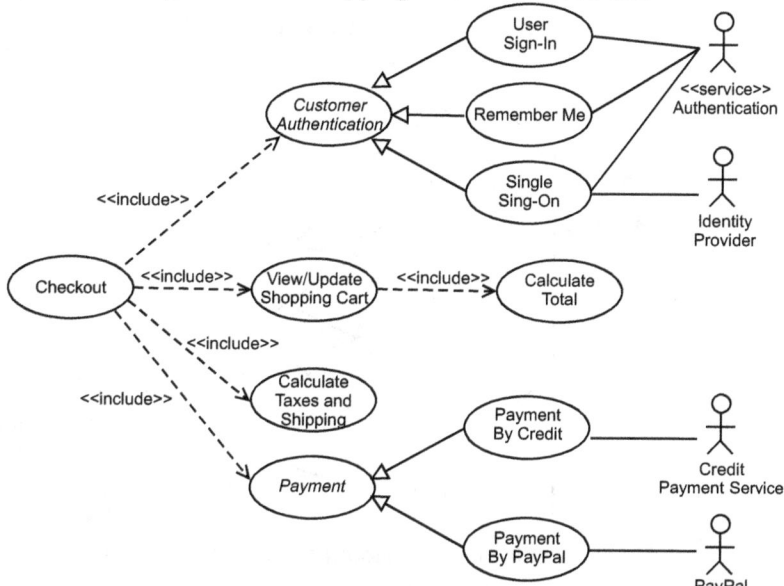

Fig. 6 : Online shopping - checkout, authentication and payment use cases

4. Use case diagram for Credit Card Processing System Use Cases

In this use cases example, Credit Card Processing System (Credit Card Payment Gateway) is a subject, i.e. system under design or consideration. Primary actor of the system is the Merchant's Credit Card Processing System. The merchant submits a credit card transaction request to the credit card payment gateway on behalf of a customer. Bank which issued customer's credit card is actor which could approve or reject the transaction. If transaction is approved, funds will be transferred to merchan't bank account.

Authorize and Capture use case is the most common type of credit card transaction. The requested amount of money should be first authorized by Customer's Credit Card Bank, and if approved, is further submitted for settlement. During the settlement funds approved for the credit card transaction are deposited into the Merchant's Bank account.

In some cases, only authorization is requested and the transaction will not be sent for settlement. In this case, usually if no further action is taken within some number of days, the authorization expires. Merchants can submit this request if they want to verify the availability of funds on the customer's credit card, if item is not currently in stock, or if merchant wants to review orders before shipping.

Capture (request to capture funds that were previously authorized) use case describes several scenarios when merchant needs to complete some previously authorized transaction - either submitted through the payment gateway or requested without using the system, For example, using voice authorization.

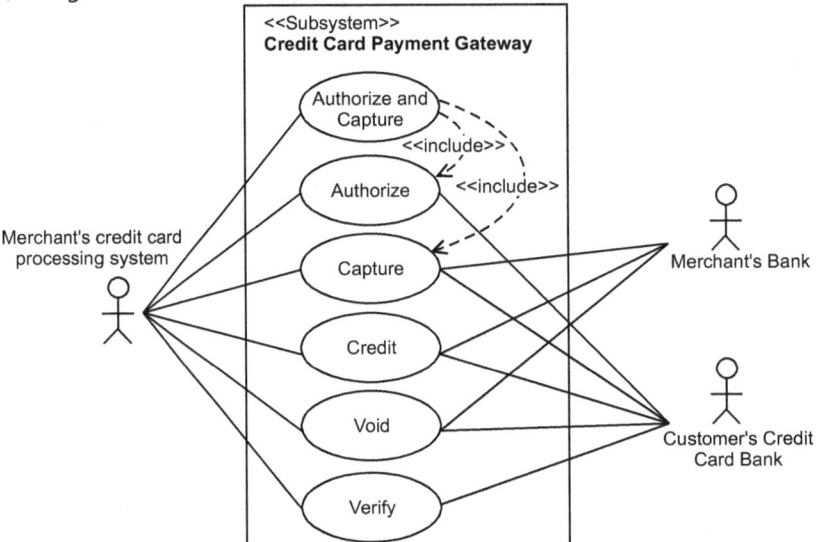

Fig. 7 : Credit card processing system use cases

Credit use case describes situations when customer should receive a refund for a transaction that was either successfully processed and settled through the system or for some transaction that was not originally submitted through the payment gateway.

Void use case describes cases when it is needed to cancel one or several related transactions that were not yet settled. If possible, the transactions will not be sent for settlement. If the Void transaction fails, the original transaction is likely already settled.

Verify use case describes zero or small amount verification transactions which could also include verification of some client's data such as address.

5. Use case diagram for Bank ATM Use Cases

An automated teller machine (ATM) or the automatic banking machine (ABM) is banking subsystem that provides bank customers with access to financial transactions in a public space without the need for a cashier, clerk or bank teller.

Customer uses bank ATM to check balances of his/her bank accounts, deposit funds, withdraw cash and/or transfer funds ATM Technician provides maintenance and repairs. All these use cases also involve Bank actor whether it is related to customer transactions or to the ATM servicing.

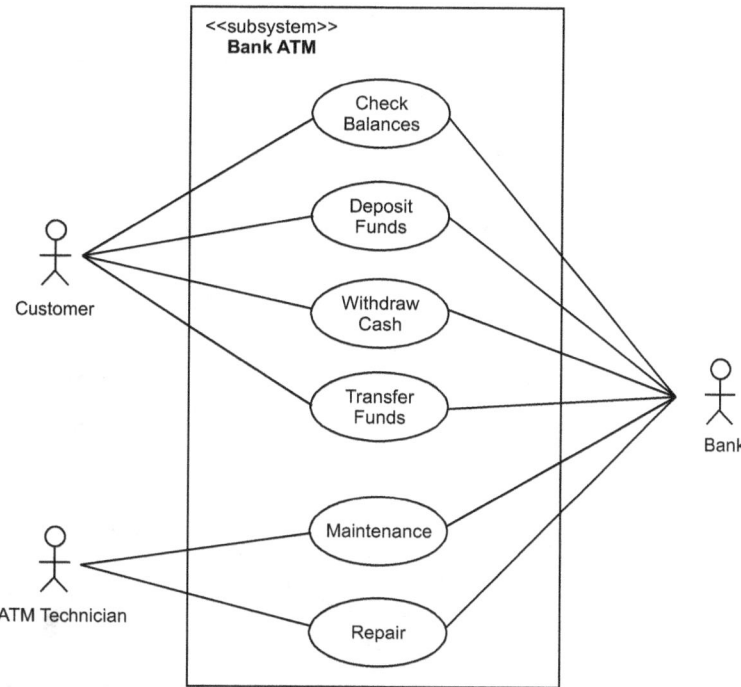

Fig. 8 : An example of use case diagram for bank ATM subsystem - top level use cases.

On most bank ATM's, the customer is authenticated by inserting a plastic ATM card and entering a personal identification number (PIN). Customer Authentication use case is required for every ATM transaction so we show it as include relationship.

Including this use case as well as transaction generalizations make the ATM Transaction an abstract use case.

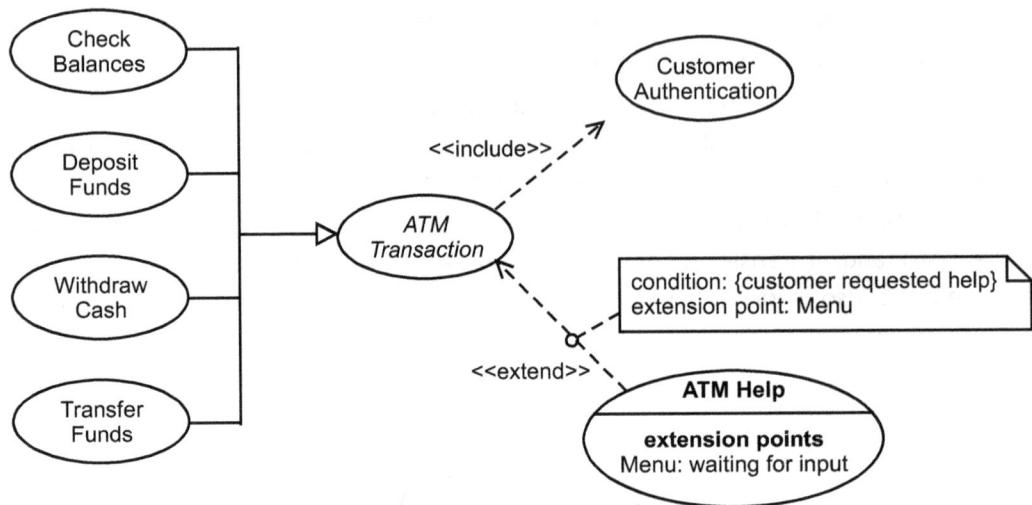

Fig. 9 : Bank ATM Transactions and Customer Authentication Use Cases Example

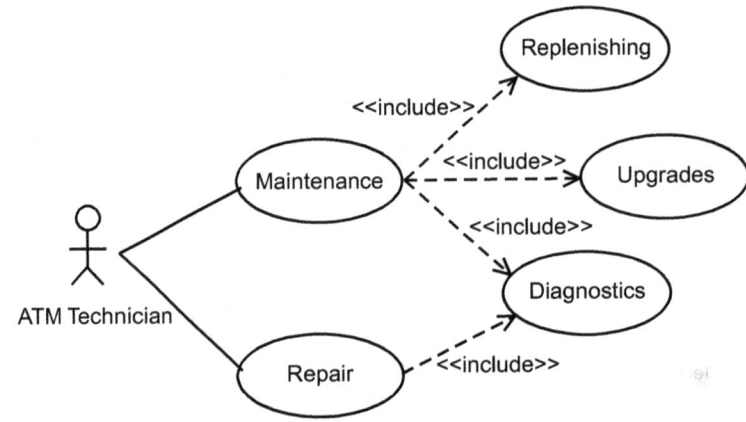

Fig. 10 : Bank ATM Maintenance, Repair, Diagnostics Use Cases Example

6. Use case diagram for Hospital Use Cases

Hospital Management System is a large system including several subsystems or modules providing variety of functions. Hospital Reception subsystem or module supports some of the many job duties of hospital receptionist. Receptionist schedules patient's appointments and admission to the hospital, collects information from patient upon patient's arrival and/or by phone. For the patient that will stay in the hospital (inpatient) s/he should have a bed allotted in a ward. Receptionists might also receive patient's payments, record them in a database and provide receipts, file insurance claims and medical reports.

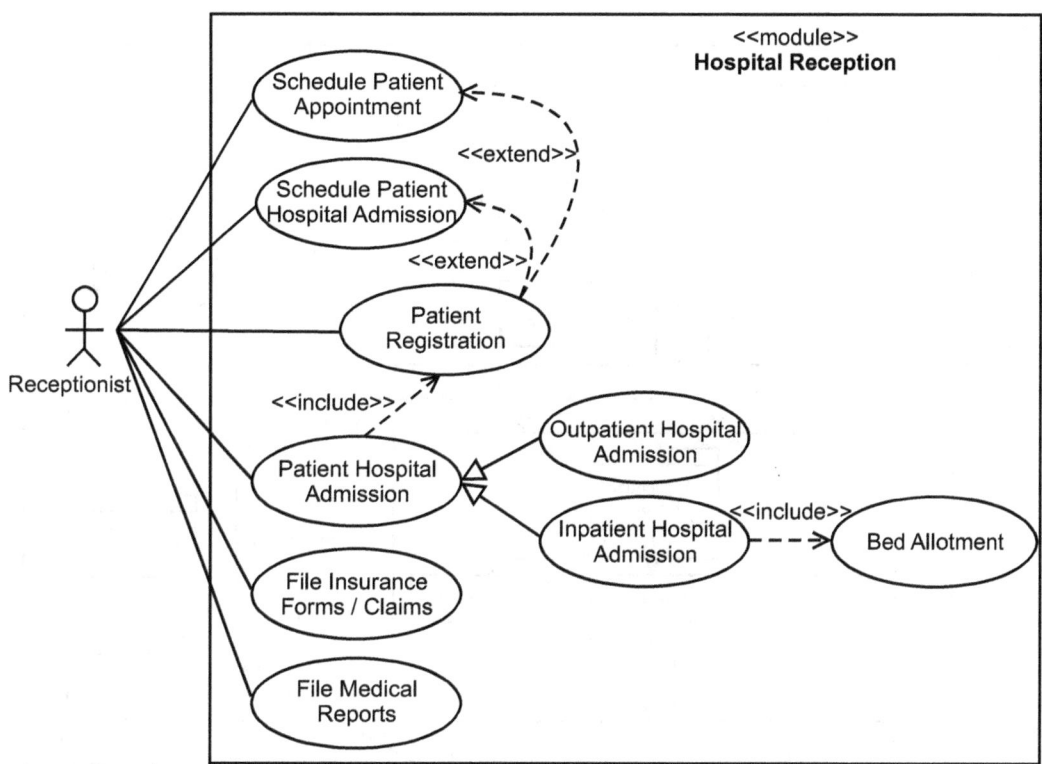

Fig. 11 : An example of use case diagram for hospital reception

PART - II

1. Package diagram for Multi-Layered Application Model

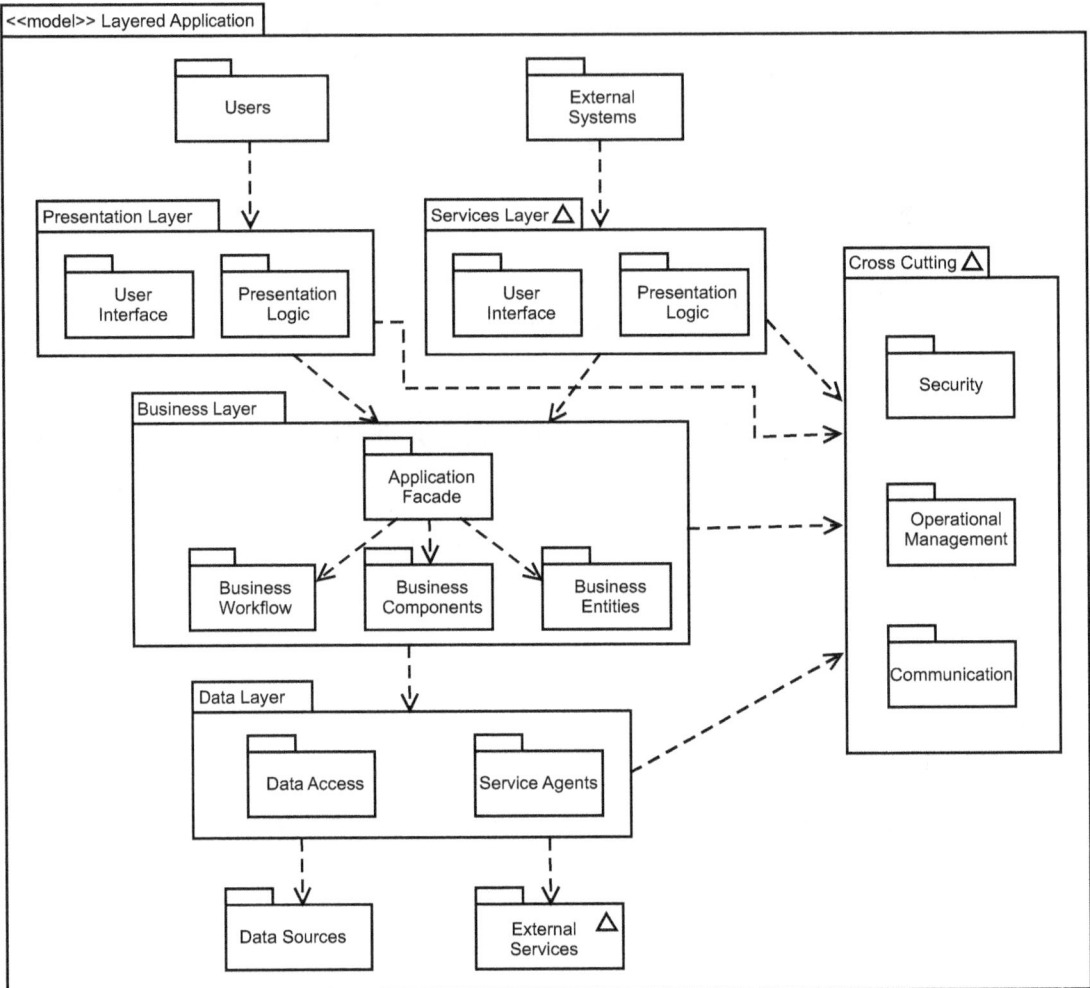

Fig. 12 : Package diagram for Multi-Layered Application Model

2. Package diagram for Shiping order

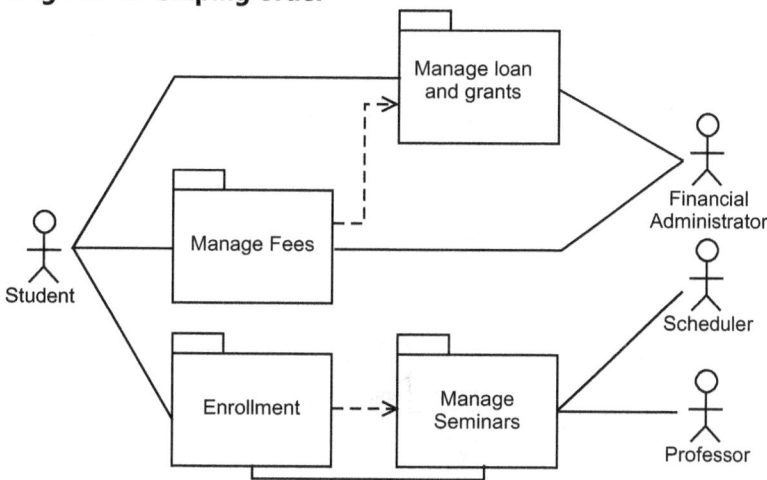

Fig. 13 : Package diagram for shiping order

3. Package diagram for Bank Domain Model

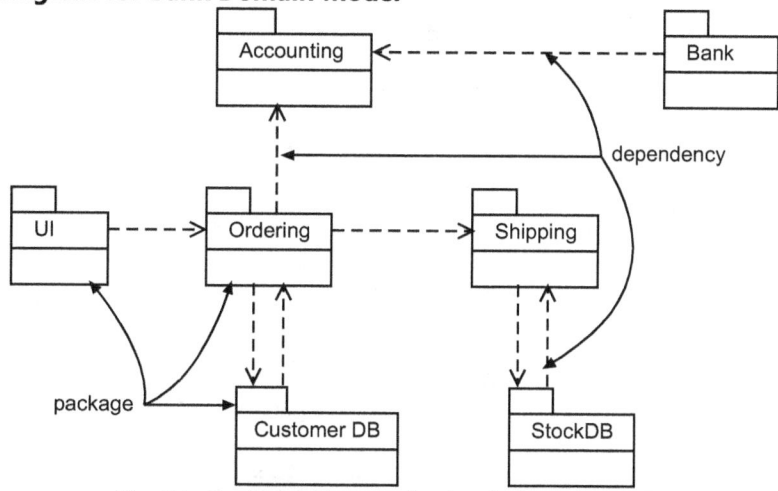

Fig. 14 : Package diagram for bank domain model

4. Class diagram Library Domain Model

It describes main classes and relationships which could be used during analysis phase to better understand domain area for Integrated Library System (ILS), also known as a Library Management System (LMS). Each physical library item - book, tape cassette, CD, DVD etc. could have its own item number. To support it, the items may be barcoded. The purpose of barcoding is to provide a unique and scannable identifier that links the barcoded physical item to the electronic record in the catalog.

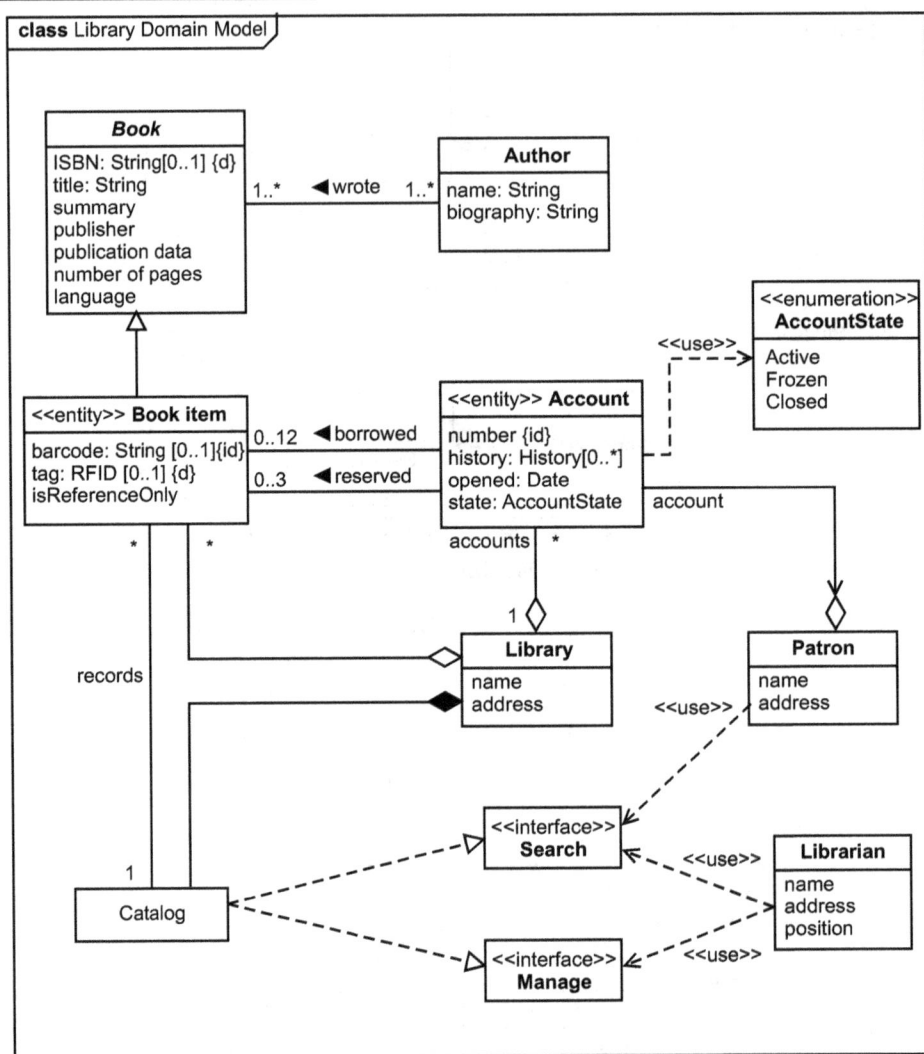

Fig. 15 : Class diagram example - library domain model

Barcode must be physically attached to the item, and barcode number is entered into the corresponding field in the electronic item record. Barcodes on library items could be replaced by RFID tags. The RFID tag can contain item's identifier, title, material type etc. It is read by an RFID reader, without the need to open a book cover or CD/DVD case to scan it with barcode reader. Library has some rules on what could be borrowed and what is for reference only. Rules are also defined on how many books could be borrowed by patrons and how many could be reserved. Library catalog provides access for the library patrons and staff to all sources of information about library items, allows to search by a particular author, on a particular topic, or in a particular format, that the library has. It tells the user where materials meeting their specific needs can be found.

5. Class diagram for Online Shopping Domain

This diagram is an example of class diagram which shows some domain model for online shopping. Each customer could have some web user identity. Web user could be in several states and could be linked to one shopping cart. Each customer has exactly one account. Account owns shopping cart and orders. Orders are sorted and unique. Each order is linked to none to several payments.

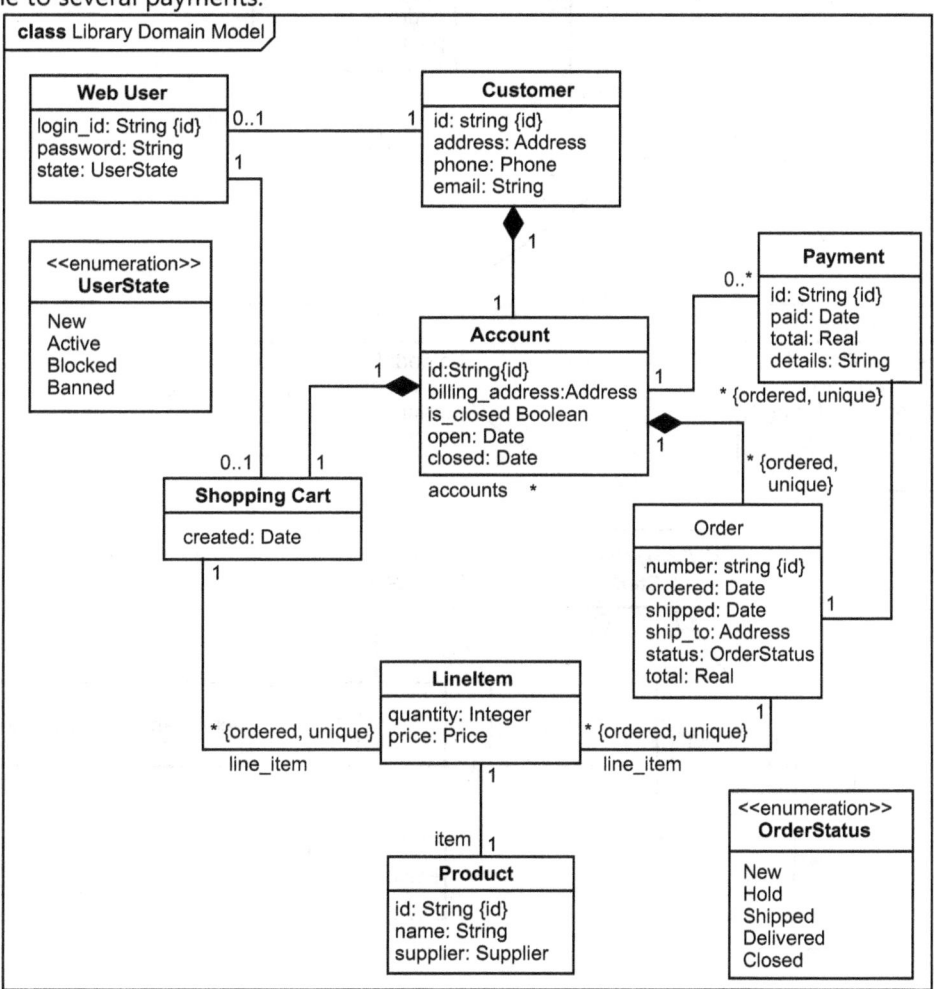

Fig. 16 : Class diagram example - online shopping domain

6. Class diagram for Hospital Management Domain Model

Domain model for the Hospital Management System is represented class diagrams.

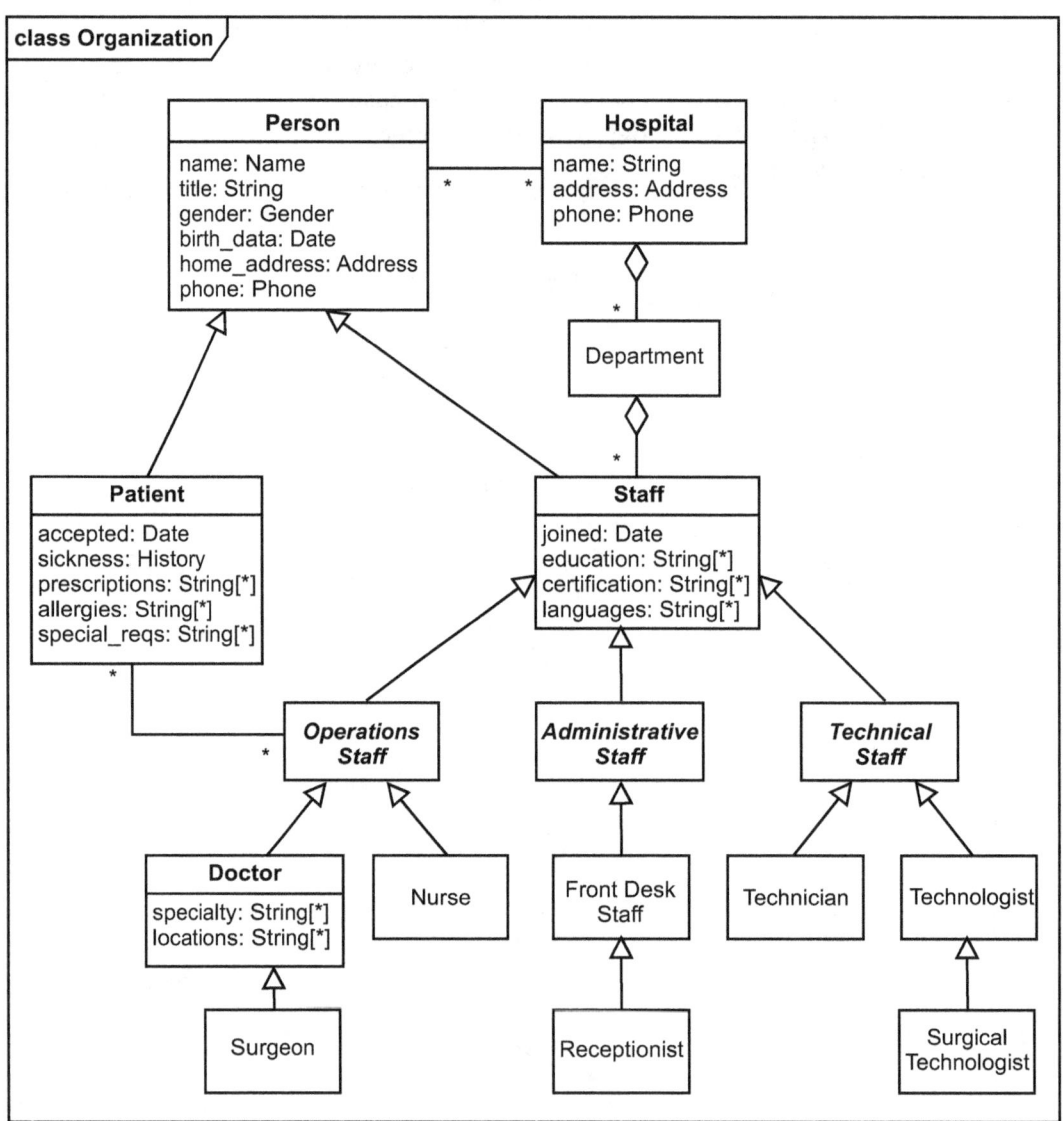

Fig. 17 : Class diagram for Hospital management domain model

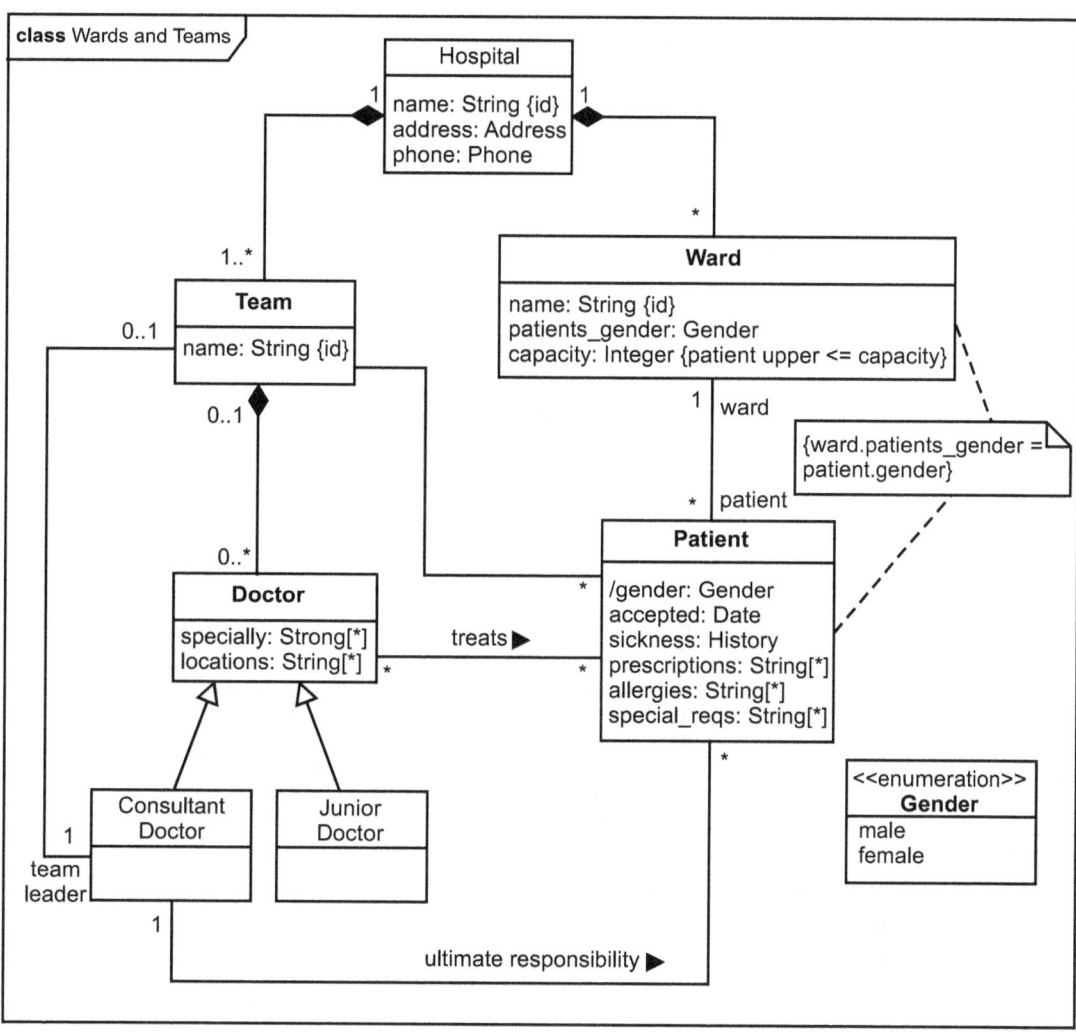

Fig. 18 : Class diagram for hospital system

7. Class diagram for Vehicle system

This diagram shows an *inheritance hierarchy* – a series of classes and their subclasses. Its for an imaginary application that must model different kinds of vehicles such as bicycles, motor bike and cars.

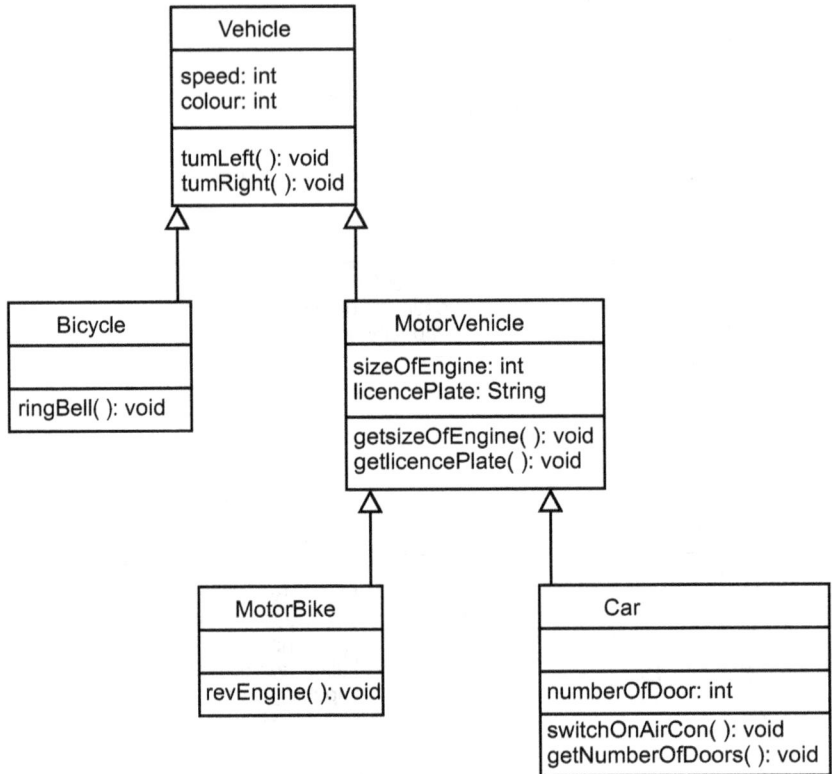

Fig. 19 : Class diagram for vehicle system

Notes:
- All Vehicles have some common attributes (speed and colour) and common behaviour (turnLeft, turnRight).
- Bicycle and MotorVehicle are both kinds of Vehicle and are therefore shown to inherit from Vehicle. To put this another way, Vehicle is the superclass of both Bicycle and MotorVehicle.
- In our model MotorVehicles have engines and license plates. Attributes have been added accordingly, along with some behaviour that allows us to examine those attributes.
- MotorVehicles is the base class of both MotorBike and Car, therefore these classes not only inherit the speed and colour properties from Vehicle, but also the additional attributes and behaviour from MotorVehicle.
- Both MotorBike and Car have additional attributes and behaviour which are specific to those kinds of object.

8. Class diagram for University Courseware Management system

This example demonstrates relationships between classes. It's from an imaginary application that models university courses.

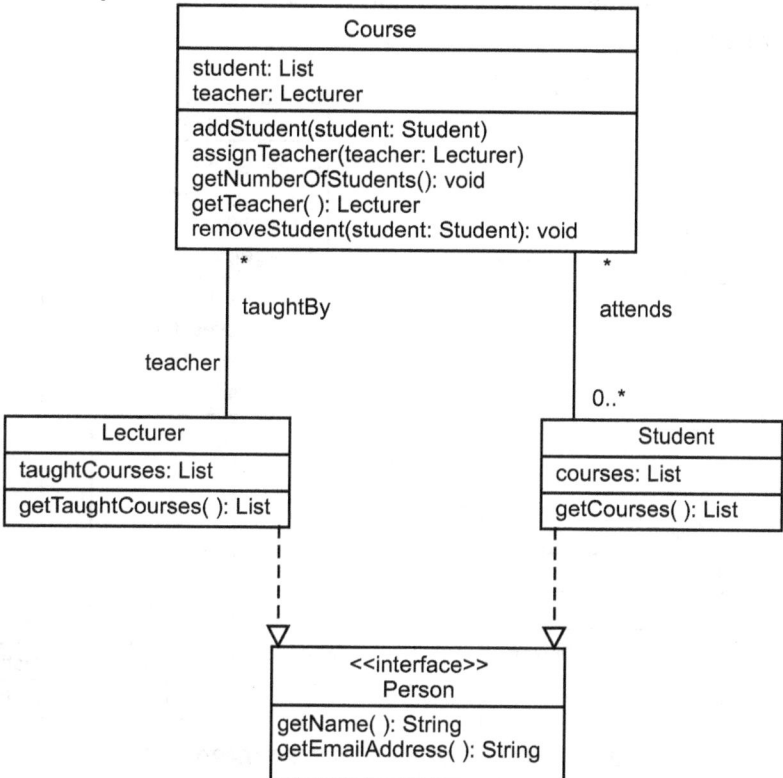

Fig. 20 : Class diagram for university courseware management system

Notes
- Each Course object maintains a list of the students on that course and the lecturer who has been assigned to teach that course
- The Course object has behaviour that allow the adding and removing of students from the course, assigning a teacher, getting a list of the currently assigned students, and the currently assigned teacher.
- Teachers are modelled as Lecturer objects. As a lecturer may teach more than one course there is an association between Course and Lecturer. The "taughtBy" relationship shows that a Course only has a single teacher, but that a lecturer may teach several Courses.
- Each Lecturer object also maintains a list of the Courses that it teaches.
- There is a similar relationship between Course and Student. A course is attended by zero or more Students, and a Student may attend multiple courses.

This example also demonstrates the use of interfaces.

The diagram shows a Person interface that stipulates that objects conforming to this interface will have a getName and getEmailAddress methods. Both Lecturer and Student are shown to be types of Person.

9. Class Diagram for Company Software

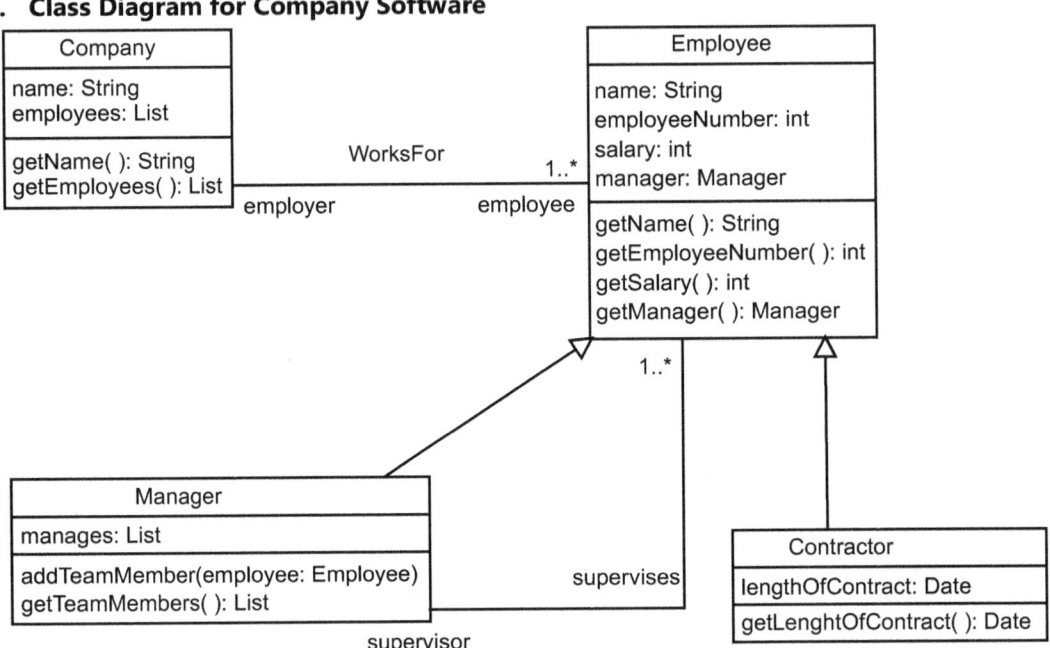

Fig. 21 : Class diagram for company software

10. Class diagram for Elevator Problem

A product is to be installed to control elevators in a building with m floors. The problem concerns the logic required to move elevators between floors according to the following constraints:

- Each elevator has a set of m buttons, one for each floor. These illuminate when pressed and cause the elevator to visit the corresponding floor.
- The illumination is canceled when the elevator visits the corresponding floor.
- Each floor, except the first floor and top floor has two buttons, one to request and up-elevator and one to request a down-elevator.
- These buttons illuminate when pressed. The illumination is canceled when an elevator visits the floor and then moves in the desired direction.
- When an elevator has no requests, it remains at its current floor with its doors closed.

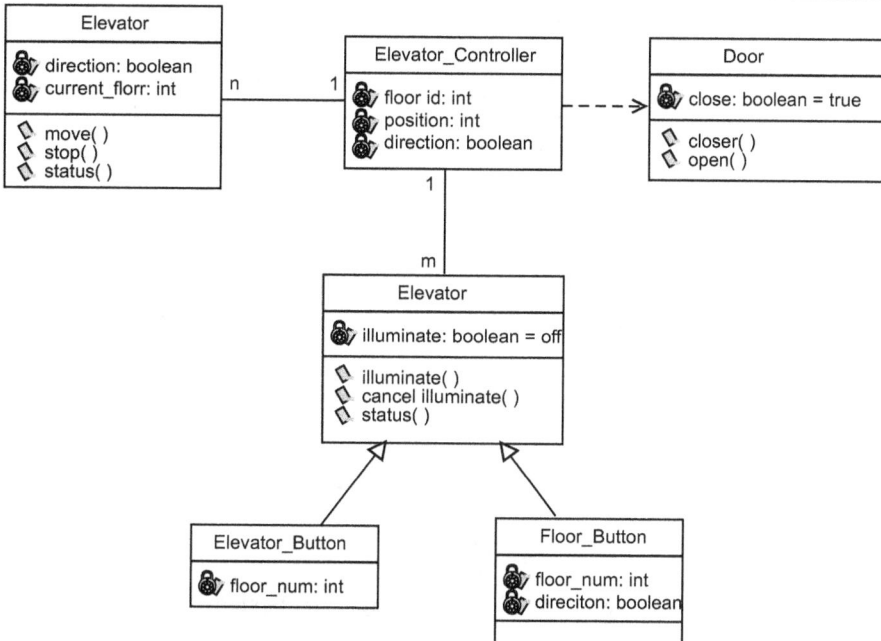

Fig. 22 : Class diagram for elevator problem

11. Class diagram for seminar Enrollment

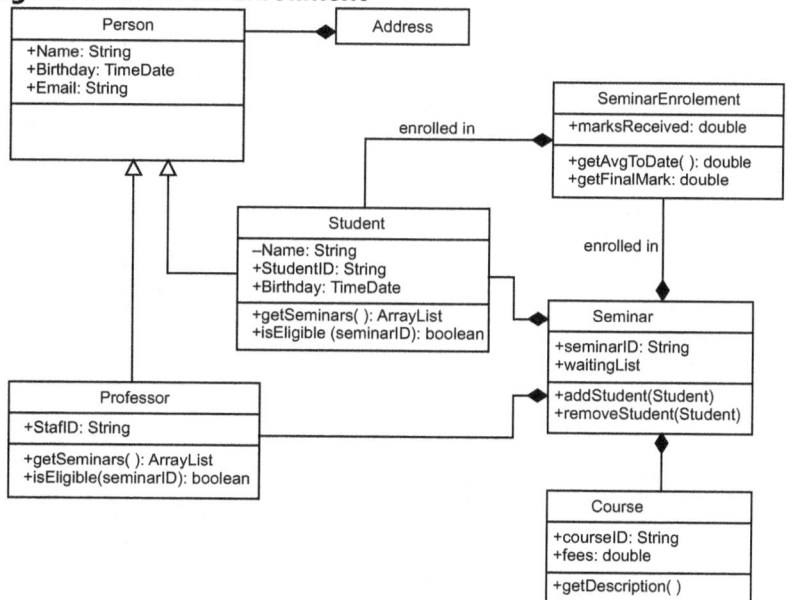

Fig. 23 : Class diagram for seminar enrollment

12. Class diagram for Auction System

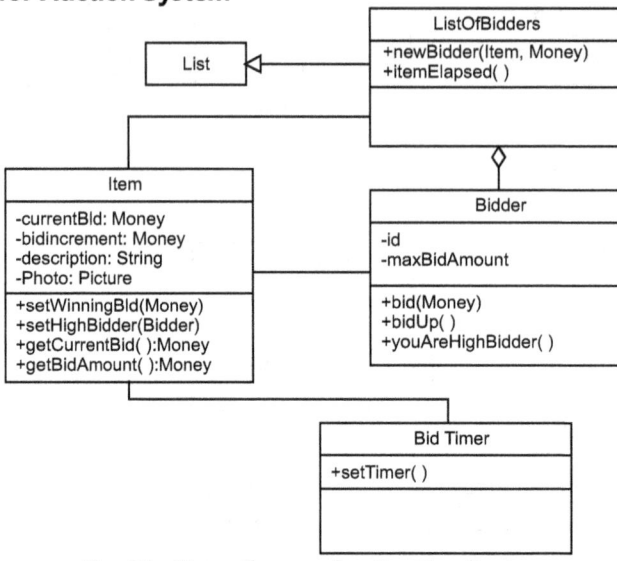

Fig. 24 : Class diagram for Auction System

13. Object diagram for Bank ATM

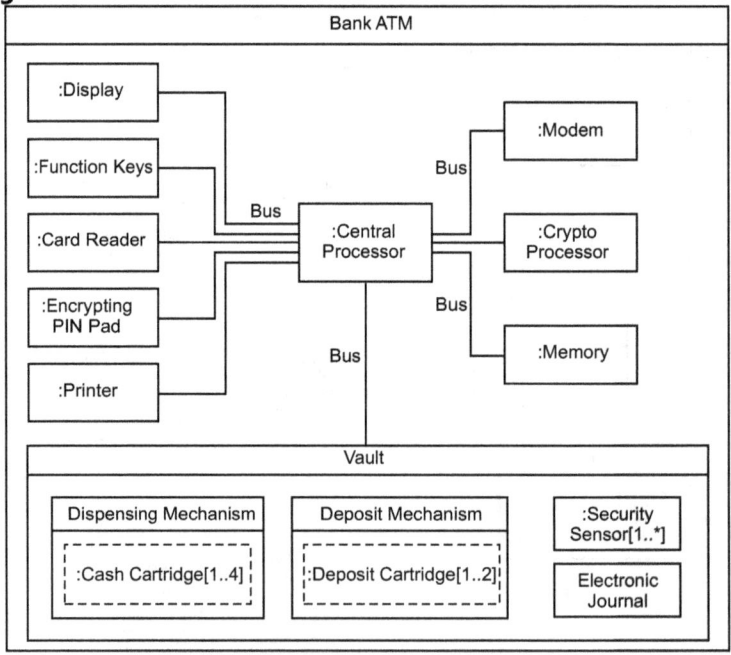

Fig. 25 : Object diagram for Bank ATM

This is an example of UML *internal structure diagram* which shows composite structure of Bank Automated Teller Machine (ATM).

Bank ATM is typically made up of several devices such as central processor unit (CPU), cryptoprocessor, memory, customer display, function key buttons (usually located near the display), magnetic and/or smartchip card reader, encrypting PIN Pad, customer receipt printer, vault, modem.

Internal structure diagram example - Bank ATM

Vault stores devices and parts which require restricted access, including cash dispensing mechanism, deposit mechanism, several security sensors (e.g. magnetic, thermal, seismic, gas), electronic journal system to maintain system log, etc. Cash dispenser includes several removable cash cartridges and deposit mechanism - removable deposite cartridges.

ATM is usually connected to the bank or interbank network via some modem (e.g. dial-up or ADSL) over a public switched telephone line or a leased line. Network interface card (NIC) could be used as a high-speed alternative in VPN connections.

14. Object diagram for order processing

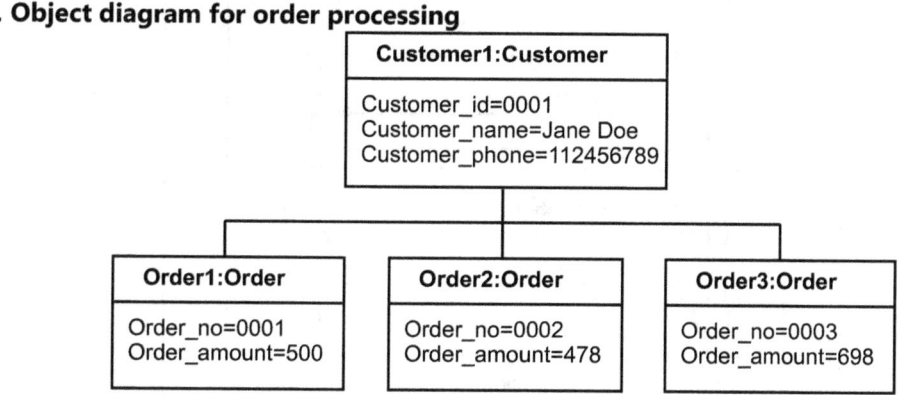

Fig. 26 : Object diagram for order processing

PART - III

1. Sequence diagram for Online Bookshop system

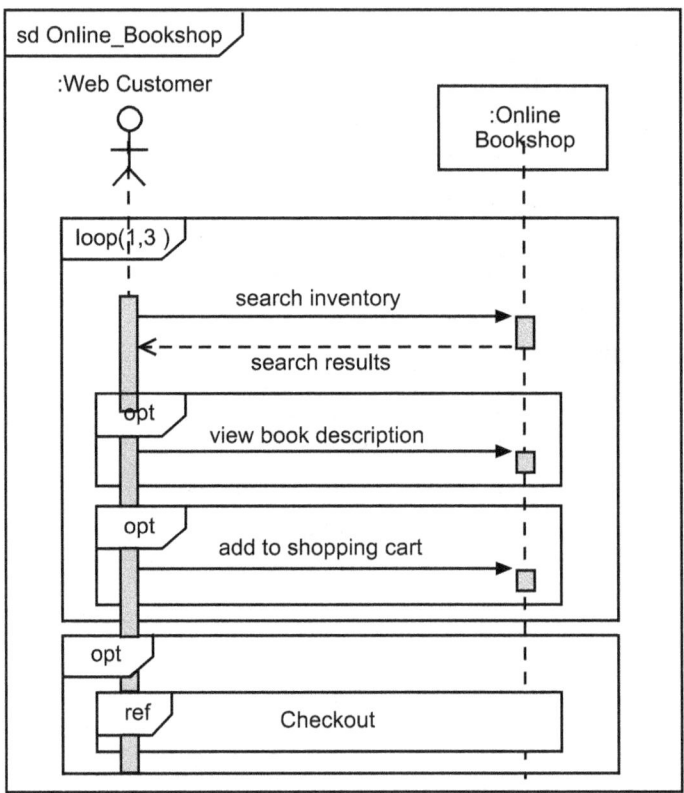

Fig. 27 : Sequence diagram for Online Bookshop system

2. Sequence diagram for Facebook User Authentication in a Web Application

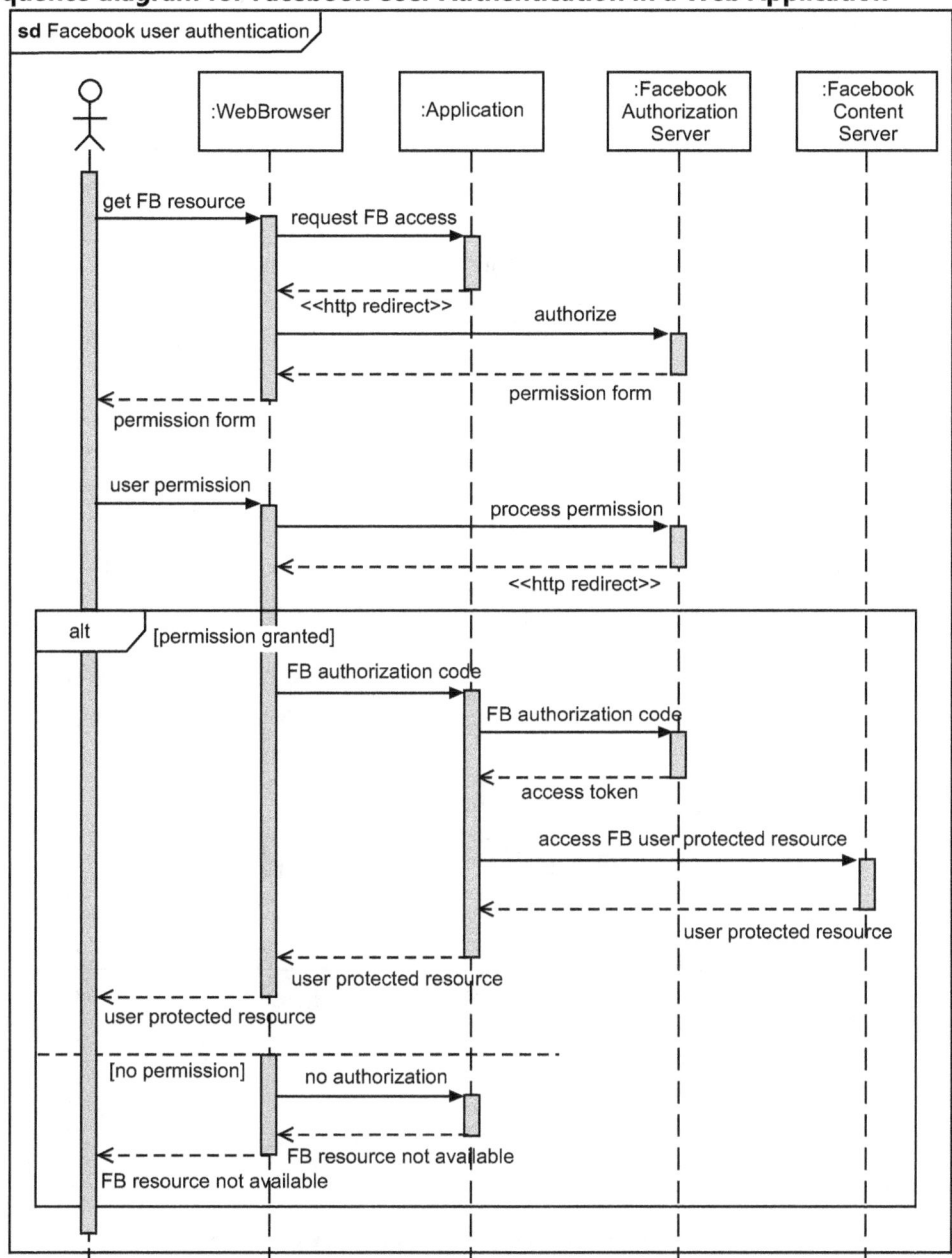

Fig. 28 : Sequence diagram for facebook user authentication in a web application

3. Sequence diagram for Elevator Problem

A product is to be installed to control elevators in a building with m floors. The problem concerns the logic required to move elevators between floors according to the following constraints:

- Each elevator has a set of m buttons, one for each floor. These illuminate when pressed and cause the elevator to visit the corresponding floor. The illumination is canceled when the elevator visits the corresponding floor.

- Each floor, except the first floor and top floor has two buttons, one to request and up-elevator and one to request a down-elevator. These buttons illuminate when pressed. The illumination is canceled when an elevator visits the floor and then moves in the desired direction.

- When an elevator has no requests, it remains at its current floor with its doors closed.

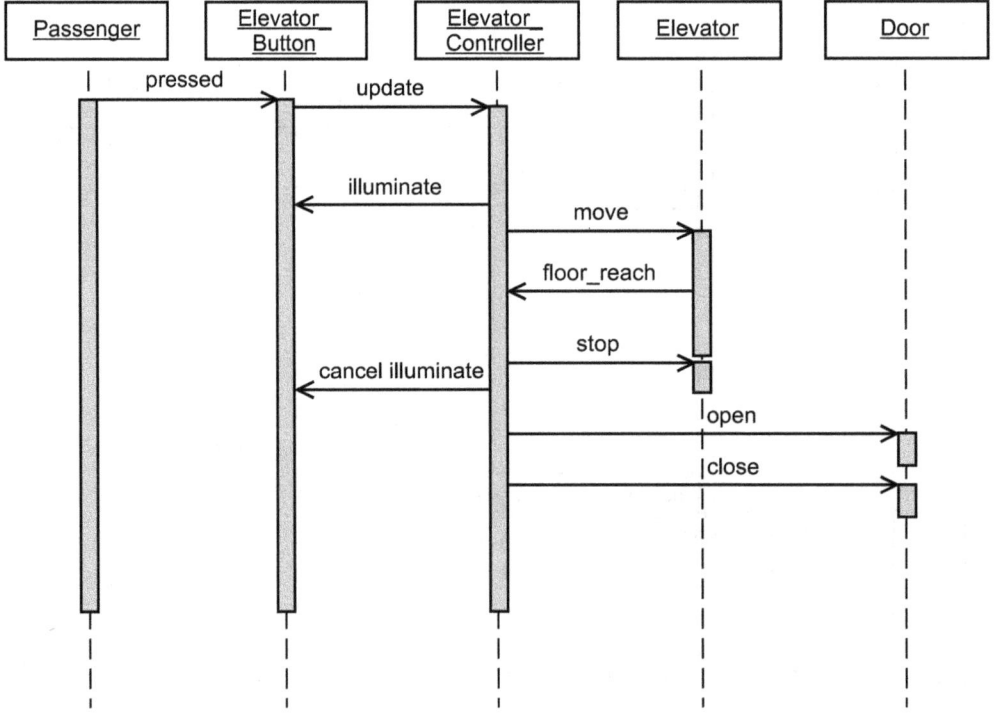

Fig. 29 : Sequence diagram for elevator problem

4. Communication diagram for Online Bookshop

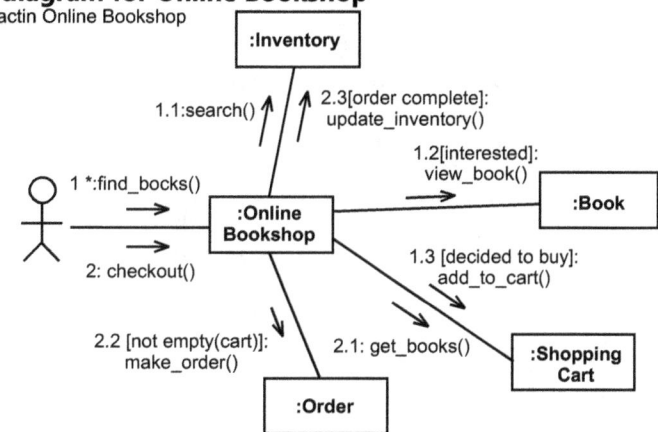

Fig. 30 : Communication diagram for Online Bookshop

A product is to be installed to control elevators in a building with m floors. The problem concerns the logic required to move elevators between floors according to the following constraints:

- Each elevator has a set of m buttons, one for each floor. These illuminate when pressed and cause the elevator to visit the corresponding floor. The illumination is canceled when the elevator visits the corresponding floor.
- Each floor, except the first floor and top floor has two buttons, one to request and up-elevator and one to request a down-elevator. These buttons illuminate when pressed. The illumination is canceled when an elevator visits the floor and then moves in the desired direction.
- When an elevator has no requests, it remains at its current floor with its doors closed.

5. Communication diagram for Elevator Problem

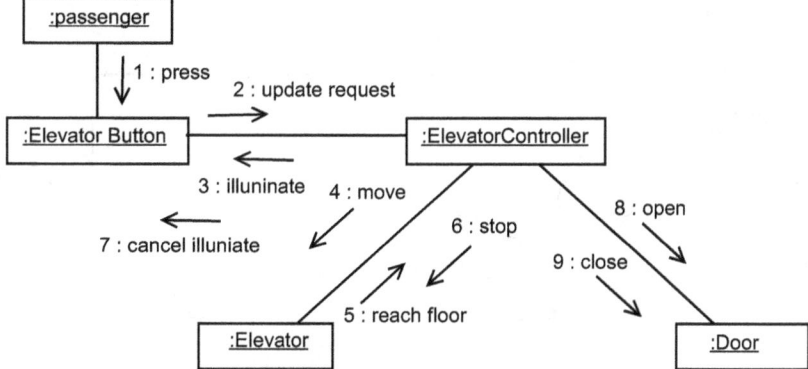

Fig. 31 : Communication diagram for elevator problem

PART - IV

1. Activity diagram for online shopping system

Online customer can browse or search items, view specific item, add it to shopping cart, view and update shopping cart, checkout. User can view shopping cart at any time. Checkout is assumed to include user registration and login.

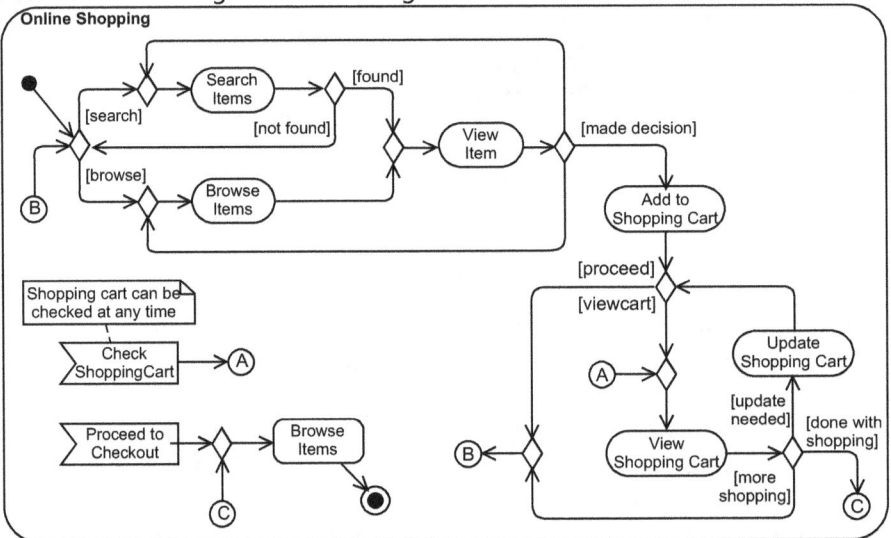

Fig. 32 : Activity diagram for online shopping system

2. Activity diagram for Process Order system

Requested order is input parameter of activity. After order is accepted and info is filled, payment processing and shipment is done **in parallel**. Note that in usual business cases shipment will only be done after payment is confirmed.

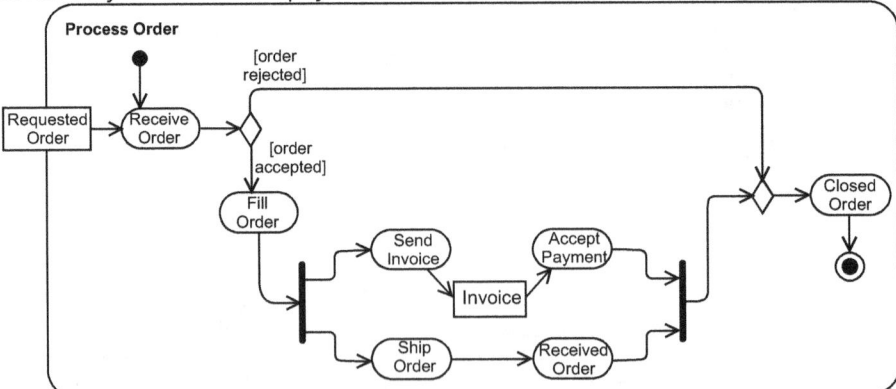

Fig. 33 : Activity diagram for process order

3. Activity diagram for Document Management Process

Partitions are shown here as horizontal **swimlanes** and represent different roles participating in the activity – Author, Reviewer, Approver, and Owner.

Document is created, reviewed, updated, approved, and at some point archived. This activity diagram shows responsibilities of different roles and flow or sequence of document changes.

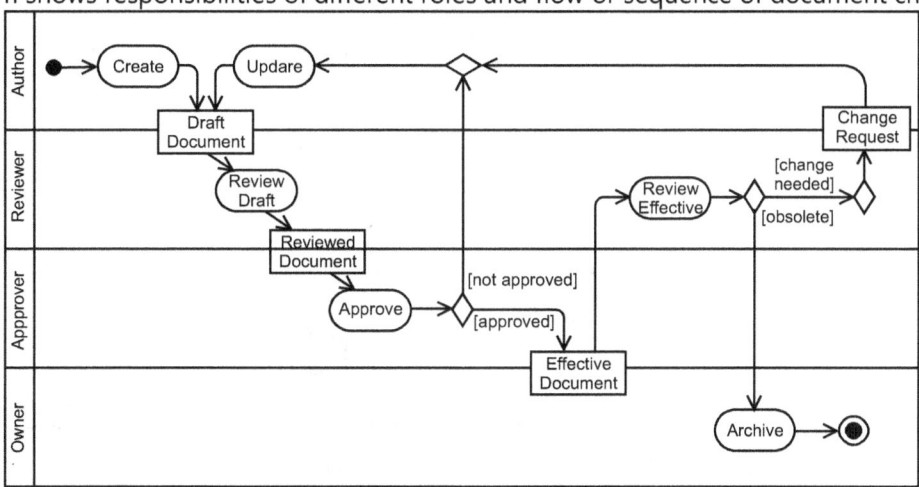

Fig. 34 : Activity diagram for document management process

4. Activity diagram for Resolve Issue

After ticket is created by some authority and the issue is reproduced, issue is identified, resolution is determined, issue is fixed and verified, and ticket is closed, if issue was resolved.

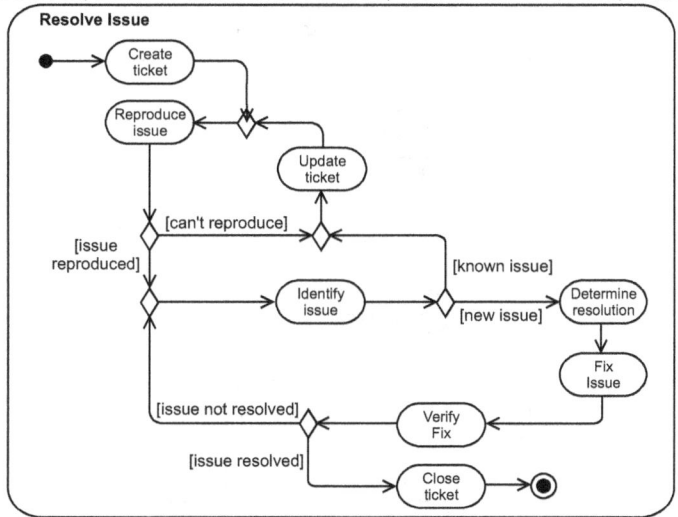

Fig. 35 : Activity diagram for resolve issue

5. Activity diagram for Withdraw money from a bank account through an ATM

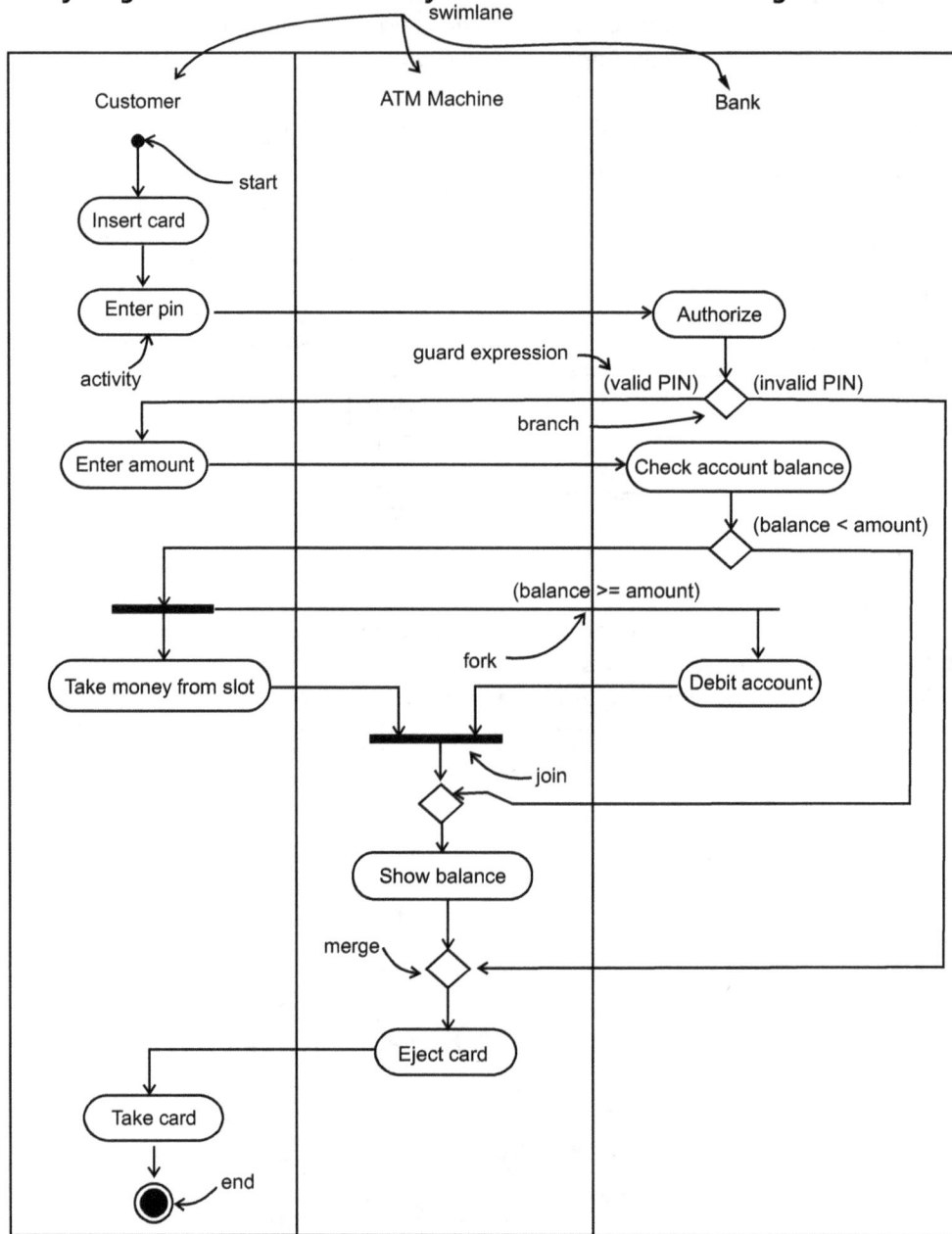

Fig. 36 : Activity diagram for withdraw money from a bank account through an ATM

6. State Machine diagram for Water Phase Diagram

Water can exist in several states - liquid, vapour, solid, and plasma. Several transitions are possible from one state to another.

For example, freezing is phase change from liquid state to ice. Condensation is phase change from vapour state to liquid. Water vapour could turn directly into frost through deposition.

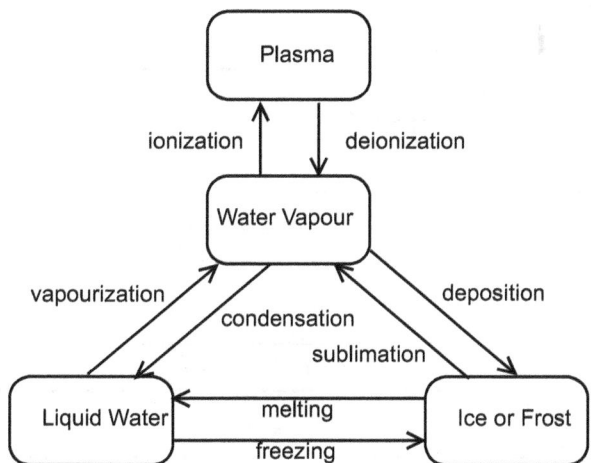

Fig. 37 : State Machine diagram for water phase diagram

7. State Machine diagram for Bank ATM State Machine

This is an example of UML behavioral state machine diagram showing Bank Automated Teller Machine (ATM) top level state machine.

ATM is initially turned off. After the power is turned on, ATM performs startup action and enters Self Test state.

If the test fails, ATM goes into Out of Service state, otherwise there is triggerless transition to the Idle state.

In this state ATM waits for customer interaction.

The ATM state changes from Idle to Serving Customer when the customer inserts banking or credit card in the ATM's card reader. On entering the Serving Customer state, the entry action readCard is performed.

Note, that transition from Serving Customer state back to the Idle state could be triggered by cancel event as the customer could cancel transaction at any time.

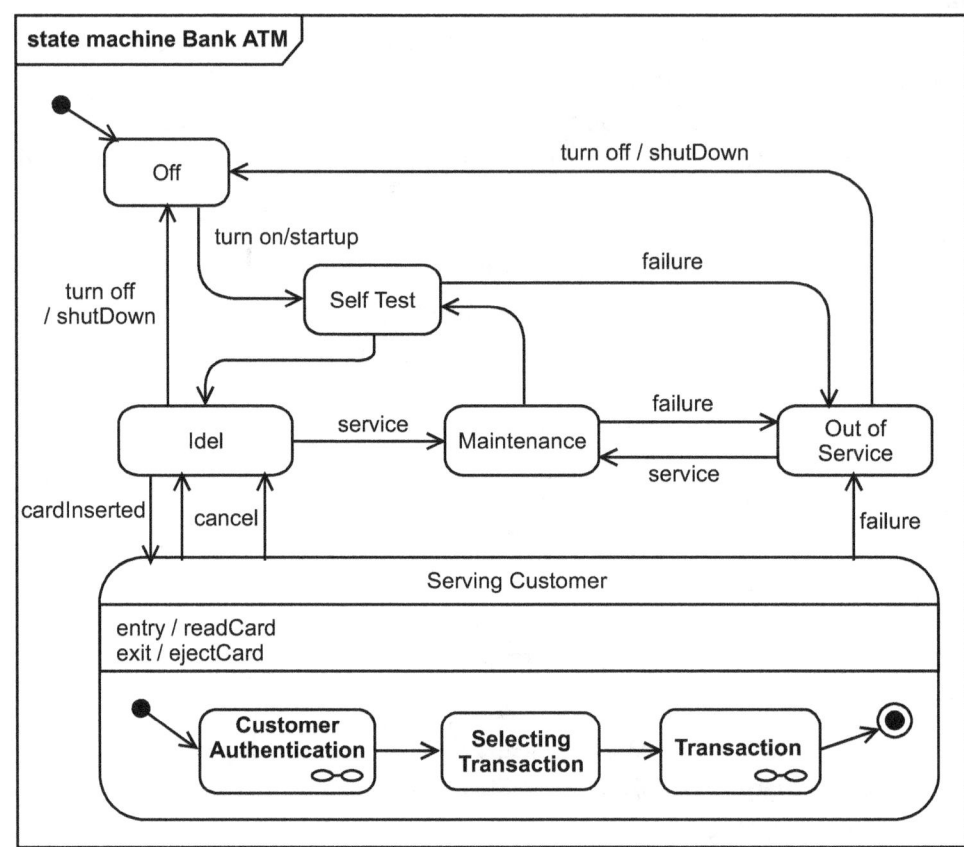

Fig. 38 : State Machine diagram for bank ATM state machine

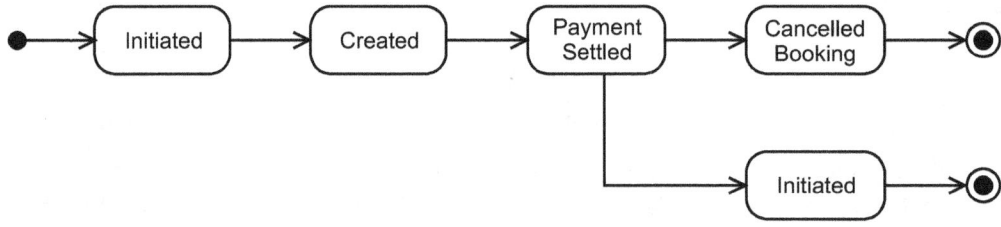

Fig. 39 : State Machine diagram for booking system

PART - V

1. Component diagram for Retail Website

An example component diagram for a retail website.

Search Engine component uses Inventory interface to allow customers to search or browse items. Shopping Cart component uses Orders component during checkout process. Authentication component allows customer to login and binds the customer to Account.

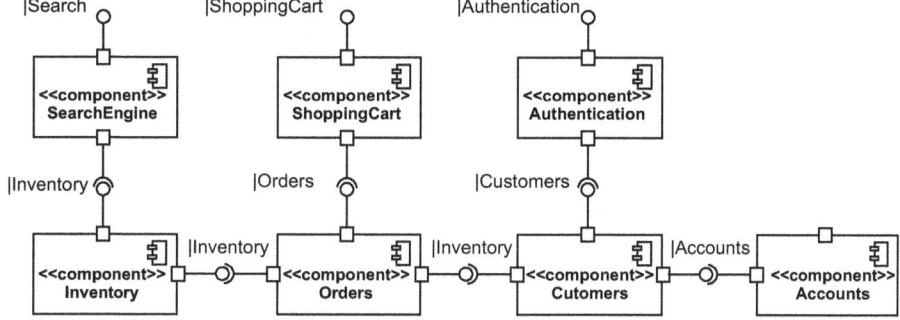

Fig. 40 : Component diagram for retail website

2. Component diagram for Student seminar scheduler

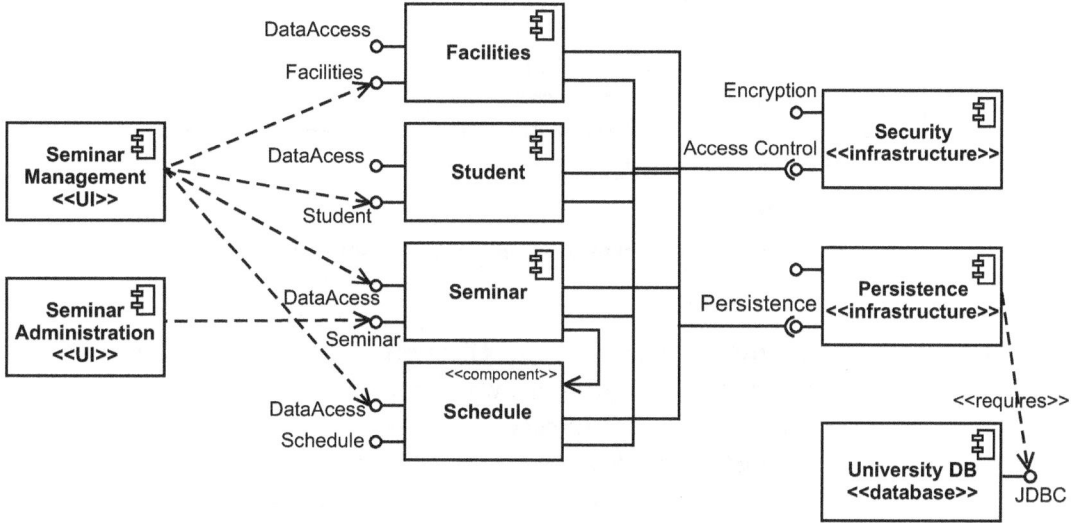

Fig. 41 : Component diagram for student seminar scheduler

3. Deployment Diagram For a Vehicle Registration System

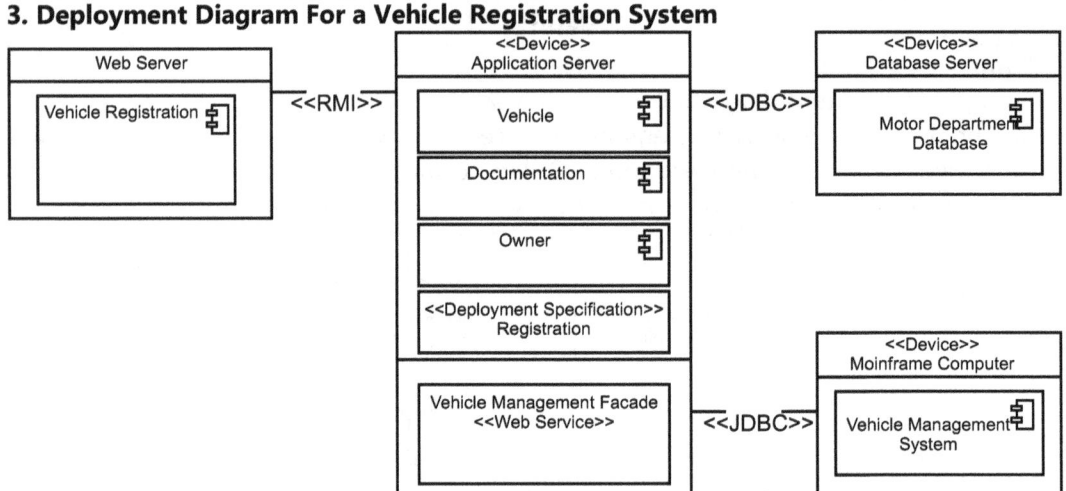

Fig. 42 : Deployment diagram For a vehicle registration system

4. Deployment Diagram For Web Application

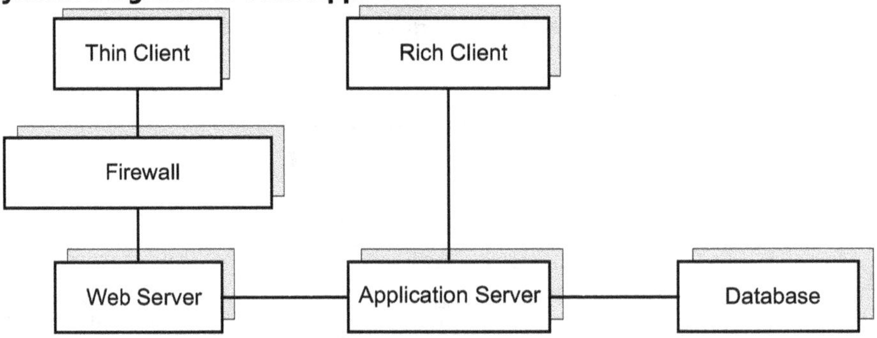

Fig. 43 : Deployment diagram for web application

5. Deployment diagram for Book club Web Application

Book club web application artifact book_club_app.war is deployed on Catalina Servlet 2.4 / JSP 2.0 Container which is part of Apache Tomcat 5.5 web server.

The book_club_app.war artifact manifests (implements) OnlineOrders component.

The artifact contains three other artifacts, one of which implements UserServices component. The Application Server «device» (computer server) has communication path to Database Server «device» (another computer server).

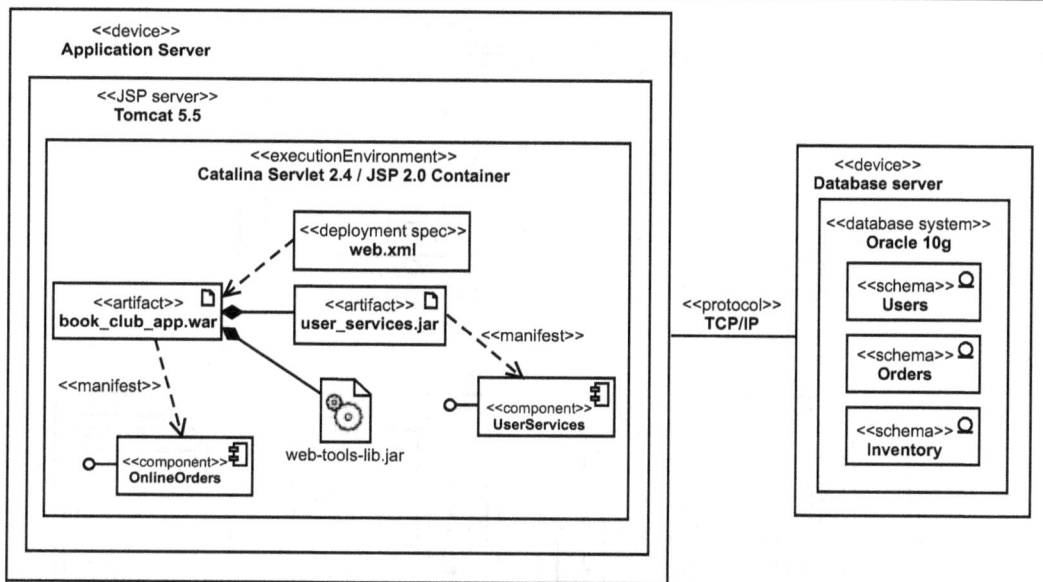

Fig. 44 : Deployment diagram for book club web application

6. **Deployment diagram for Multilayered Load Balancing**

A network load balancer is an appliance device that is used to split network load across multiple servers. An example shows jetNEXUS ALB-X hardware load balancer. It combines the functions of OSI Layer 7 (Application Layer) load balancing, HTTP compression, SSL offload and content caching in one solution.

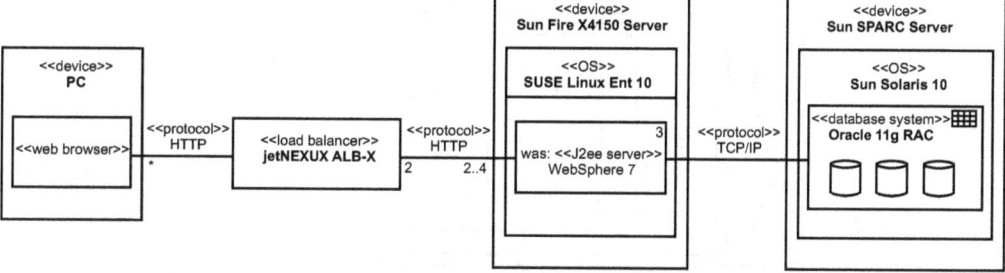

Fig. 45 : Deployment diagram for multilayered load balancing

7. **Deployment diagram for Clustered Deployment of J2EE Web Application**

Another example of deployment diagram for J2EE web application with load balancing and clustering which shows specific server instances involved. Incoming HTTP requests are first processed by Apache web server. Static content such as HTML pages, images, CSS, and JavaScript is served by the web server. Requests to JSP pages are load balanced and forwarded to 2x2 Apache Tomcat servers using both vertical and horizontal clustering.

All 4 instances of Apache Tomcat servers save/receive data to/from a single instance of Oracle 11g DBMS, which could become a performance bottleneck if web application is data-intensive.

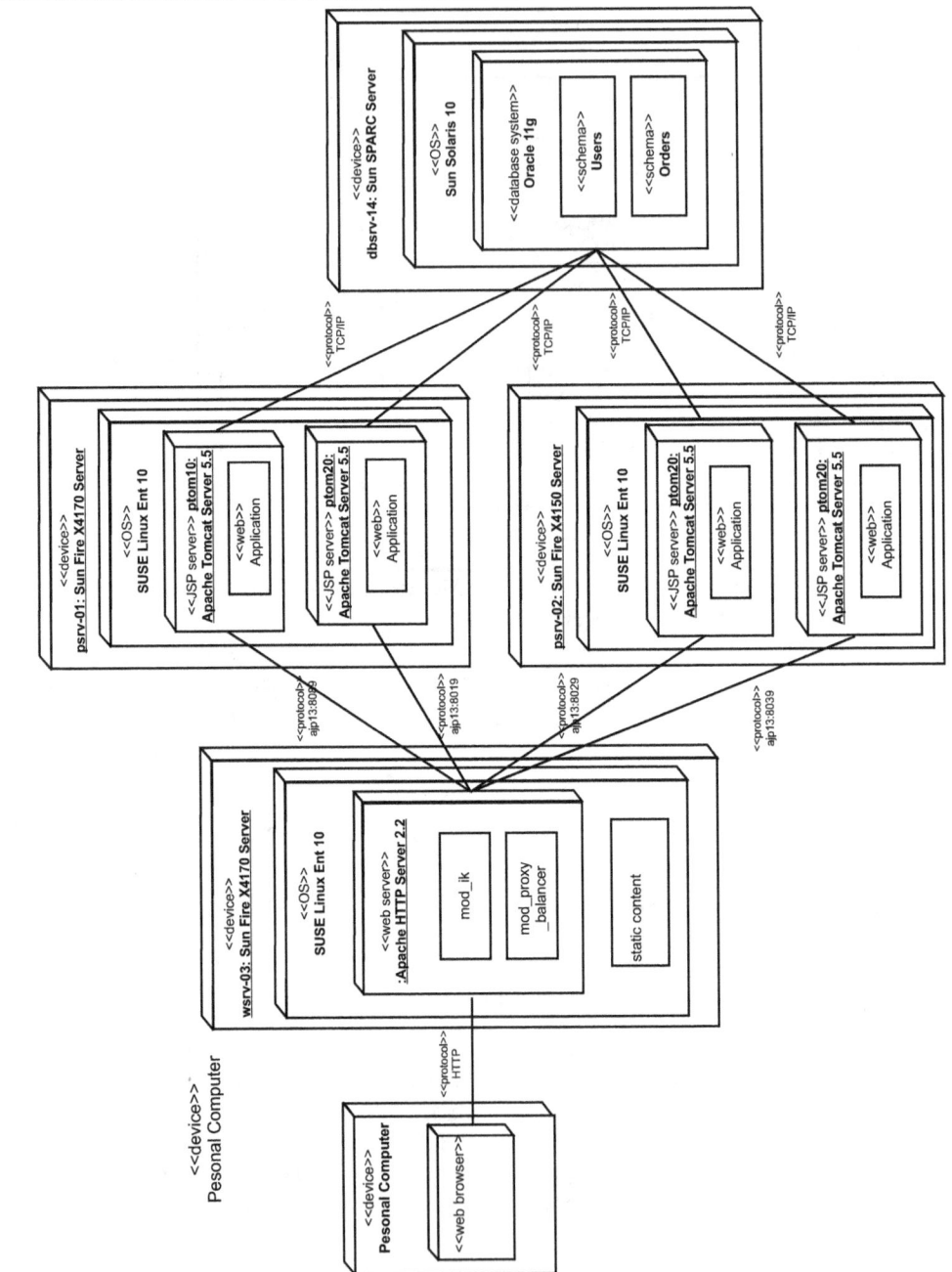

Fig. 46 : Deployment diagram for clustered deployment of J2EE web application

8. Deployment diagram for Apple iTunes Deployment

The iTunes setup application could be downloaded from iTunes website and installed on a home computer. After installation and registration iTunes application could communicate with Apple iTunes Store. Customer can buy and download music, video, TV shows, audiobooks, etc. and store it in media library.

Mobile devices like Apple iPod Touch and Apple iPhone could update own media libraries from home computer with iTunes through USB, or could download media directly from Apple iTunes Store using some wireless protocol like Wi-Fi, 3G, or EDGE.

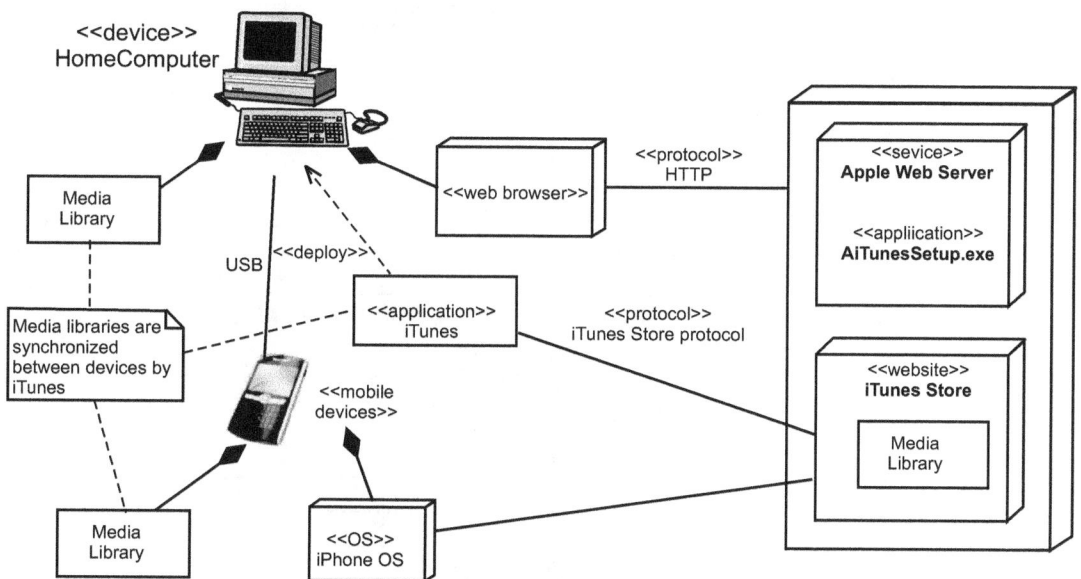

Fig. 47 : Deployment diagram for apple itunes deployment

9. Deployment diagram for Android Application Deployment

Android is a software stack for mobile devices that includes an operating system, middleware and key applications.

Android relies on Linux OS for core system services such as security, memory management, process management, network stack, and driver model. The Linux kernel also acts as an abstraction layer between the hardware and the rest of the software stack.

Android applications are written in Java. Android SDK tools compile and package the code along with any required data and resource files into Android application archive file having .apk suffix.

The .apk file represents one Android application to be deployed to the Android-enabled mobile devices.

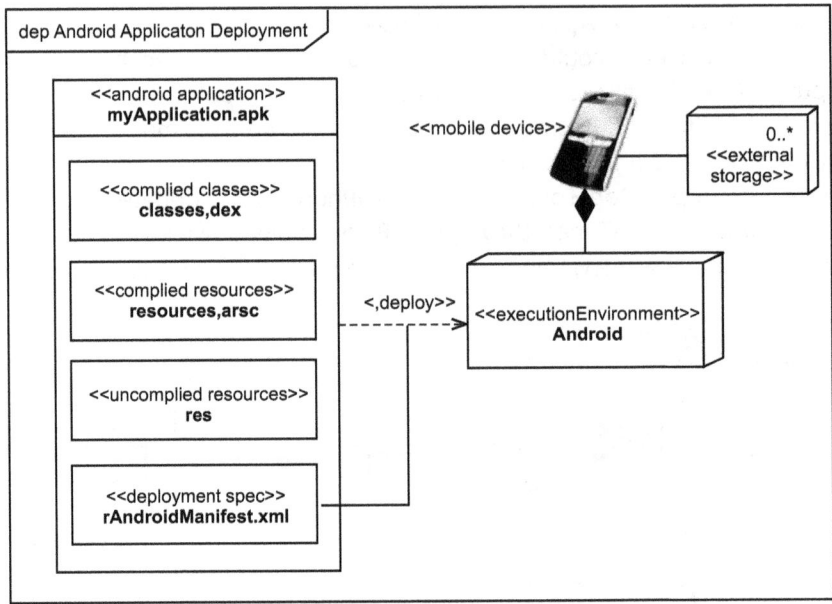

Fig. 48 : Deployment diagram for android application deployment

Acronyms

UML	Unified Modeling Language
OMG	Object Management Group
MDA	Model Driven Architecture
MOF	Meta Object Facility
RUP	Rational Unified Process
OCL	Object Constraint Language
CIM	Computation Independent Model
PIM	Platform Independent Model
PSM	Platform Specific Model
XMI	XML Metadata Interchange
CORBA	Common Object Request Broker Architecture
ORB	Object Request Broker
DII	Dynamic Invocation Interface
DSI	Dynamic Skeleton Interface
GIOP	General Inter-ORB Protocol
CRC	Class Responsibility Collaborator
OOAD	Object Oriented Analysis and Design

www.ingramcontent.com/pod-product-compliance
Lightning Source LLC
Chambersburg PA
CBHW080243170426
43192CB00014BA/2549